Carl Lostritto

Compu Drawin

tational

g

From foundational exercises to theories of representation

APPLIED RESEARCH +DESIGN PUBLISHING

Table of Contents

8 **Acknowledgments**

10 **Preface**
12 Additional Notes for the Beginning Programmer
12 Architecture and Other Disciplines
12 Start

15 **Chapter 1 Definitions**
18 What drawing is not and what computing cannot do
20 A drawing cannot be edited
25 A computer cannot draw
28 A drawing is not final
29 Misunderstandings about Computing
32 Image Formats in this Book
33 Exercise 1.1 / Coding a mark
35 Exercise 1.2 / Draw from a function library

79 **Chapter 2 Structures**
79 From Dirty Marks to Lines, Shapes & Representations
90 A Taxonomy of Taxonomies of Lines
92 The existence taxonomy
102 The temporal taxonomy
108 The geometry-material taxonomy
110 The behavior scope taxonomy
114 The auto-what? Taxonomy
114 Exercise 2.1 / One mark, two readings
114 Exercise 2.2 / Line Finder
114 Exercise 2.3 / Line-Maker+Line-Finder+Line-Maker

173 **Chapter 3 Strategies**
174 From Willful Misuse to Opportunistic Surprise
174 Exercise 3.1 / Re-Code a Common Digital Tool
178 Misplacing Intelligence
178 Exercise 3.3 / Dumb Algorithm
182 The Computational Underlay
182 Exercise 3.4 / Non-Grid Graph Paper

215 **Chapter 4 Form**
215 Objects and Space / matter and machines
216 Depth & Projection
218 Exercise 4.1 / **Automatic Drawing**
218 Depth is Inherently Difficult
219 Depth Cues
220 Exercise 4.2 / The depthy line
220 Exercise 4.3 / Pursuit of flatness
221 Objects
222 Surfaces
223 Two and a half dimensional objects and pseudo-spaces
220 The Form of Ink

277 **Chapter 5 Futures**
279 Still on Paper, Still Difficult, Slower, Longer
280 Craft
281 Drawing Discipline
282 Making and Re-making Technology

287 **Appendix**
289 Index

To Anna.

Without you my drawings would have very boring titles. Thank you for the motivation.

Acknowledgments

For four years in a row, in the spring, I taught iterations of a computational drawing research studio at RISD in the Department of Architecture. Many of the ideas, frameworks, and theories in this book were fleshed out under the influence of the advanced students in these courses: *Computing Drawing: Animating the Thick Surface* (2013), *Computing Drawing: Inhabiting Surface* (2014), *Computing Drawing: Similarly Different Lines* (2015), and *Architecture Based On Drawing Buildings* (2016).

I am indebted to one colleague in particular, Chelsea Limbird, whose enthusiasm for experimental drawing methods, pedagogies and cultures amazes me. Her pivotal close read of this text was profoundly helpful and influential. I also want to acknowledge Amy Kulper for modeling a style of leadership, scholarship and disciplined inquiry that fueled this project.

Preface

Computing and drawing have intertwined histories. The first computer art was drawn. Limits on processing power and memory storage precluded pixels and images. Instead, computers were programmed to control machines that moved pens to make marks on paper.[1] Soon thereafter, the trajectories of computing and drawing diverged. The aim of this book, and the work within it, is to explore the implications of bringing them back together. Besides what computing and drawing mean, this book will explore what computing and drawing can collectively do. In most cases, merging computing and drawing involves merging cultures and methods. The territory within which we compute and the territory within which we draw are—with a few exciting exceptions—largely distinct. For these reasons, deciding to "make a drawing with a computer" or "compute in the space of the drawing" are no simple tasks. But they are exciting, productive, and creative.

I did not intend to set out on this line of inquiry. In January 2010 I was researching the role of computational media in the design process. My focus was animation, and I was seeking computational methods that might inform architecture by way of provoking animation to perform in ways other than the simulation or the diagram. I was programming using the Python programming language and animating the formation of path lines. In an online repository for drawing libraries in Python I stumbled upon Chiplotle,[2] a library for controlling HPGL-era pen plotters that were salvageable thanks to the open nature of the HPGL protocol and some other libraries that allowed serial-port communication via USB adapter. It looked interesting, and because we were between semesters I had the luxury of a tangent. I checked Craigslist and there happened to be one large format pen plotter for sale about ten miles from my apartment for $50—including pens and even some vintage paper. I would learn later that this was an extremely lucky and rare find. But at the time I thought, why not test it out? I remarked to a colleague that I'd give the pen plotter two weekends before moving back to my "serious" research. The first weekend went well. The Chiplotle developers were right, bleeding ink is incredibly seductive. The machines, beautifully engineered, were not exactly easy to use, but every challenge was an opportunity. Eight years have passed and nearly all my work relates to these drawing machines in some way.

This is not a textbook, nor is this a portfolio. However, like many in academia, my teaching and practice convolve. To some extent I bring my own interests to teaching, but much more significantly, my teaching influences my practice. As I mention later in the book, computer programming is like teaching to a computer. Moreover, teaching is ingrained in how I think about making. As a result, without even trying I often create pedagogical threads through my professional art practice. Though writing *about* my work is difficult for me, writing prompts or exercises that run parallel to it seems natural.

I've developed and experimented with many different methods for artists, designers, and architects learning to code. I think everyone should code, at least a little, and I *know* everyone can do it. However, the best way to learn in any creative field, no matter what type of learner one is, involves a messy integration with an existing creative practice. In that spirit, the exercises that make up the core of this book do not form a "learn to code" course. Rather, in concert with other technical resources, they will guide the reader on a path that keeps the technical aspect of coding while drawing tethered to creative inquiry.

If you're an experienced programmer, my aim in writing this book is to bring a theoretical perspective unique to my background within (and perhaps at times, near the boundaries of) the discipline of architecture. For the artist, architect, or designer who has dabbled in programming, you can dive right in with whatever environments and languages you're comfortable with. The algorithms are programming language agnostic. They can be implemented in object-oriented languages, procedural languages, web-based languages, scripting languages, and often can be performed without a digital computer at all. For the beginning programmer (and others), I've provided an appendix with some resources. Those suitable for the complete novice are tagged as such.

Additional Notes for the Beginning Programmer

Some advice: you already are 99% of the way to learning how to program. If you can read and write, you have the foundations already. Contemporary programming languages, along with libraries that augment their basic capacities, establish environments that require very little of the fussy and obscurely symbolic conditions you may be associating with the word, "code." Indeed, coding is a particularly misleading colloquialism for writing in a language that can be interpreted or executed by computers. That language can also be read (and interpreted and executed) by humans. Second, you can start making computational art immediately. You do not need to be an expert in computer programming before you can start applying computation to drawing. In fact, the opposite is true, learning to code within the context of drawing will help you—artist, architect, or designer—learn to code faster and better. It will be more fun and you'll feel the satisfaction of creation.

Architecture and Other Disciplines

This book often approaches drawing from within the disciplinary bounds of architecture. Readers within the discipline–architects and architecture students–will recognize particular concerns and questions: an interest in space and form, the question of scale, or the capacity of the drawing to become a work of architecture through mental inhabitation. Those are not unique to architecture, of course. Those outside the discipline may not even recognize the quirks, hang-ups and particular obsessions of architecture when they appear, and may be surprised at the lack of buildings in this book. Rather than strictly define when something is architectural vs. artistic it is largely avoided with the hope that readers, architects, and others may assert or resist their own disciplines at their own discretion.

Start

In the spirit of exercises that serve a practical purpose and fuel discourse, here's a warm up one to start.

Exercise 0.1 *Make Some Lists*

List all the reasons you draw. List all the reasons you write code. What items are on one list and not the other? How would drawing/coding in your practice be different if their roles were more similar?

Notes

1. As a note of clarification, first, "draw" in this context is defined as lines marked on paper as opposed to pixels rendered in a digital image format. One account of the '60s era cultural clash between architects and computer scientists at the Architectural Academy in London can be found in Paul Brown's *White Heat Cold Logic: British Computer Art 1960-1980.* Cambridge, MA: MIT Press, 2008. Grant D. Taylor's *When the Machine Made Art: The Troubled History of Computer Art*, documents the first winners of the trade journal *Computers and Automation* "Computer Art Contest" of 1963. The winners, scientists at the US Army Ballistic Research Laboratories, produced "Splatter Pattern" using a "Dataplotter," a massive table-sized apparatus first released by "Electronic Associates Incorporated" in the 1950s that produced small drawings by moving a pen across a fixed piece of paper based on analog input–which could be generated by computer.
2. Víctor Adán and Douglas Repetto, "Chiplotle: An HPGL (Hewlett-Packard Graphics Language) Python API," Chiplotle! , accessed February 09, 2018, http://sites.music.columbia.edu/cmc/chiplotle/

Chapter 1
Definitions

This is a book about the hybridity of computing and drawing. It would seem prudent, therefore, to begin by addressing, simply, "what is drawing?" and "what is computing?" However, both of those terms are associated with contested histories, multiple creative and scientific cultures, and various colloquial and literal definitions, which are often at odds with each other. Both computing and drawing are disciplines in their own right, and both terms define sub-cultures within the discipline of architecture. As a result, it is not possible to exhaustively explore both terms here, though it is possible for the hybridity between computing and drawing to bring clarity to each in terms of method, meaning, and knowledge.

Many of the most complete tomes about drawing in art and architectural history do not presume a single definition of such a vast and ever-evolving term. The gold standard for such a tome is Deanna Petherbridge's *The Primacy of Drawing, Histories and Theories of Practice.*[1] Petherbridge, an artist and curator as well as a scholar, agrees, noting at the onset that,

> "It would be reasonable to expect that a book devoted to the exploration of drawing should begin with an authoritative definition of its subject. However, my examination of the many definitions of drawing, both contemporary and historical, has proved to me the futility of attempting such a task. Any formula would have to encompass the indefinable status and contradictory aspects of drawing, and therefore would immediately dissolve into a web of disclaimers."[2]

The difficulty involved when demarcating a clean line between painting and drawing, for example, is a perennial discussion. In contemporary discourse, matters are further complicated by computing's looming presence over the evolving definition of drawing. This presence pulls drawing away from matters of critical inquiry into an un-winnable and often personal debate over technology verses tradition. Thanks to the rise of digital technology, drawing is often understood as at risk of being supplanted by the computer. That discourse only serves, ironically, to dilute the already open boundary of "drawing." A 2012 symposium at the Yale School of Architecture titled, "Is Drawing Dead?" exposed many strong opinions on the future and past of representational practice in architecture,[3] but a working definition was never articulated by the participants. Various meanings could be inferred by the speakers and their work, but their wide variation rendered the eponymous question of the symposium moot. Effectively, many of the participants were implying, "your way—the old way—of drawing is dead, but my way of drawing is alive." At one point, a member of the audience held up a pencil case while protesting computers. His defensive comments seemed to reference drafting rather than drawing. (But isn't drafting a kind of drawing?) A member of the panel clarified, he was more concerned with sketching.

Further adding fuel to the fire of ambiguity surrounding the definition of drawing is rooted in language. The previous paragraph could have used multiple forms of "draw" in place of *"demarcating," "pulls," "articulated," and "rendered"* to describe actions and relationships that have nothing to do with lines on paper. At this moment it can be tempting to indulge in a cliché: a trip to the dictionary. However, the Oxford English Dictionary lists seventeen definitions of draw as a noun,[4] seventy-five as a verb,[5] and even more for "drawing" as noun and adjective (distinct from the verb form). All are relevant, even those that deal with archery and horse racing, and many are delightfully oblique to one another. Consider two verb forms of draw, "To bear, endure, suffer, undergo,"[6] and "To attract by moral force, persuasion, inclination, etc.; to induce to come (to a place); to attract by sympathy (to a person)."[7] One can hear drawing, as in a "drawing set," used in a professional architectural context to refer to digital output on paper. Drawing is an ordered collection of lines. Drawing is the pulling of an idea into material being. A drawing is an abstraction or a drawing is a neutral truth. A drawing is form.

Attempting to clarify any of those definitions leads us to Petherbridge's web. However, without limits, it's easy to see how almost anything can be a drawing. While Petherbridge proceeds by identifying a drawing continuum, another option is the definition of drawing not in terms of what it can be, mean, or do, but what it cannot.

What drawing is not and what computing cannot do

The choice to define in the negative, to create anti-definitions, is itself a philosophical and ideological position. It implies a recognition that either the term in question, at the moment, drawing, covers more ground than that which is not drawing, or that the term has become so loose that it is no longer possible to create a single working definition. Though the intellectual exercise of defining what drawing is not can become operative, from a cultural standpoint it nonetheless risks offending, because drawing—in most of its creative forms—is an elite activity that requires skill. The voice of the enforcer that proclaims, "That's not a drawing," is likely to be received as insult rather than critique because drawing places contemporary practice on an historic continuum. Furthermore, drawing implies difficulty. Drawing's anti-definitions are potentially problematic, conceits, and incomplete thought experiments. Nonetheless, they are necessary.

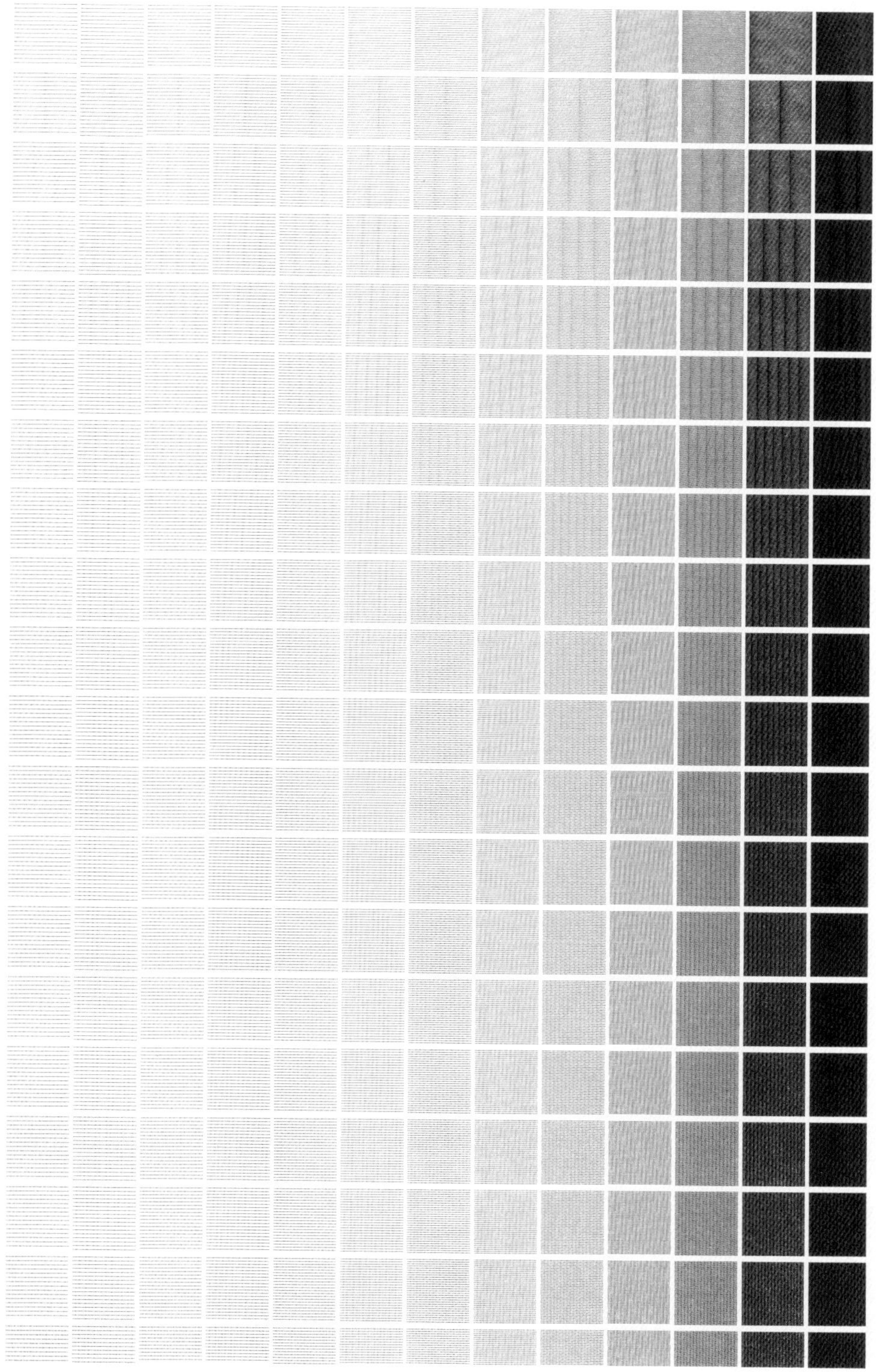

A drawing cannot be edited

Or, more specifically, it cannot be edited down or operated on, only built up. When one marks on paper, for example, one can erase those marks, but that is actually another kind of marking that involves the interaction of material. The pencil eraser is very different from what we might think of in digital software when we use the "undo" function. Although drawing involves the gradual evolution of effects and content, this adjustment is a matter of building up rather than editing down. Think about the difference, for example, between the layering up of many marks to refine the perceived geometry of a line as opposed to the editing of control points of a curve in digital drafting software. When drawing, one cannot post facto adjust the start point, end point, pressure, or speed of a mark. Once the mark is made, there is no going back.

This anti-definition is closely aligned with another term, "model." Both models and drawings can serve as representations, but while models exist for the purposes of operation, drawings exist for the purposes of perception. Most so called "digital drawings," in design software, are in fact models of lines, not drawings at all. What we see on the screen is not the actual drawing, but a stand in that allows us to manipulate, edit, create and delete lines. This brings some clarity about the role of drawing, but how does it help in practice? Thinking about drawing in this way suggests that computing technology can augment, but not replace, drawing technology. Rather than construct a virtual drawing and "print" it out, digital media can provide a model that can be used to compute, simulate or resolve geometry or procedures that can lead to or analyze drawing.

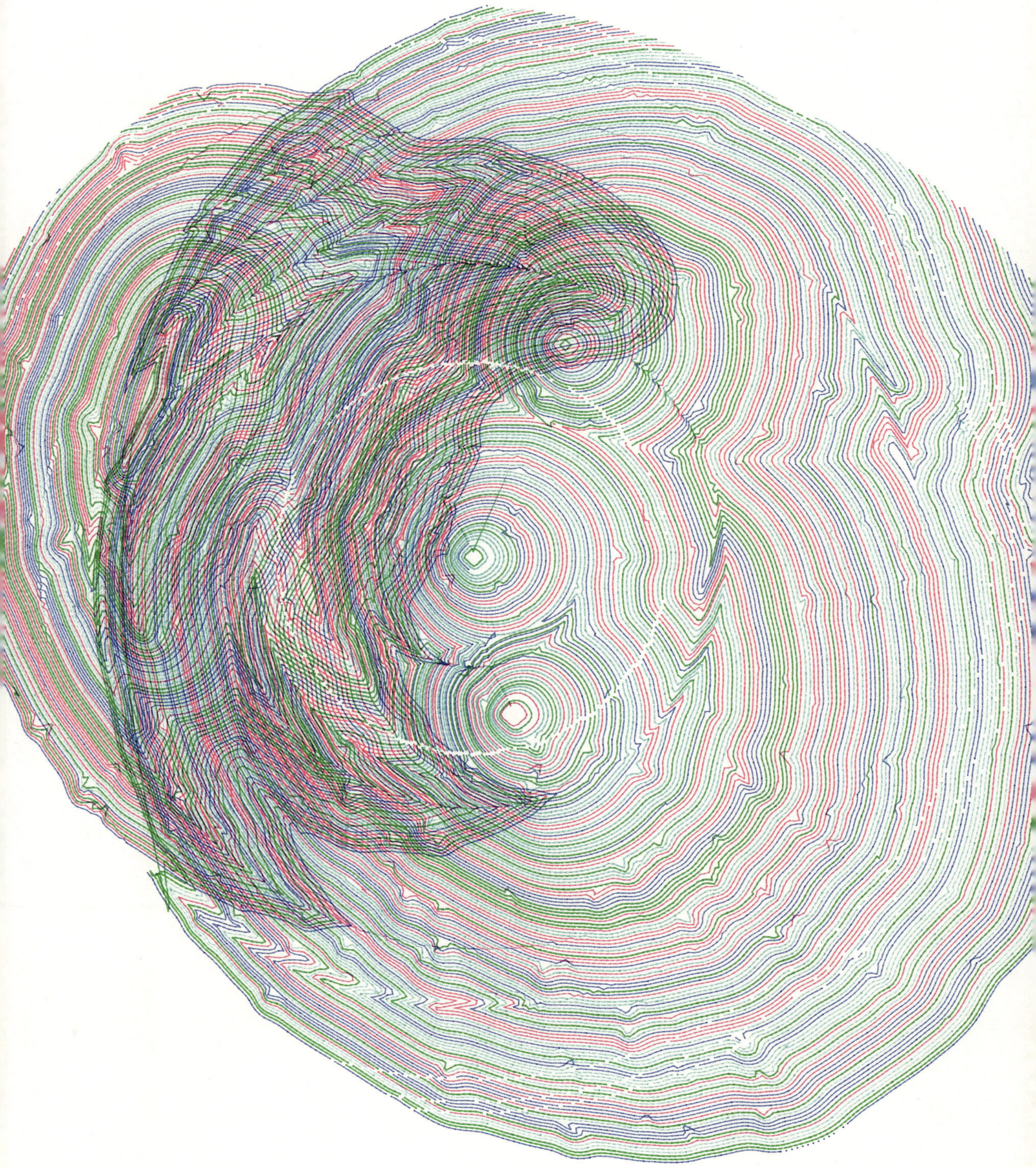

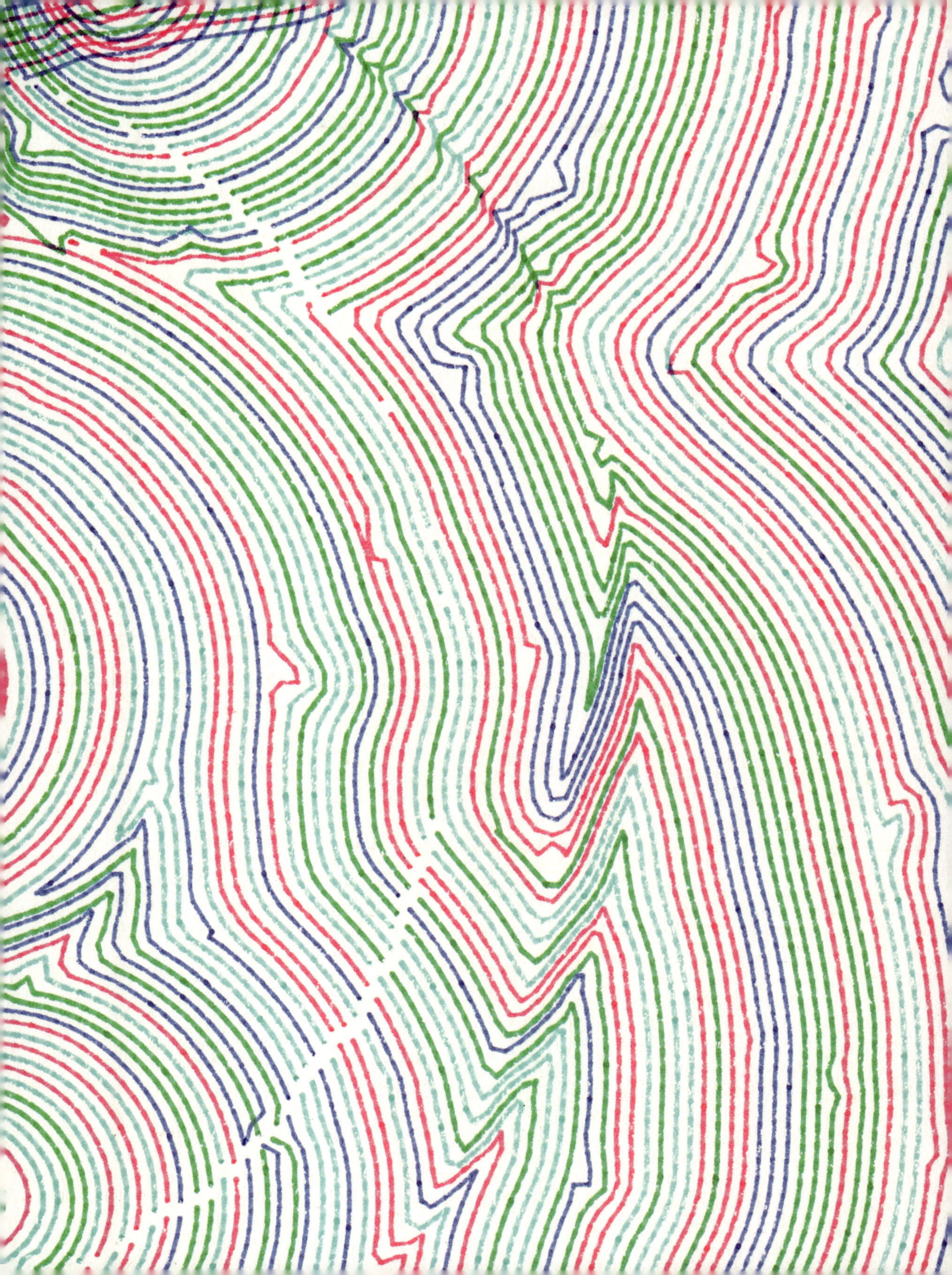

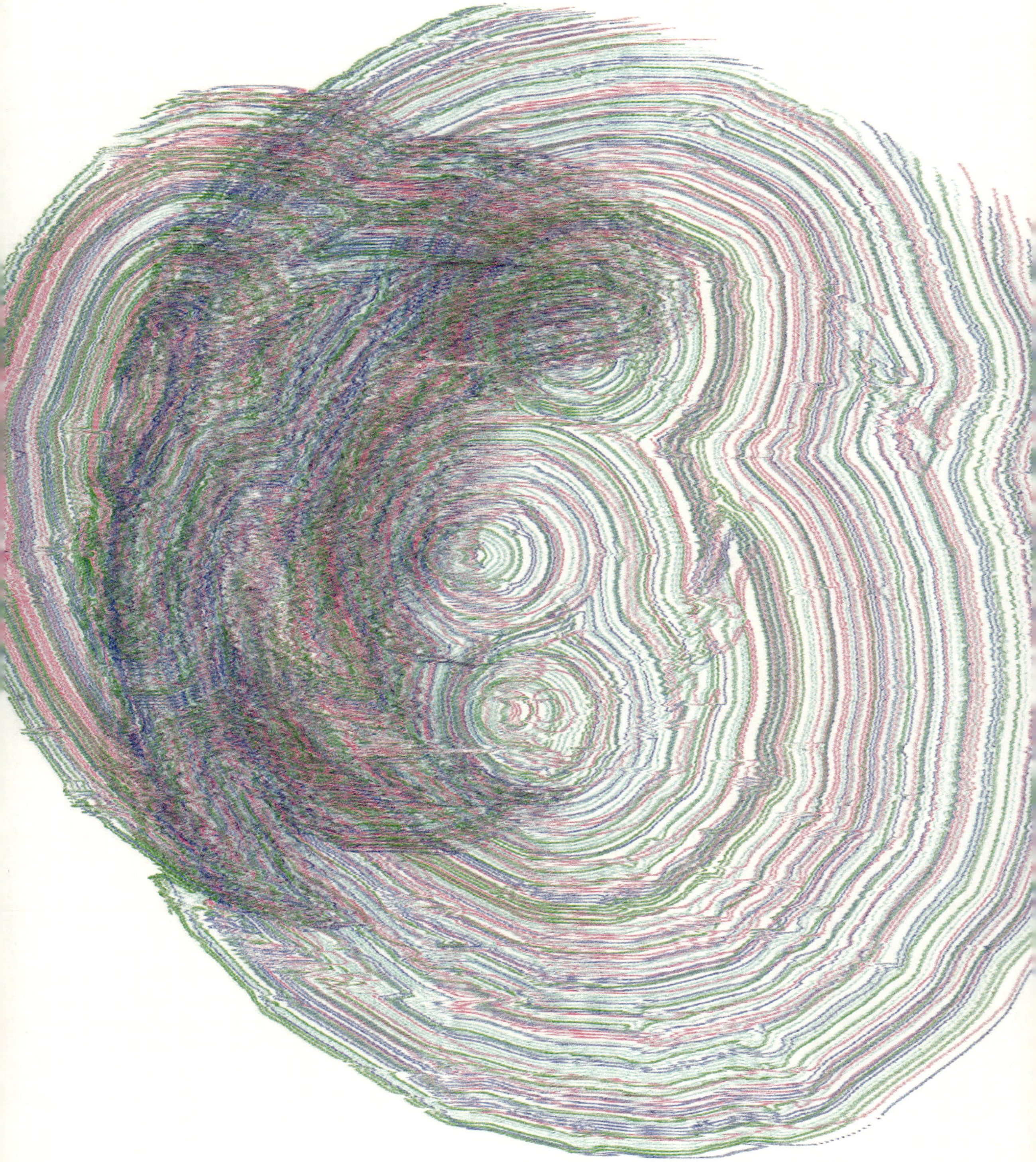

A computer cannot draw

A corollary of the "drawing cannot be edited" anti-definition is that drawings exist to be perceived, and that perception is often a key part of a drawing's making cycle. If drawing is understood as a formation, then a reading of a drawing must form in the mind, including the mind of the drawing maker. The drawing is never merely the collection of matter. In this way, a drawing is unlike a building, it must be read, or at least interpreted, for it to function. Many so-called "drawing machines," even those that process data from sensors, produce drawing matter, but because the apparatus does not have an internal representation of a reading of the drawing, the apparatus is not drawing.

Computers are neither fully autonomous nor do they meet most of the many definitions of intelligence.[8] This is not an anti-computational perspective, but an optimistic reality check. Computers are programmed by humans. A drawing can be mediated by computer, but ultimately a drawing is a human activity. This is one key difference between drawings and images. Ultimately, a drawing cannot be reduced to discrete elements, unlike the digital image, which is organized by pixels. Many millions of digital images are generated for computers by other computers. Even though programmed by humans, the majority of images exist to transmit information to computers and will never be seen directly by human eyes.

The pixels of the scan have begun to be sorted within each row based on hue.

A drawing is not final

All drawings are works in progress. Even when a drawing is done it's open to interpretation. The ambiguity of a line leaves open the capacity for multiple interpretations. This means that if one is working to "get it right," articulate something perfectly, or achieve an exact result, one may be "rendering," "communicating," "computing," or "simulating," but one is not drawing. Does this anti-definition mean that drawing can not be a disciplinary practice, that drawing is always in service of something else, a thing to think with, prepare with, or work out prior to the ultimate work? No, it does not. Drawing can certainly function as a discipline, but such a disciplinary practice would seem to require a conception of a work, or a project broader than an individual drawing.

The anti-definitions of drawing posited here expose a friction with contemporary ways of practicing architecture, art, or design. The non-operative nature of drawing would seem to make it less valuable to architects than a model. Its capacity to surprise can disrupt a goal-oriented design process; yet the reality that drawing always involves human engagement means that drawing demands a degree of design intention, especially with respect to drawing's position in the linage of a project.

Misunderstandings about Computing

Computing is also a complex and often misused term. Though the definition itself does not engender the same ambiguity as drawing, computing is often conflated with the personal computing era. Computing was used in literature as early as 1579,[9] which reinforces the notion that the kind of processing, calculation, procedures, reckoning, or reasoning that are normally associated with personal computers need not involve any machines whatsoever, and it certainly need not involve a digital personal computer. In architectural discourse, the digital turn often accurately describes the strategies and techniques associated with mainstream software and mass-customization that emerged for architects in the '90s and soon thereafter become ubiquitous. Mario Carpo uses an analogy of identification of currency to saliently position the digitally made relative to the machine made and hand made.

"The signature, the banknote, and the credit card: when objects are handmade, as a signature is, variability in the process of production generates differences and similarities between copies and identification is based on visual resemblance; when objects are machine-made as a banknote is, mass-produced, exactly repeatable mechanical imprints generate standardized products and identification is based on visual identicalness; when objects are digitally made, as are the latest machine-readable or chip-based credit cards, identification is based on the recognition of hidden patterns, on computational algorithms, or on other non-visual features."[10]

This analogy is unusually prescient to the realm of drawing, in that the digital marks the end of the visual, suggesting that a return trajectory to a re-engagement with the hand might flow in reverse, through machine-based production. In writing about the rise of electronic media in 1964, Marshall McLuhan posits,

"The effect of electronic technology had first been anxiety. Now it appears to create boredom. We have been through the three stages of alarm, resistance, and exhaustion that occur in every disease or stress of life, whether individual or collective. At least, our exhausted slump after the first encounter with the electric has inclined us to expect new problems."[11]

Can the same pattern apply to the state of digital media? Currently, conceptual practices that profess to be post-digital dominate much of the discourse, a signal that architecture has moved on from the digital as topic, digital as provocation, or predominantly digital project (aka "paperless") as a feat. Perhaps we are bored. However, in recognizing the propensity for the post-digital to describe an aesthetic rather than an idea,[12] and by contrast to that reaction, this book uses computation rather than digital to make a connection to ideas and methods that pre-date mainstream use of digital technology in architecture, art, and design.

Another reason this book uses the term computation and embraces the cultural, historical, and ideological frameworks that go with it involves the dichotomy that digital media tends to bring to discourse. There is no doubt that digital media changed architecture and design. One can debate whether this change constitutes a revolution or a relatively minor shift in methods and practice. One can debate whether this change was positive, negative, or neutral. Unfortunately, these debates tend to occur with strong gravity. The digital turn happened relatively fast in architecture, over the course of less than a generation. Today, it's not uncommon for an institution to be made up of those who were educated and started to practice before, during, and after the digital turn. These three groups can have dramatically different takes on the role and meaning of digital tools and media. The debates that arise both from these frictions, while academically or intellectually interesting (and necessary from an historical perspective), do little to inform or motivate the way we make. This avoidance of the "digital versus x" (where x can be manual, transnational, hand, analog, or physical) does align with some of the principles of post-digital practice. However, this book deviates from the idea that moving on from an obsession over the digital means moving on from focused inquiry and attention towards craft, media, and methods.

It is important to note that contemporary computation does often involve the personal computer and is often digital in nature. The pixel-based image—a model, not a drawing, as has already been outlined—does play a substantial role in this work. The digital will be explored in depth in this chapter as a foil to the line and, later, pixel-based representations will transform, animate, and activate material drawings. But in this work the digital image comes before and after the material drawings. The drawings here are computational in nature but not inherently digital and they are not about being digital. Furthermore, they do not aim to participate in an argument about the role of the digital.

The definition-oriented discourse continues now with a focus on pixels and their relationship to drawings. Likely, readers will be comfortable with the idea and nature of a pixel, a term that was coined to mean "picture element."[13] It is hard to function in a digital world without encountering a pixel, even for those who do not work in the visual arts. Though pixels have no dimension, their legibility is related to the size they are rendered. If drawing is distinct from a model in that it cannot be edited, we are most likely to encounter a drawing as a material artifact. The material can me moved around (including off the page) with new marks, but we cannot edit the marks on the terms of their perception. Pixels exist for just the opposite purpose—they can be changed infinitely with no implications on the appearance of the image.

Every computer screen, that is every collection of pixels, is a moving (or movable) image. In this sense, it can never be a drawing. As personal computers become more powerful, the quantity of pixels increases. Though increasingly rare, early computer artists operated on individual pixels. Computer programming functions that do nothing other than set or reference single pixels can be extremely valuable relative to drawings. Though digital images are not drawings, they can expose, transform or inform drawings because they are nimble in ways material cannot be: they are easily transformed, parsed, and transmitted. Pixels, in their nature, are elements of images, not elements of drawing. Even the highest resolution digital image, a digital scan of a material drawing for example, might capture detail finer than the human eye can perceive, but is structurally different from the original drawing. But this is not reason to shun the digital. Rather, the opposite is true: it is precisely because of this contrast in nature that we will find pixels a productive ally in drawing discourse.

Image Formats in this Book

There are two kinds of graphics in this book: vector graphics and pixel-based graphics. Upon even a quick skim, however, readers might identify three types of imagery: first, the crisp lines of the vector graphics, which are the result of file formats that describe geometry and appearances of shapes. These formats passed from author to graphic designer to printer without ever being translated into pixels. (Only at the last moment was the geometry converted into droplets of ink.) Second, the results of the pixel-based algorithms, which, because of the pedagogical thread to this project, are purposefully low resolution so as to expose their structure. These grossly pixelated images harken back to an era of personal computer technology in which the relatively low resolution of even high end screens were emblematic of a particular technological moment. Rendered lines at irregular angles manifest the pixel grid in their patterned steps. Mitigated early on by anti-aliasing,[14] this condition is still present but largely unperceivable at extremely high resolutions. The third kind of graphic is the material drawings made by computer-controlled pen plotters. However, within the scope of this book, the actual drawings do not appear. Rather, they are scans that capture the originals at the highest resolution possible. This technicality might not seem to be worth mentioning, but because these graphics are collections of pixels—models—that represent a drawing, they can be edited as such. This becomes an opportunity when the two-dimensional structure of the pixel-based image misaligns with the order of the drawing. The pixel based image, for example, is conducive to linear sorting of rows and columns based on color values in the image. The drawing on page 24 is subject to precisely that process.

The final term that requires defining is algorithm. This book will focus on the craft of writing computer code, but it is not the programming language—or the literal code—that is important, but the underlying procedures, logic, and rules. Those constitute an algorithm. At least in theory, algorithms are independent of programming language, even computers. Sol LeWitt, for example, wrote hundreds of algorithms for drawings intended for humans to execute with pen or pencil.[15] Algorithms have a practical benefit in this context because we can transmit procedures, logic, and rules without the need for author or reader to be fluent in the same programming language. More importantly, it is the algorithm that gives rise to new kinds of thinking that change and expand what a drawing can be.

Writing algorithms does require the use of some computational vocabulary unique to the action being performed. This is a situation in which drawing and computing are inherently aligned and sympathetic to one another. Both drawing and computing are at their foundations a set of actions. When coding, the actions are called functions. (Some languages call them methods.) Functions, essentially, do something based on some input or prompting. It is likely that drawing without a computer, especially drawing as part of a disciplined practice, already involves thinking about marks in terms of consistent families or types. A mark may have a different appearance, dimension or geometry than another mark of the same type, but being in the same family means that it shares some of the same traits, orders, or behavioral logic. Thinking this way about drawing is inherently computational.

In the first exercise of this book, computational thinking will become codified by simply writing that logic down as a function. The only prerequisite for this exercise is to consider, "What are the fundamental actions necessary to draw?" This question is not meant to have a universal answer. In fact, the degree to which answers to that question may vary from person to person reflects a principle position of this pedagogy: the apparatuses we build are not making drawings for us, we are making drawings with them.

Exercise 1.1 *Coding a mark*

Reference an existing drawing. Without concern for the composition of the marks in that drawing, articulate, in plain English, the underlying logic of each kind of mark as a text document, a library of drawing actions necessary to create the marks in that work. Each mark function entry in the library should include: a name; the inputs, if any, that the function requires including a description of the inputs, whether any are optional, what are the limits or bounds of the inputs, what is the format of the input; a description of what the function produces; and finally, an example of the mark. Keep in mind that the text library is a collection of the rules and actions necessary to make the drawing, which is very different from a description of the drawing.

As much as the first exercise is designed to correspond neatly to the way many artists, architects, and designers think about drawing, there are also likely some aspects to this exercise that will feel alien to many. Before dissecting the meaning of this exercise, consider some very basic examples. A straight mark might take two coordinates, a start point and an end point, as input. The speed at which the mark is made might significantly affect its appearance. Therefore, a third input might then be the speed of the marking in inches per second. It might be named "hatch." Another kind of mark might take a list of points as an input and travel between them. Yet another kind of mark might be radial in nature, organized in terms of radii and angular length.

Perhaps a mark changes thickness at certain moments. Perhaps the mark is governed by goals or patterns rather than determined by reference points. There's no limit to the detail, or simplicity of any mark-making function. So how do we evaluate the functions? One answer would be to say that we shouldn't. Instead, we should focus on the drawing made with the functions. The elegance of the algorithm or the nuance of the name of the function are ultimately immaterial compared to the work—the drawing itself. Thinking through this further, what if the library of functions is the work?

An ordered collection of marks is certainly one definition of drawing. Even if the text library is separated from the outcome of that text, which is a clear and valid distinction to make, most will find that they can defend and discuss the creative decisions made in authoring the text. A group critique of mark-making function libraries is possible. This small acknowledgment has large implications: writing functions is a creative act. Occasionally, one might even stumble on, or purposefully write, a function that can be read as poetry. For this reason, the term used to describe the text written by a programmer, "code," is not always apt. Although sometimes arcane and symbolic, the text written to control an apparatus—whether human or computer—is meant to be read and understood. To a non-programmer, computer code can appear to obfuscate, but its actual purpose is to explain. In some cases, it can evoke.

Regardless of the status we ascribe to it, the mark-making library is analogous to many libraries available to the programmer. Programming languages have built in libraries that perform functions for marking and many other tasks. Even the most expert programmer does not use their own code exclusively. Libraries written by others are an essential part of creating a drawing (or any work). Though exercises 1.1 and 1.2 prompt the exploration of computational drawing without a digital computer, when moving into coding digitally, most artists and designers will start with an existing library for marking. Even still, none of the functions are fixed. They can be extended, modified, augmented, or custom-created to suit specific or personal intentions. The appendix of this book lists multiple existing libraries for a variety of programming languages that you might want to explore.

With marking functions defined—by oneself or provided by others—those functions can be used without worrying about their inner logic. This separation into "layers," the inner layer of the function and the outer layer in which the function is deployed, or called, is referred to as "abstraction" in computer science. At the layer outside a marking function, one can create marks by calling the function and not consider, or re-write, the code within it. Another way to think of this layering of abstraction in the context of drawing is that each mark need not be a reinvention of a new mark type. Once a kind of mark is defined, many instances of that mark can be made without invention of new mark types. As a corollary, the definition of a mark is not the same as the creation of a mark. The outer layer—the "calling"—of functions is necessary to deploy the actions that have been articulated.

Both conditional statements and loops allow functions and other operations to be performed based on a logical order. If you are fluent in English, you already implicitly understand how these constructs work. Similar logic is built into our spoken and written language. A conditional statement is an if-then argument: if a condition is true, then do something. A variant on the if-then statement is the if-then-else statement, which, in more verbose terms can be articulated as, if a condition is true, then do something—otherwise—do something else. In an if-then statement, the "do something" part can be any number of things, it could be one line of code calling one of your marking functions or multiple lines of code that do anything else. A "while" construct is shorthand for while a condition is true, do something. A very basic drawing algorithm might read something like:

```
While the number of marks made so far is less than 100, "make a mark".
```

Of course, make a mark, could be any one of your marking functions.

Exercise 1.2 *Draw from a function library*

Using nothing more than loops and conditional statements, call your marking functions from your library by writing in plain English. Then, make another drawing using a library made by someone else.

The algorithm just given as an example is simple enough to write out as a sentence. However, when the algorithms get even slightly more layered, with loops within loops and multiple functions within each conditional, it becomes necessary to organize the code a bit more. Different programming languages do this in different ways. This book does not adhere to the conventions of any one language. Instead, algorithms are written something called "pseudocode," which uses plain English, but is structured like a programming language. Indentations are used to group code together in segments associated with each conditional or loop. For example, the example algorithm in pseudocode is:

```
while the number of marks is less than 100
  mark
```

If the marking function was called, say, "squiggle" and it took as input to numbers, an average radius and a length, we can write:

```
while the number of marks is less than 100
  squiggle (10, 100)
```

How would "the number of marks" be calculated? It is important to remember that unlike humans, the computer does not "see" marks or understand what a drawing is. The programmer needs to keep track of the number of marks made in order to compare that number to a datum. So when implemented, most likely the code would look something like this:

```
set count to 0
while count is less than 100:
  squiggle (10, 100)
  increment count by 1
```

Count is a variable created by the author of the code. It starts at zero, and each time the loop iterates, it increases by one, effectively counting how many marks have been created.

An example that is slightly more complex and uses if-then statements and loops together:

```
set count to 0
while count is less than 100:
  if count is even, then
    squiggle (10, 100)
  else
    squiggle (5, 100)
  increment count by 1
```

To conclude this chapter, consider some custom computational marks:

```
A squiggle is created in terms of radius, length, and the following actions
  currentLength starts at 0
  currentAngle starts at 0
```

```
  points starts as an empty list
  x starts as radius
  y starts at 0
  while currentLength is less than or equal to length:
    newX is set to radius × cos(currentAngle)
    newY is set to radius × sin(currentAngle)
    add the (newX, newY) to points list
    currentLength is set to be the length of a line through points list
    currentAngle is modified by a random value between 1 and 5
    radius is modified by a random value between -3 and 3
  create a smooth line through the points list
```

```
A variablyThickLine is created in terms of startPoint, endPoint and a list of thinMoments
  vector is established between startPoint and endPoint
  hatchMark is made at the start of vector and oriented parallel to vector
  for each thickMoment
    determine rotationAmount by dividing 180 by the number of copies needed
    while the thickMoment has not been reached
      copy hatchMark in the direction of vector and rotate by rotationAmount
  determine rotationAmount to reach endPoint
    while the endPoint has not been reached
      copy hatchMark in the direction of vector and rotate by rotationAmount
```

```
A drunkenAntPath is created in terms of startPoint, numberDrinks, and length
  create currentPoint based on startPoint
  set currentLength to 0
  create velocity and set it to be a random vector (x, y) of amplitude 1
  create acceleration and set it to 0
  create angularAcceleration and set it to be a random number between -1 and 1
  while currentLength is less than length
    create nextPoint by adding velocity to currentPoint
    adjust currentLength by adding the amplitude of velocity
    create a line between currentPoint and nextPoint
    set currentPoint to the same value as nextPoint
    adjust velocity by rotating velocity by angularAcceleration
    scale velocity so that its amplitude is its previous amplitude + acceleration
    adjust acceleration by adding (random value between -.1 and .1) × numberDrinks
    adjust angularAcceleration by adding a random value between -1 and 1
```

a *driftingDashPolyline* is created in terms of a list of *points, dash, gap, driftTime,* and *trace*

(note that *points* is a list of x and y values, *dash* is a number that refers to the length of the dash segment, *gap* is a number that refers to the length of the gap between the dashes, *driftTime* is the amount of time recorded in steps that the segments are allowed to drift, and *trace* is a true or false value that the indicates whether the segments should be copied as the move)

```
create an empty list of segments
between each sequential pair of points
  set currentPoint to be the first point of the pair
  determine vector from the first point to the second point of the pair
  calculate dashVector by scaling vector so that its length is dash
  calculate gapVector by scaling vector so that its length is gap
  while currentPoint is far from the second point of the pair
    create a line from currentPoint to currentPoint+dashVector
    insert line into segments list
    adjust currentPoint by adding dashVector and adding gapVector
for driftTime number of steps
  for each segment in list of segments
    if trace then
      make a copy of segment and move it slightly in a random direction
      replace segment it in the list with the copy
    else
      move segment slightly in a random direction
```

Notes

1. Petherbridge, Deanna. *The Primacy of Drawing, Histories and Theories of Practice*. New Haven: Yale University Press, 2010.
2. Ibid., 3.
3. *Is Drawing Dead?* Yale School of Architecture, New Haven, February 9, 2012. In case there was any doubt about drawing's accused murderer, the symposium material noted, "However, as the promise of digital technology is increasingly fulfilled by sophisticated methodologies, such as parametric modeling, computational design, digital design and fabrication, and Building Information Management (BIM), drawing has come under stress and become ill-defined and moribund."
4. "draw, n." OED Online. February 2018. Oxford University Press. http://0-www.oed.com.librarycat.risd.edu/viewdictionaryentry/Entry/57533 (accessed January 05, 2018).
5. "draw, v." OED Online. February 2018. Oxford University Press. http://0-www.oed.com.librarycat.risd.edu/view/Entry/ 57534 (accessed January 05, 2018).
6. Ibid.
7. Ibid.
8. Legg, Shane, and Marcus Hutter. "A Collection of Definitions of Intelligence." In *Advances in Artificial General Intelligence: Concepts, Architectures and Algorithms*, 17–24. IOS Press, 2007.
9. "If men respect their fickle date of time/ Now in delight, then drowned in dark annoy/ Computing Age with their unbridled time/ Of all estates how brittle is their Joy." Is quoted in "compute, v." OED Online. March 2018. Oxford University Press. http://0-www.oed.com.librarycat.risd.edu/view/Entry/37974?rskey=sWruE9&result=1&isAdvanced=false (accessed April 09, 2018) from A. Munday's, Mirrour Mutabilitie, 1579.
10. Carpo, Mario. *The Alphabet and the Algorithm*. Cambridge, MA: MIT Press, 2011, 4.
11. McLuhan, Marshall. *Understanding Media: The Extensions of Man*. Cambridge: MIT Press, 1994, 26.
12. Carpo, Mario. "Post-Digital 'Quitters': Why the Shift Toward Collage Is Worrying." Metropolis. March 26, 2018. Accessed March 30, 2018. http://www.metropolismag.com/architecture/post-digital-collage/
13. Lyon, Richard F. "A Brief History of 'Pixel'." IS&T/SPIE Symposium on Electronic Imaging, January 15, 2006.
14. Leler, William J. "Human Vision, Anti-aliasing, and the Cheap 4000 Line Display." ACM SIGGRAPH Computer Graphics 14, no. 3 (1980): 308–13. doi:10.1145/965105.807509.
15. LeWitt, Sol. *Sol LeWitt: 100 Views*. Edited by Susan Cross and Denise Markintosh. North Adams: MASS MoCA in Yale University Press, 2009. This book accompanies an exhibit of LeWitt's wall drawings at a MASS MoCA installation, in which the drawings, and the drawing instructions are both given appropriate treatment.

OPPOSITE The pixels of the scan are partially re-arranged as a result of a sorting algorithm that is about halfway complete.

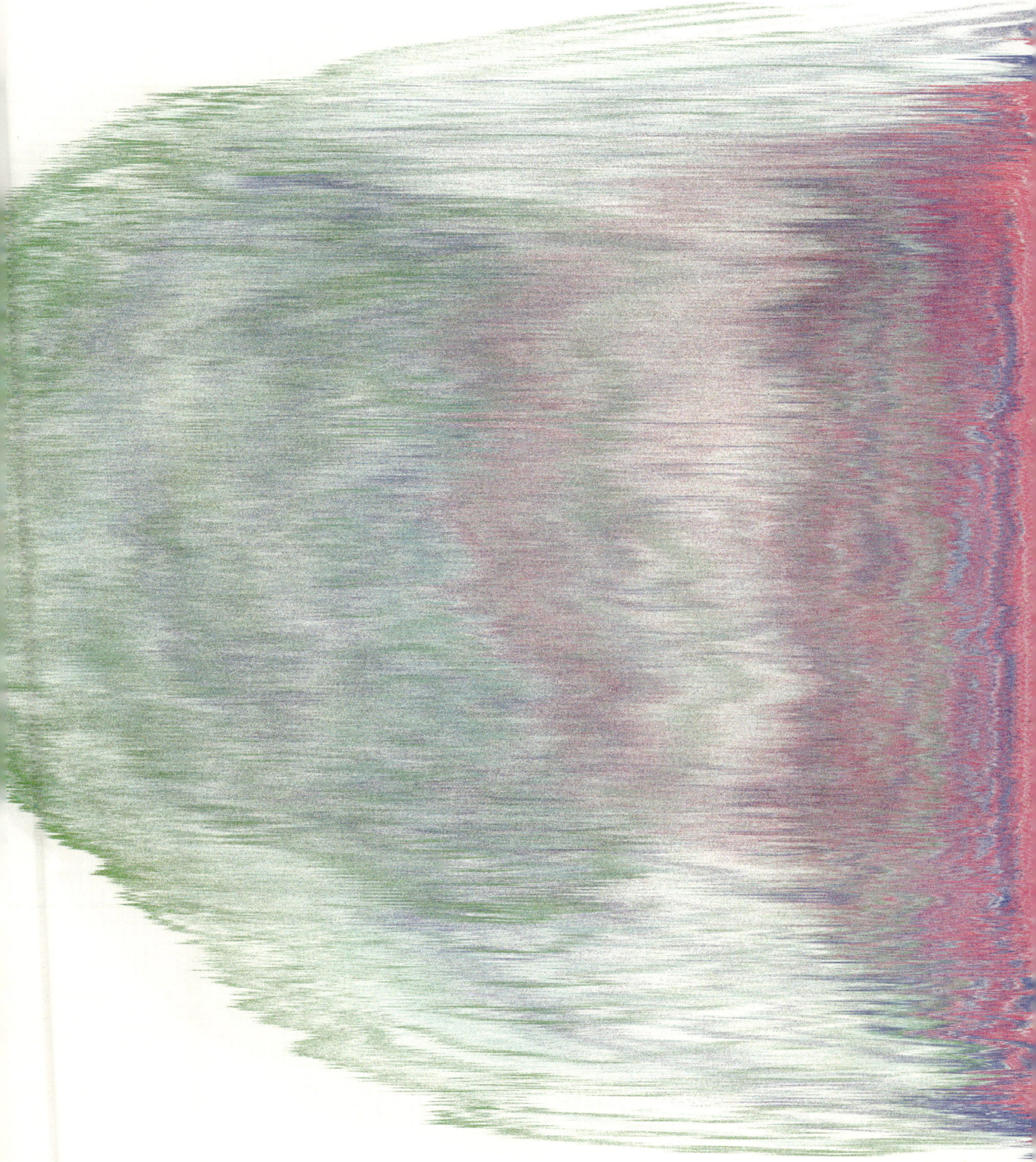

ABOVE The pixels of the scan are are completely sorted within each row.

OPPOSTE PAGE The pixels of the scan are now sorted by hue within each column.

A squiggle.

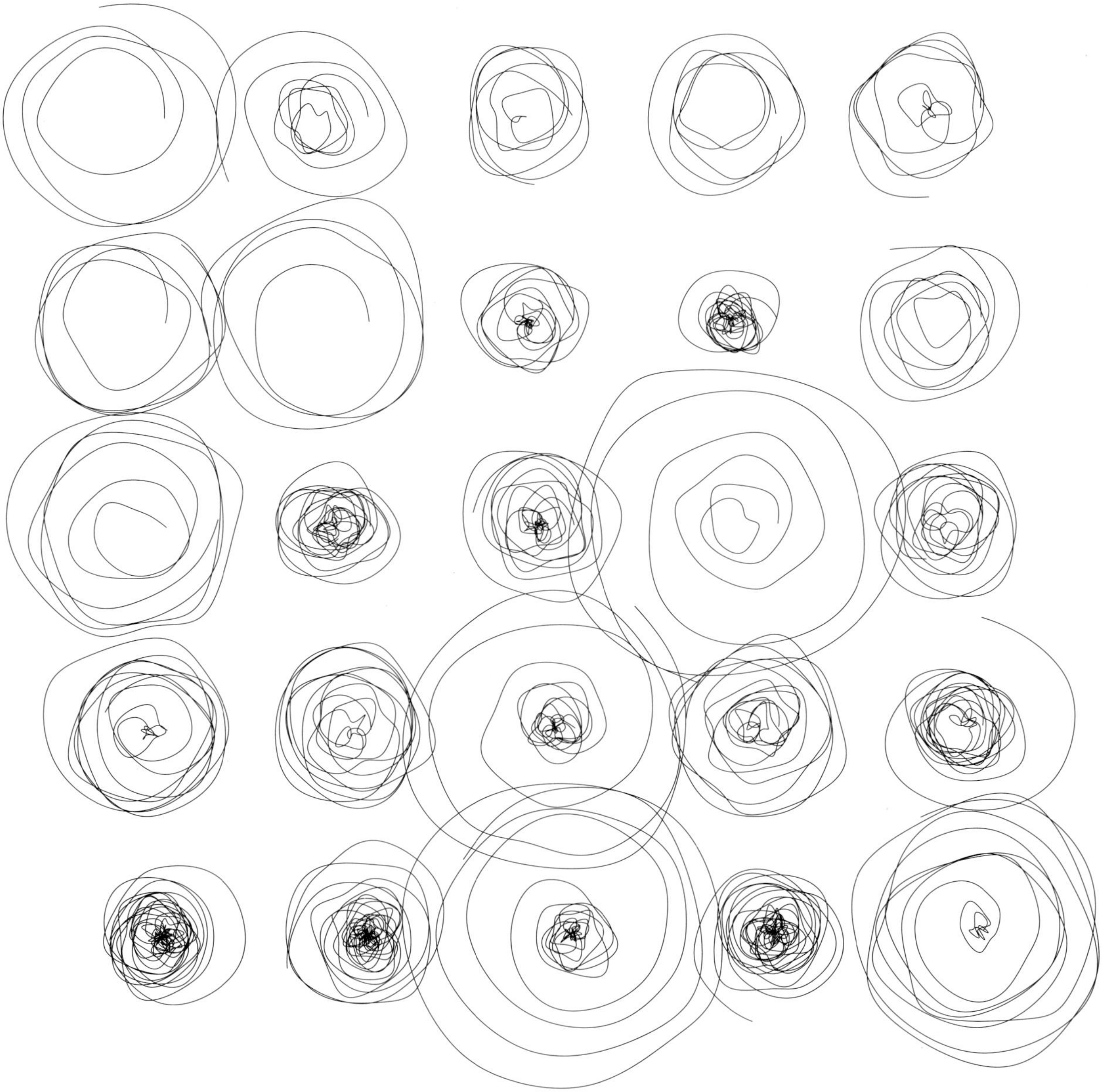

A collection of squiggles, each created with the identical function given different input.

TOP A *variablyThickLine* with evenly spaced *thinMoments*.

BOTTOM A collection of *variablyThickLines* with a range of quantity and spacing of *thinMoments*.

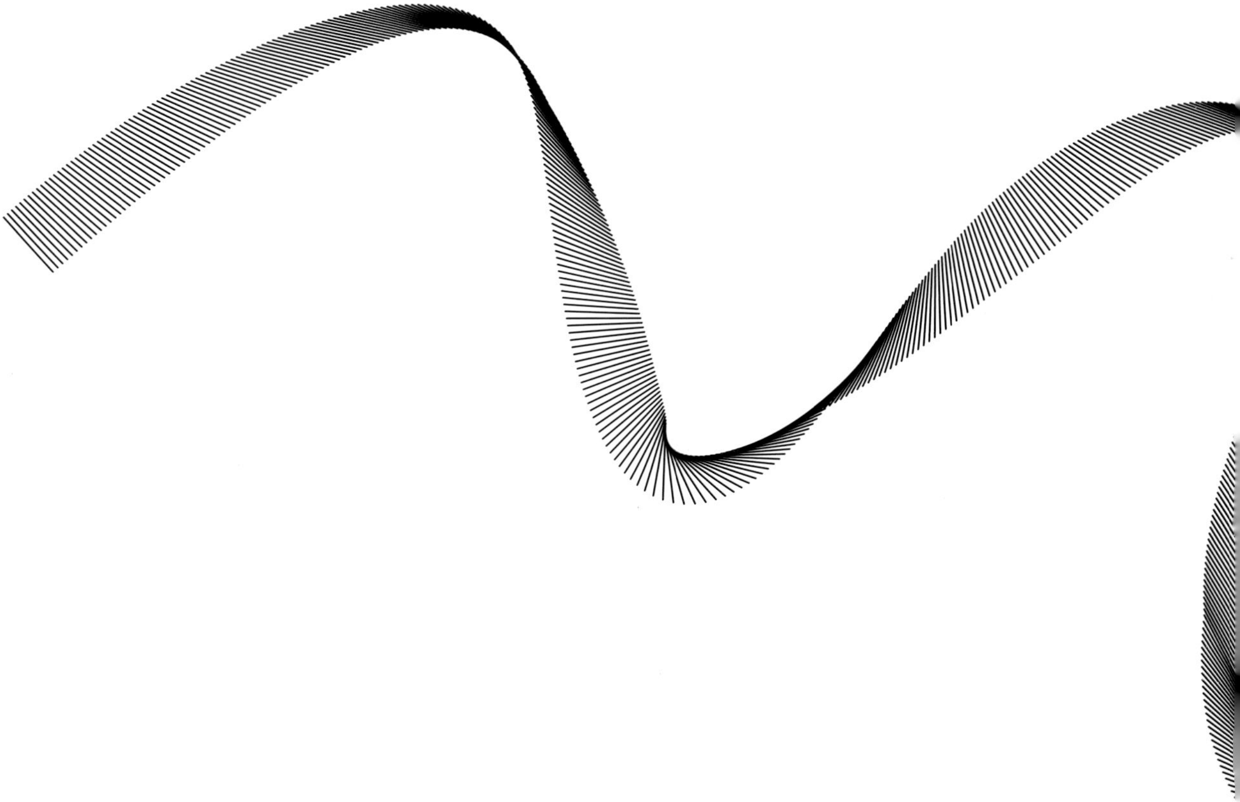

ABOVE AND FOLLOWING SPREAD An adaption of the *variablyThickLines* function that takes an existing curve as an input rather than a single start and end point.

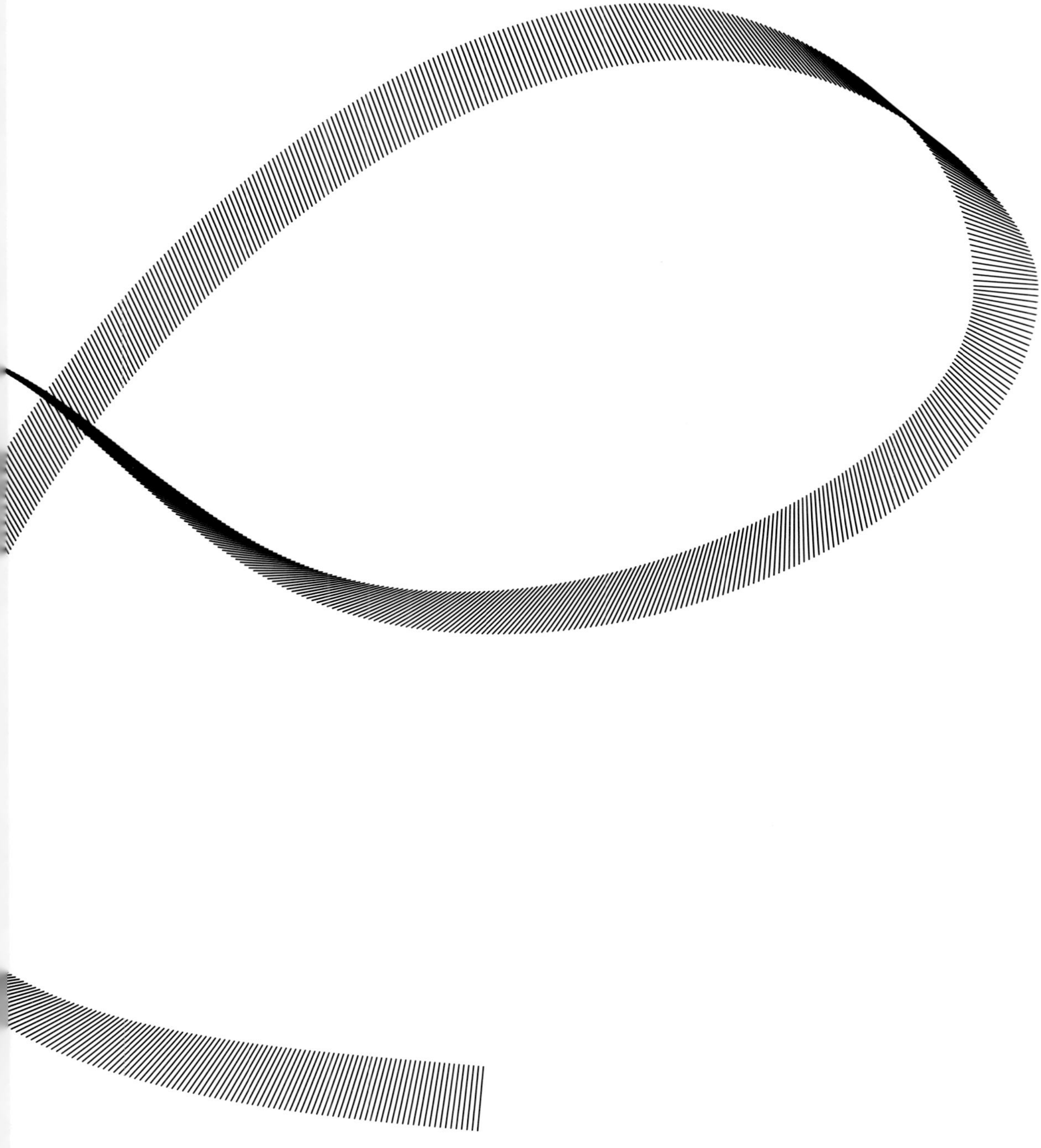

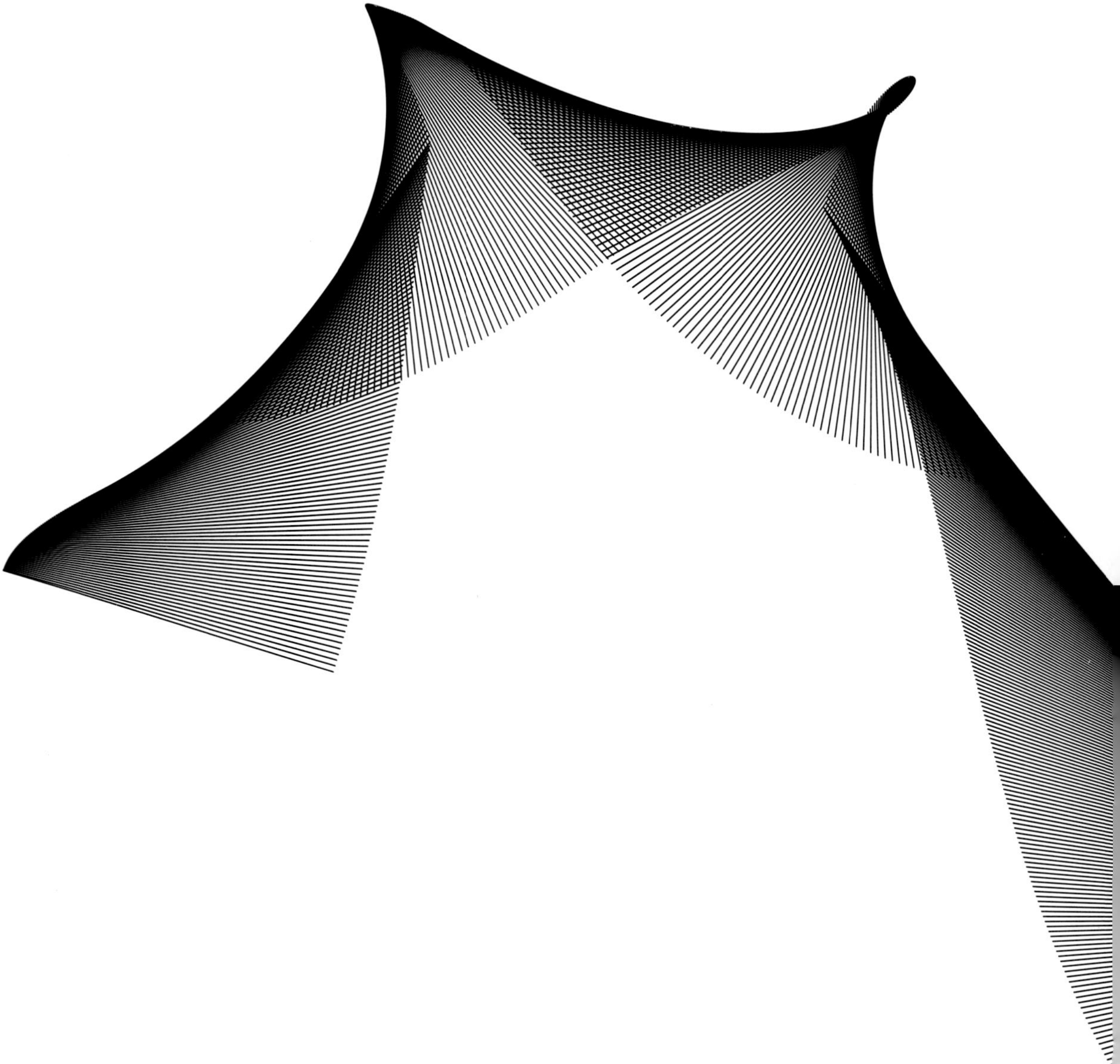

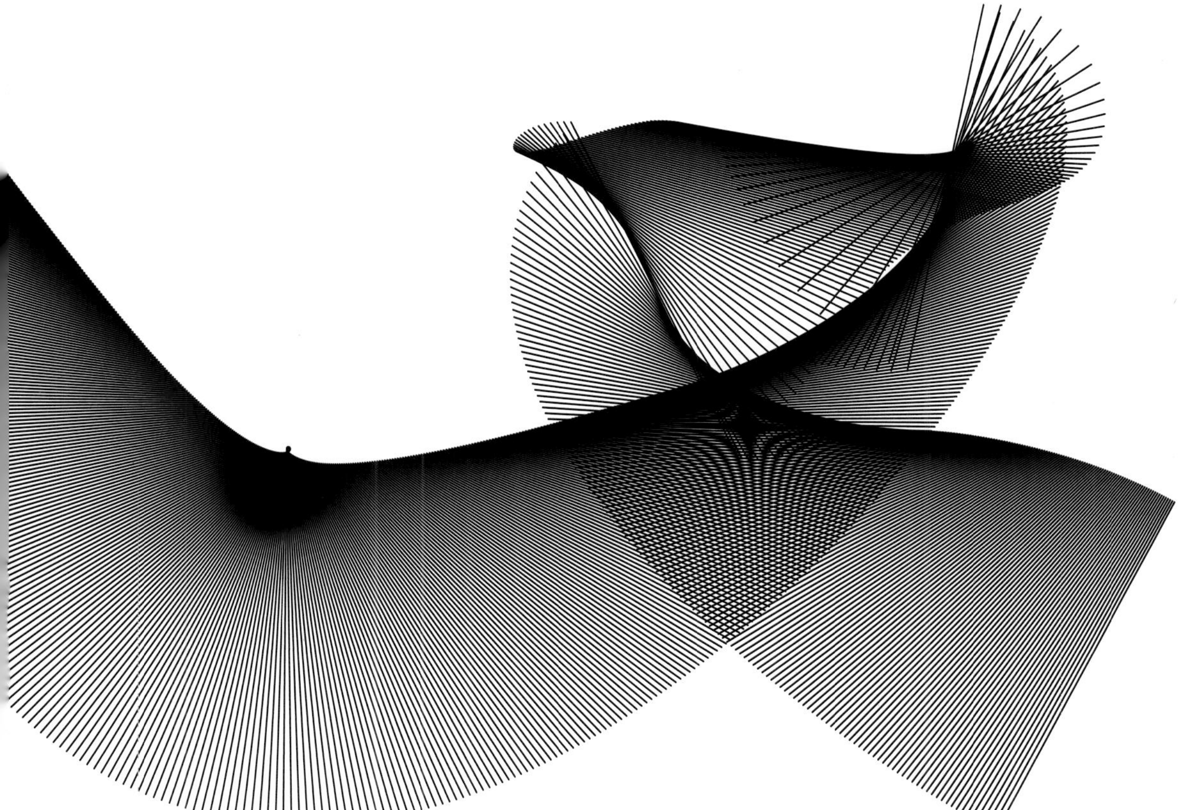

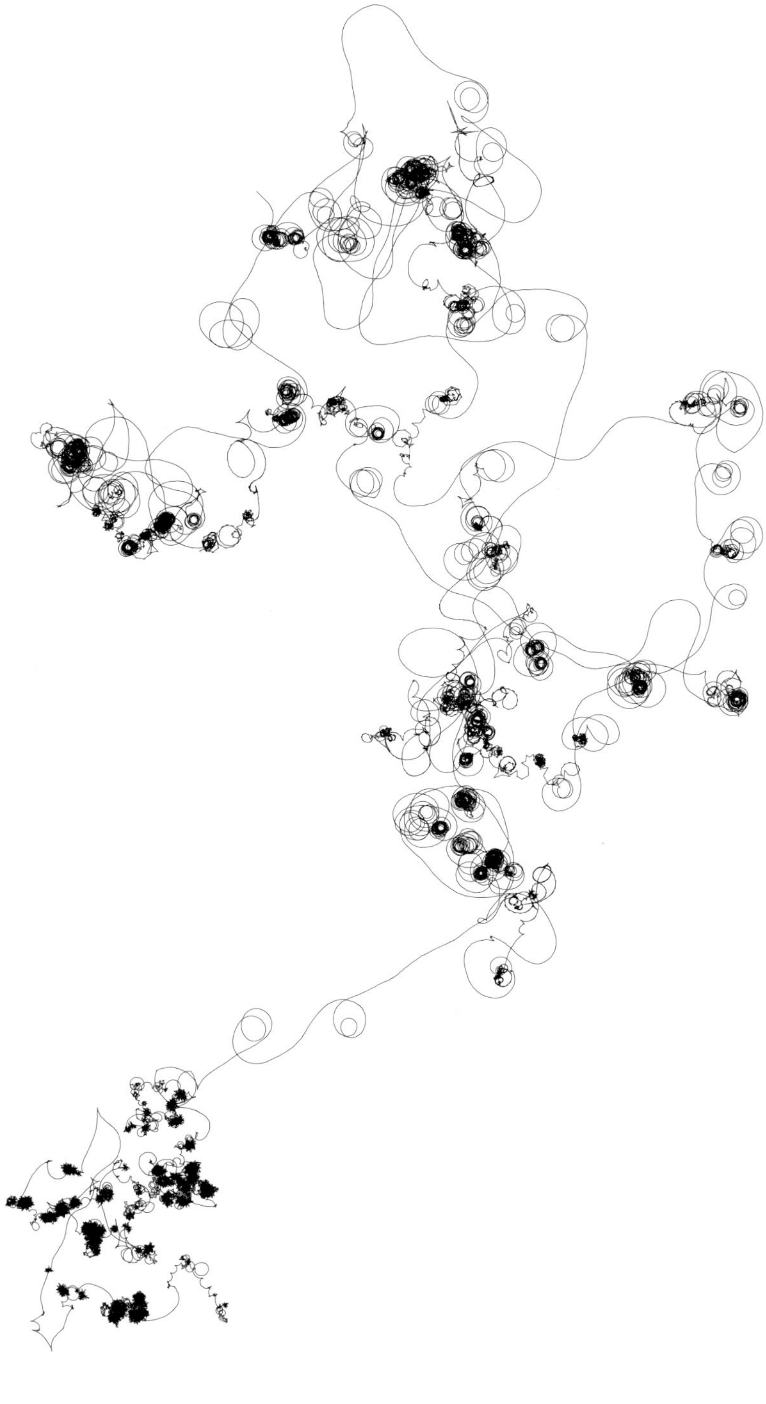

A *drunkenAntPath*

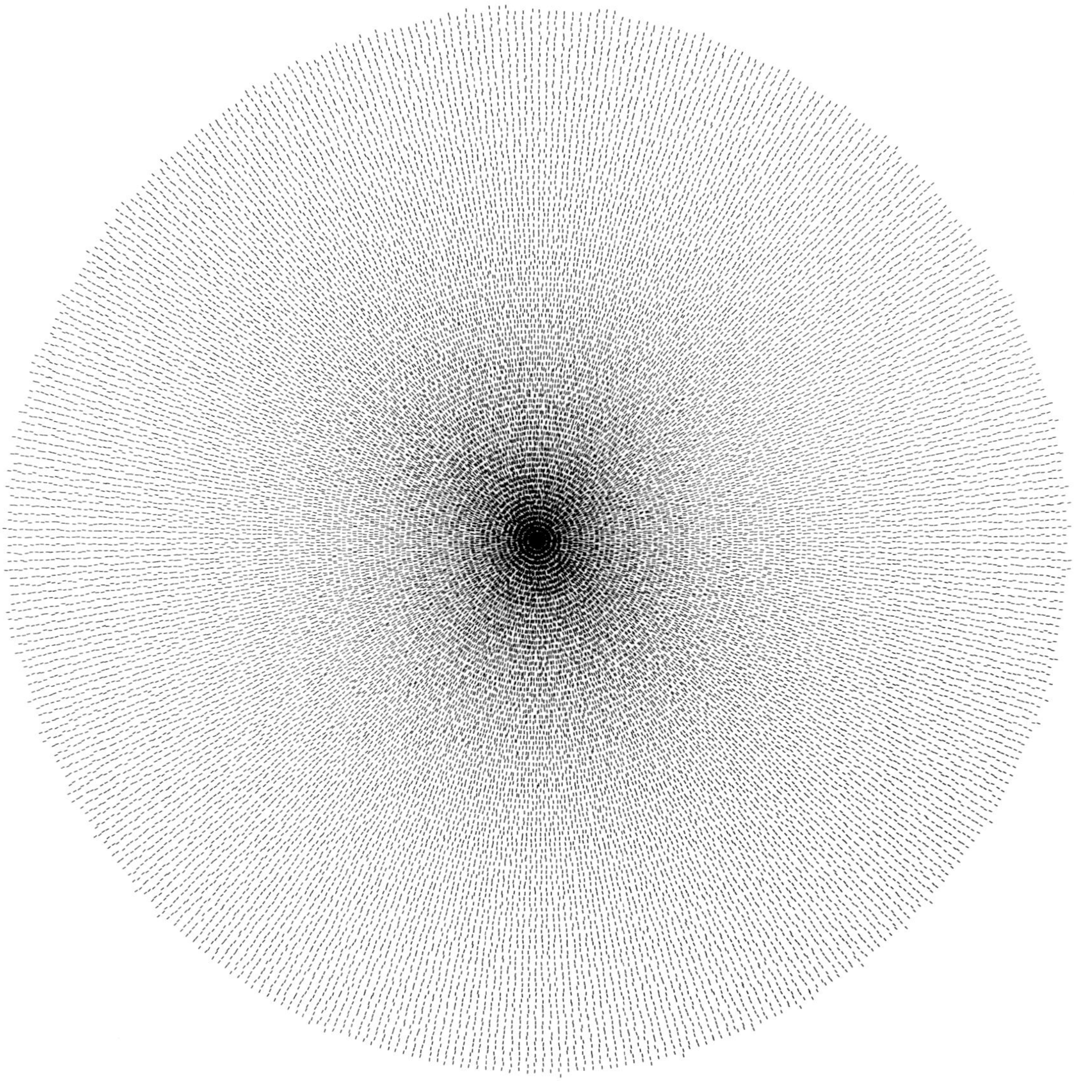

A *driftingDashPolylines* with a spiral as input. The curve is so dense that the dash segments tend to correspond to segments other than their neighbor on the spiral creating the appearance of lines traveling from the center outwards.

ABOVE AND OPPOSITE PAGE A collection of *driftingDashPolylines* with the same input curve and different numeric inputs.

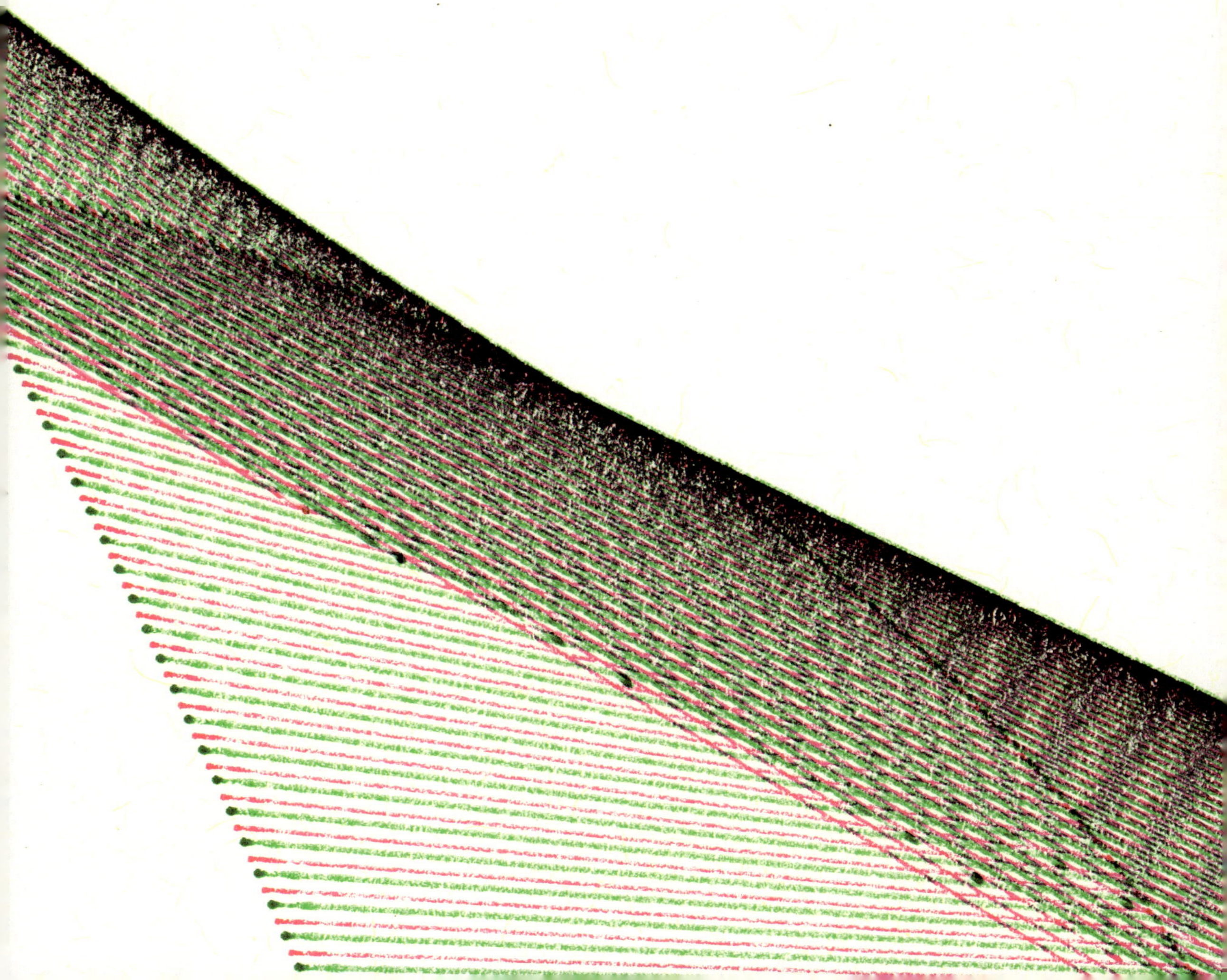

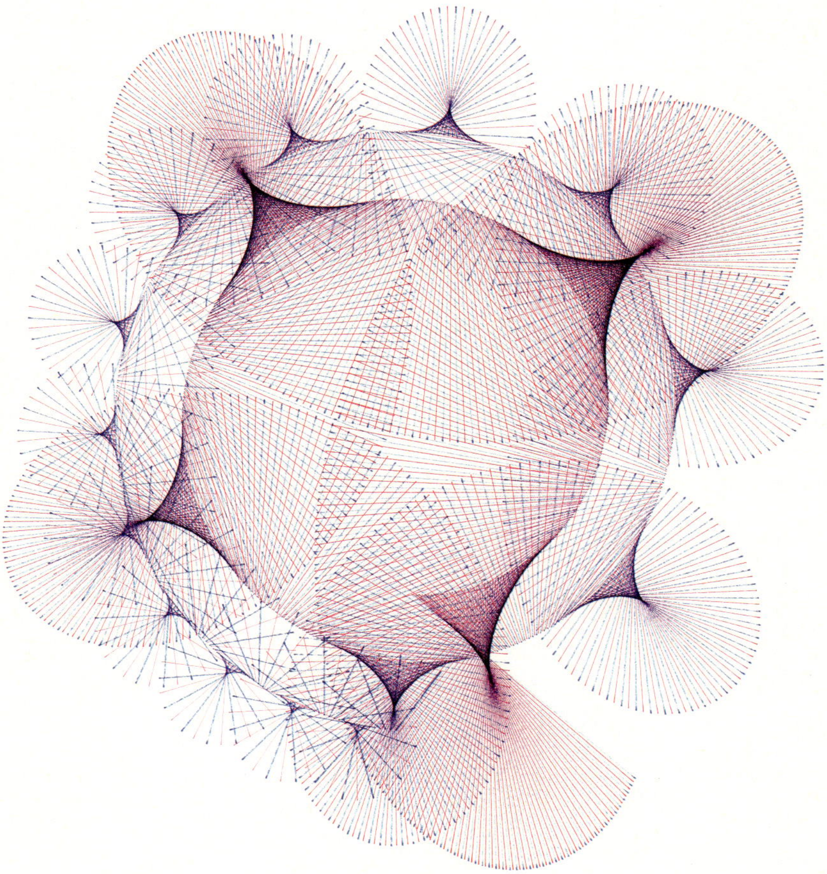

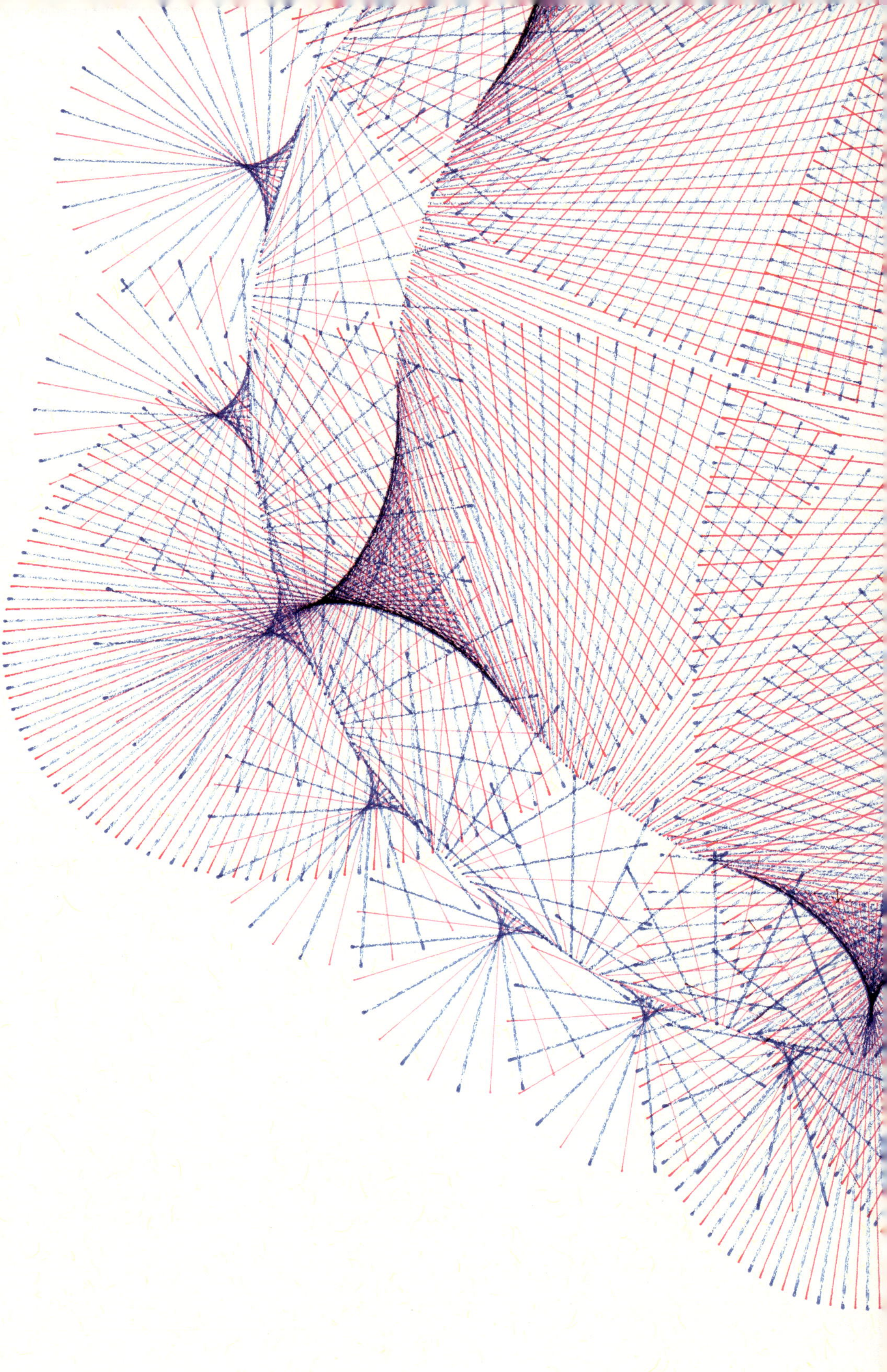

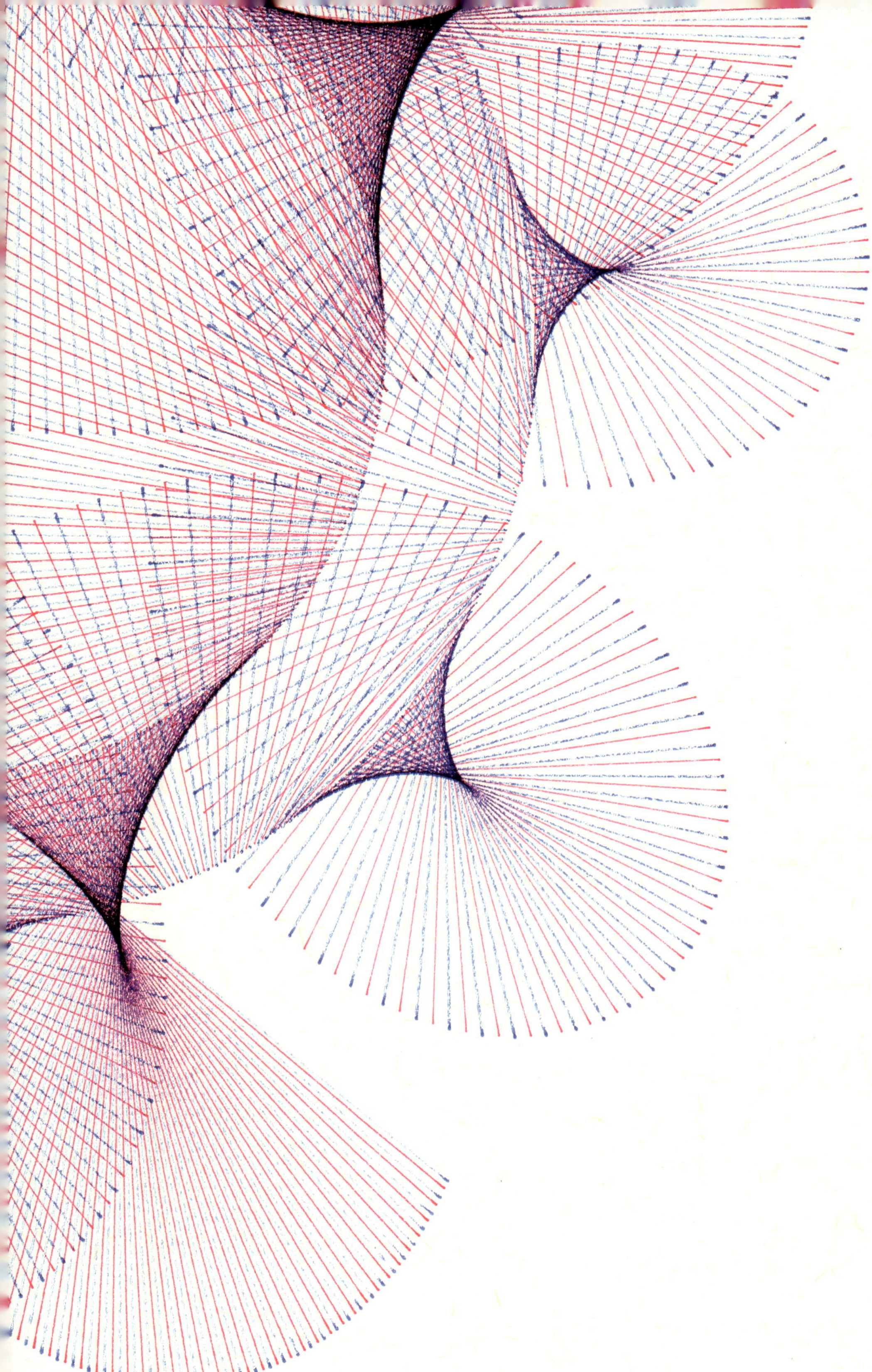

Chapter 2
Structures

From Dirty Marks to Lines, Shapes & Representations

What is the difference between a mark and a line? A mark is literal, direct, and unambiguous in its creation. In the previous chapter, exercises prompted the codification of marks, but in some cases, it is important to note, the marks were not lines. This is not a matter of nomenclature, extremity or classification. No matter how bombastic, trail-like, curvy or straight the mark, it might not always register as a line. This is because lines are relational mental constructs. A line is what we read into marks. Sometimes, the association between marks and lines is not one to one. Consider two marks made by a pen in exactly the same location. Consider 100 such marks. The line read by those marks may be different depending on the number of marks, but it is still only one line. Consider the horizon line. The horizon line is real; it can be measured, photographed, described, and defined, but it is not a thing. It can be perceived without association with a single mark. A mark does not always lead to a line and a line is not always made up of one mark. Consider, further, that a line can exist because of the tension between marks—as in when our mind literally connects the dots—or a complete lack of marks—as in when marks fill an area to maximum density except for a small sliver of space.

A shift from marks to lines is important, first, because disciplined drawing requires that the artist, designer, or architect consider not just the actions performed, but the implications of those actions on the perception of the work. Second, the concept of the line puts some productive pressure on computation. Marco Frascari, in *Eleven Exercises in the Art of Architectural Drawing* defines a theory of the "non-trivial architectural drawing." Not unlike "non-trivial" in mathematics or computer science, non-trivial drawings,

> "are the very condition of architectural experimentations; they exist before all other kinds of architectural experiences. If properly done, these drawings are quite different from artistic or illustrative drawing ... Non-trivial architectural drawings offer idiosyncratic approaches, which controvert the presence of the entity presented in the drawing yet elaborate it further. In that respect, the authority of this construction is a matter of apprehending a reference system between what is internal to the frame and what is external to it."[1]

Computing with respect to marks is relatively trivial compared to computing with respect to lines, especially if we treat the line as Frascari's drawing "entity." A non-trivial computational drawing apparatus, therefore, must be in command of the drawing media, drawing content, and perceptual logic—or frame—of the drawing. Interestingly, Frascari extends this theory into a critique of the digital and its tendency to speed up production and arrest the image. However, Frascari's digital apparently refers to application-oriented software, not custom computer code. Ironically, a computational approach that involves writing code as part of a drawing apparatus provides exactly what Frascari suggests that the digital circumvents: a slowness of conception that favors inquiry into the nature of architecture and a resistance to the urges of the technical. To achieve a non-trivial computational drawing, we need to do more than make marks that happen to be read as lines. We need to design the structure of the code with respect to the structure of lines. Put another way, we need to code with respect to how a drawing looks, in addition to how it is made.

George Stiny, a prolific architectural mathematician and creator of "Shape Grammars"—a discipline in its own right that simultaneously offers a structure for organizing the world, being creative, and computing with lines and rules—relishes in ambiguity and notably has made design computation career that involves the digital computer very little (excluding the hypothetical Turing Machine). Explained in *Shape, Talking about Seeing and Doing,* Stiny uses the example of three intersecting non-parallel lines,

"You probably see the same triangle as I do. It's obvious. And this seems perfectly natural. Only there's a big discrepancy between the actual lines I've drawn and what's potentially there to see. I didn't draw the sides of the triangle on purpose. They're all defined as I draw the last line ... The three sides of the triangle are shorter than my lines. They're formed when my lines intersect. No one intentionally put the triangle where it is. Yet it's there anyway, patiently waiting to be seen ... There are plenty of other ways to embed lines in my lines, so that these segments interact meaningfully."[2]

The idea of "embedding relationships" is key to Stiny's method. Anticipating the conflict with digital models of drawing, Stiny reminds us that when embedding, "The ambiguity is inevitable, but this isn't a problem. I've learned to go on from what I've done without hesitating every time I see something new."[3] It is also important to note that Stiny uses the term embedd*ing* rather than embedd*ed*. This subtle distinction suggests that the triangle is not actually there waiting to be found, but is actually something we, as humans, assert as we read (though Stiny would insist, "see") the drawing. Indeed it is very difficult for a model to contain all possible ways one might embed relationships. Clearly, Stiny enjoys being human,

"I trust my eyes. In fact, changes can be so rapid and smooth that I don't notice them. Then if I want to check what's happening, I have to stop what I'm doing in midcourse. I have to remember everything that's transpired. But I may forget ... It's lucky—what's lost in my head can't bother me."[4]

But what is lost in a digital construct *does* bother the computer programmer, and should bother the computer user even more. Later in *Shape,* Stiny quotes Ivan Sutherland, computer graphics pioneer and creator of the Sketchpad, the first ever computational drawing apparatus (it is not appropriate to call it merely software because the 1962 program was an invented interface as well as program) as saying,

"To a large extent it has turned out that the usefulness of computer drawings is precisely their structured nature, and that this structured nature is precisely the difficulty in making them ... An ordinary draftsman is unconcerned with the structure of his drawing material. Pen and ink or pencil and paper have no inherent structure. They only make dirty marks on paper. The draftsman is concerned principally with the drawings as a representation of the evolving design. The behavior of the computer-produced drawing, on the other hand, is critically dependent upon the topological and geometric structure built up in the commuter memory as a result of drawing operations. The drawing itself has properties quite independent of the properties of the object it is describing."[5]

Many artists, designers, and architects will take issue with Sutherland's claim that the drafted line, drawn by hand, is without structure. Nonetheless, his point stands if we pivot slightly to note that material drawing does not *require* structure, when the computational drawing demands it.

Sutherland encountered the conflict between drawing and computing in terms of structure in the early '60s. It is important to note that the most advanced software today still does not smoothly transition between various ways of organizing lines. If we draw two squares overlapping, we can see a third shape, *and* the two squares, and can operate on either, but we must make certain committal decisions first. For example, if we want to rotate just the middle overlapping square it would likely be necessary to perform some kind of splitting operation followed by a joining operation of relevant four segments. These methods would create a new square object, but would not alter the appearance of the marks. Although we can use software to recreate any geometric organization that we can see, to operate on a digital model of a drawing means we must decide between readings.

In the last chapter, levels of abstraction were articulated as a necessary part of the craft of computer programming. Levels of abstraction are also a key opportunity. As Stiny and Sutherland elucidate, computing and drawing—in the traditional, material sense—are at odds with each other when it comes to structure. When writing code, the mark and the relationships between the marks can be designed. If we code the marks and code the structure of the marks, there need not be a fixed relationship between conceptions of lines, nor a predetermined topology of line. This means ambiguity can be constructed. Would Stiny be satisfied with this approach? Likely not, as we are not resolving the fundamental issue he has with language and the digital model. However, we can still take Stiny's position as a motivator, even while acknowledging that, like Sutherland, the digital drawings we create will be self-contradictory in some ways. Digital constructs are inherently ambiguity-averse. However, it still might be fair to conclude that when coding as part of a drawing apparatus, we can work to achieve ambiguity despite the impossibility of representing the ambiguity-prone nature of human perception.

Can we expect to do better than Sutherland? Certainly not. However, if we pivot from the goal of making tools for others to draw with and instead make (and re-make) custom apparatuses for our own projects, we can re-cast the problem that Sutherland identified as a charge: computational drawing is problematic when universally applied, but opportune as a custom project. Hopefully, readers of this book will take seriously this claim. What is proposed here is not a single model for how to learn or practice, but seeds that, if cultivated, are almost certainly guaranteed to bear fruit. Computational drawing is always hard, because it is always problematic, but those problems are always opportunities. A drawing in which square marks overlap and the overlapping quadrilaterals are then transformed is a compelling, if esoteric, non-trivial project that *requires* computation.

Consider a line that travels in straight segments and at a grid, turns 90 degrees or keeps going straight.

```
A spaceFillingLine is created in terms of allPreviousLines and a startPoint
   create anyIntersections and set it to False
   create currentPoint and set it to startPoint
   create myLine as an empty variable
   while not anyIntersections
      create possibleDirections (north, south, east, and west) that are within bounds of image
      pick a random direction from possibleDirections
      create mark between currentPoint and currentPoint + direction
      check each line in allPreviousLines
         if line intersects mark
            set anyIntersections to True
      if mark intersects myLine
         set anyIntersections to True
      if not anyIntersections
         add mark to the end of myLine
```

This line is unique compared to those that we have considered previously in that the creation of the line is dependent upon, and therefore takes as input, all the previous lines in the drawing. Also unique is how the line would be created. For example,

```
create a list, allLines
repeat 1,000 times
   create newLine as a spaceFillingLine (allLines, random empty grid point)
   add newLine to allLines
```

versus

```
create a list, allLines
while there are more than 5 empty grid points
   create newLine as a spaceFillingLine (allLines, random empty grid point)
   add newLine to allLines
```

A common drawing structure involves nested loops to create a grid. Let's call this simple algorithm *gridSegments.*

```
set x to be 0
while x is less than 600
  set y to be 0
  while y is less than 600
    create a segment that starts at (x, y) and ends at (x+random Value, y+random Value)
    set y to y + 5
  set x to x + 5
```

To avoid becoming too esoteric in the etymological analysis of drawing structure, lets pause to consider the implementation of one of the first significant computationally structured personal computer drawings, which is cryptically, but accurately articulated as "*10 PRINT.*" The title is an excerpt of a single line of code written in the BASIC programming language, "10 PRINT CHR$(205.5+RND(1)); : GOTO 10." That single line of code, which references itself in order to constantly repeat, is the entire program. A testament to the cultural significance of that code, and that moment, is the 300+ page software studies book,[6] published in 2013, that shares its title with the canonical program. It traces the cultural significance of the technology, concepts, and motivations that carry through from the command line interface of the Commodore 64 through today. Though elegant in its short length, the implementation in the BASIC programming language is cryptic to the point of near incomprehensibility by the non-programmer. In the spirit of algorithmic communication, it can be translated to:

```
constantly repeat
  randomly choose value between 0 and 1
  if value is 0
    make a downward sloping 45-degree mark
  else
    make an upward sloping 45-degree mark
```

Though certainly not the first award-winning computer art, a distinction earned, somewhat surprisingly, by the work out of the United States Army Ballistic Research Laboratory,[7] and certainly not the first computer graphics project, 10PRINT is an important early work of computational *drawing* in the sense that as an algorithm, it structures lines that can be read ambiguously. The code is calibrated to the resulting appearance. In the typography of the Commodore 64 world, the monospaced characters form a perfect square grid in which characters similar to the "/" and the "\" span precisely from corner to corner of each cell. This allows a stream of text to function as a drawing. Individual cells become invisible as lines read spanning much longer than one cell. Without that particular condition, (if the font were different, or the characters changed to, say "*" and "#") the output would be a stream of characters rather than structured, ambiguous lines. There are infinite variations of this algorithm, many are explored in the text.[8] It is possible to implement the algorithm with pixels in a digital image so long as the two (or more) variations of the cell have correspondences, visually, to the left, right, top, or bottom.

Interestingly, there is never a model of the lines that are legible in the resulting drawings. We can see them, but Stiny would be quick to point out that we cannot operate on them. It is fair, then, to note that the code determines the drawn lines, but does not represent the drawing, nor does the drawing represent the code. Both must be considered collectively and respected for their procedural distance between one another. We cannot tweak a particular line in the drawing, but we can read the drawing, edit the code, and run it again and again and again. We can also begin to think about evolving the algorithm to involve the analysis of the correspondences between cells. Consider, for example, an algorithm that analyzes the first iteration of an output from that algorithm and makes offset copies of the longest lines. This would require the imposition of a structure to the results of the initial output. Within the *10 PRINT* book, the authors do not discuss this explicitly in terms of drawing. However, they do nonetheless address what this would mean in terms of computational craft, as they explore a program to treat the resulting drawing as a maze. They discuss, "walking" the maze, "touching" the maze, and "testing" the maze. These operations immediately change the scope of inquiry from drawing to a functional game. However, they map precisely to the kinds of analytical operations we might want to perform in the output for the purposes of a spatial, figural, or narrative agenda. Walking the maze is a kind of reading of the drawing in a way that only makes sense if the drawing and the initial code are considered together.

Mentioning that a drawing can be read differently than the code opens the door to analogies with poetry and literature. If literature is used as an analogy, it can be theorized that computational drawing is like writing a short story. More developed, longer, and more immersive than how poetry is often treated, short stories do not need to come to a clear conclusion, and not every aspect of the story needs resolution or even explanation. The author is in control of frame, bounds, content, and structure, but does not invent new linguistic rules. If necessary, the content and structure can convolve. In keeping with this analogy, one can be critical of *using* software developed by others for their intended application. Simply put, using drawing software is not drawing. One can produce a drawing with drawing software in the same way that when reading a choose your own adventure[9] novel one is creating a story. However, this analogy becomes interesting again if we consider the implications of creating a choose your own adventure novel. There are certainly many who write code to make tools for others to use. The implicit argument here is that writing the story would be a more significant contribution.

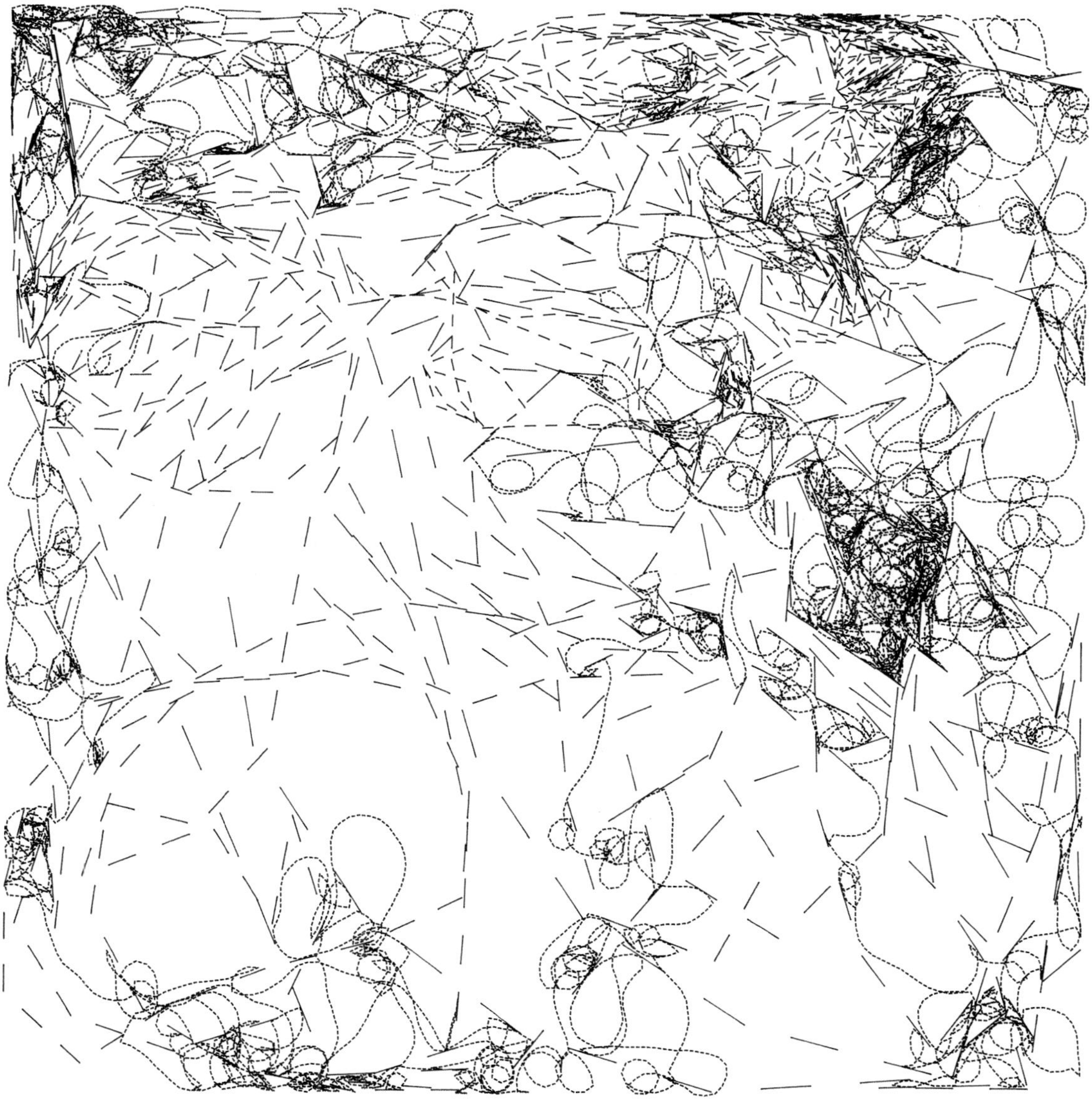

A Taxonomy of Taxonomies of Lines

William Empson, a British literary critic, is renowned for his exhaustively close readings of text. His approach is analogous to an artisanal, technical, and critical inquiry into the individual marks in the creation of drawing. Empson is best known for his *Seven Types of Ambiguity*,[10] which meticulously defines, explains, and categorizes purposeful linguistic double-meaning and contradictions. As a work of critical analysis, Empson's *Seven Types* is beautiful in its discipline, though laborious in tone. Later, a few of Epson's types will be explored in more detail in the context of material and form. For now, it will suffice to note that Empson's distinction between ambiguities is not ambiguous. With meticulous precision, he establishes seven absolutely unique and distict kinds of literary ambiguity and parses a range of examples to clarify his taxonomy. But can Empson's structure serve as a manual for writing? The fiction author, Elliot Perlman, gives an answer: yes, but not in the way Empson intended. Perlman is also the author of a very different *Seven Types of Ambiguity*.[11] In Perlman's *Seven Types*, the reader is treated to seven versions of the same story told by six different characters. The ambiguity is profoundly different from that elucidated by Empson, but the matching title is not a coincidence. Perlman's ambiguity is a matter of voice, perspective, bias, personal identity, sexuality, and psychology. Repeatedly, however, Perlman references Empson's types explicitly in his novel, using them regularly as a foil to the opinions of the protagonist, also a writer. The lesson from Perlman's work is that artists often thrive by working with, and against taxonomies rather than working within taxonomies. That should come as a bit of a relief. It is not possible to list all the types of lines, nor do most drawings conform to a limited definition of line. Though a computational approach will require a structure, that structure can (and should) flow between more than one way of thinking about line. Therefore, although a taxonomy of lines[12] is futile for the architect, artist, or designer, a taxonomy of taxonomies of lines allows for a structured ambiguity. Neither complete open-endedness, nor straightforward structure, it is somewhere in-between. And now, let's consider four types of line taxonomy.

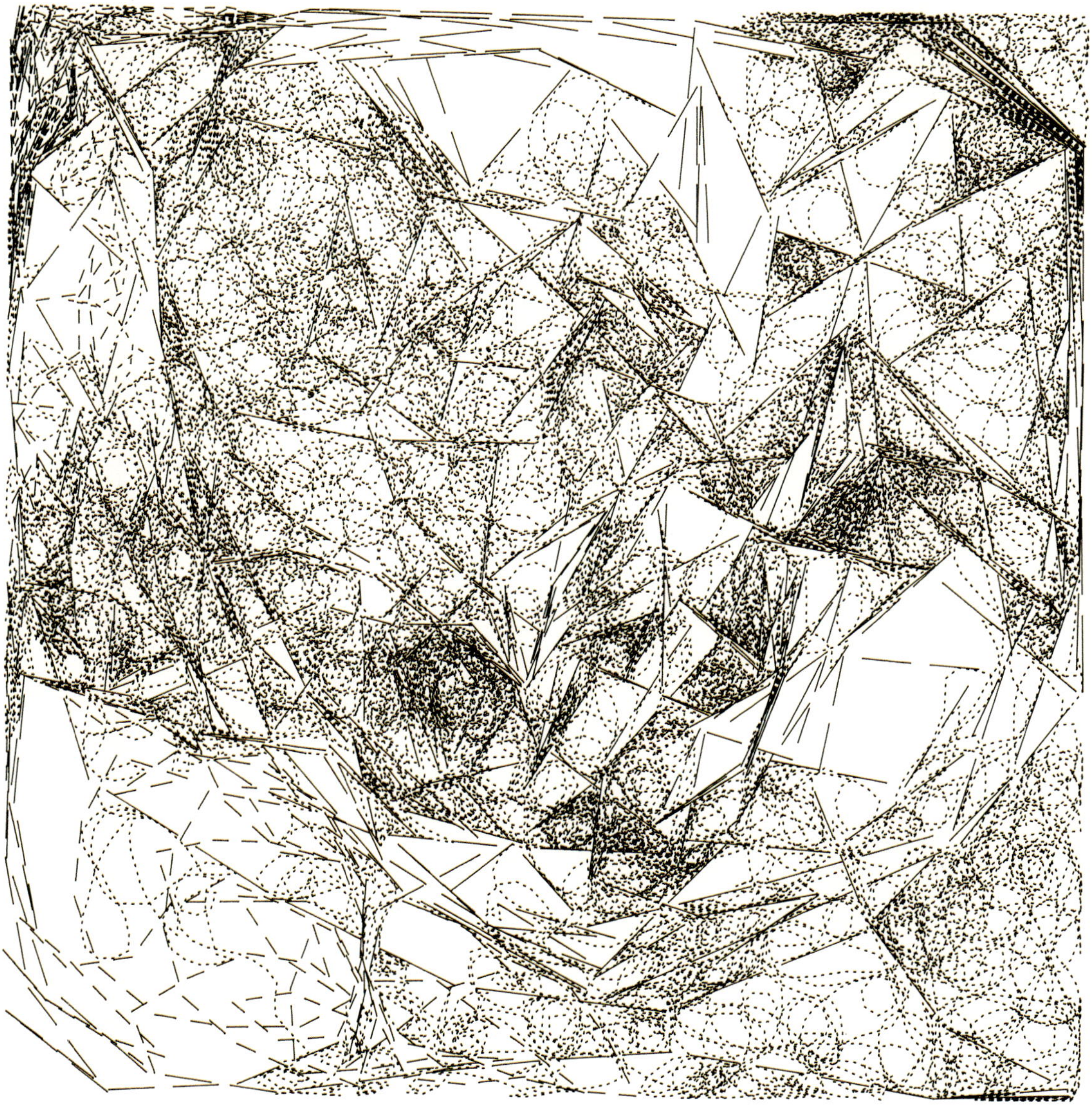

The existence taxonomy

In this taxonomy, lines are organized based on whether and how they correspond directly to things that exist materially. For example, this taxonomy would organize lines that were the objects of the drawing that corresponded to, say, a particle in a field, different from hatch lines that worked together to render an object visible or articulate its form. In this taxonomy, one can ask whether the lines are limits of form—like an outline—or the limits of perception of form—like a horizon. In this taxonomy light can be used to distinguish between types. For example, we might ask whether light in a drawing can be understood as particles. Are light rays, for example, articulated as segments? Or, is light the activator, rendering shadows cast or the hatching of a surface differently depending on the amount of transmission of light from the object? Or is light completely absent, ubiquitous, or irrelevant as is common in the "outline style"?[13]

Let's revisit one of our algorithm examples. Instead of drawing a segment in a random orientation, draw it toward a focal point. Then, gradually adjust that focal point and create a very visible, very real line. This line does not actually exist as a mark, but rather as the trail of the focal point.

```
set focusPoint to (100, 400)
create list allLines
set x to be 0
while x is less than 600
   set y to be 0
   while y is less than 600
      create segment from (x, y) to focusPoint
      find all the intersection points between segment and allLines
      if any intersection points found
         delete segment
         create newSegment from (x, y) to the closest intersection point to (x, y)
         add newSegment to allLines
      set y to y + 5
   set x to x + 5
```

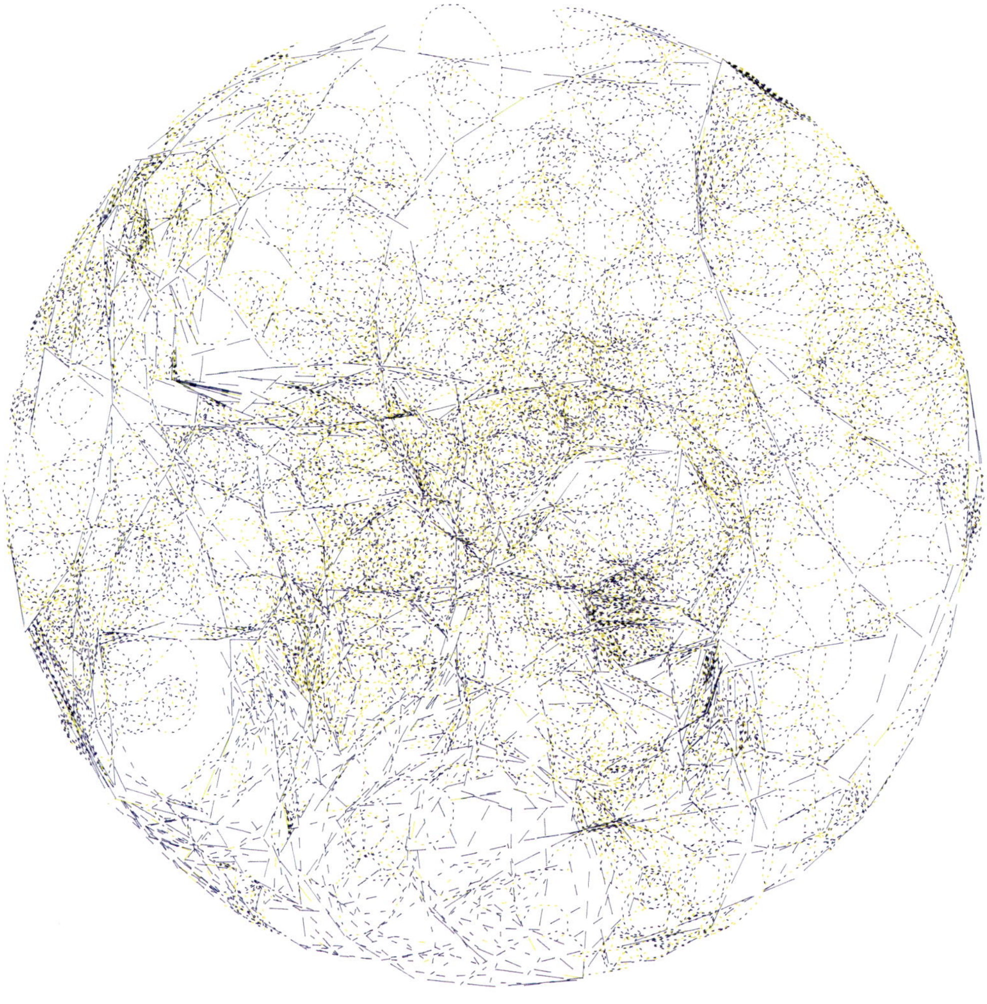

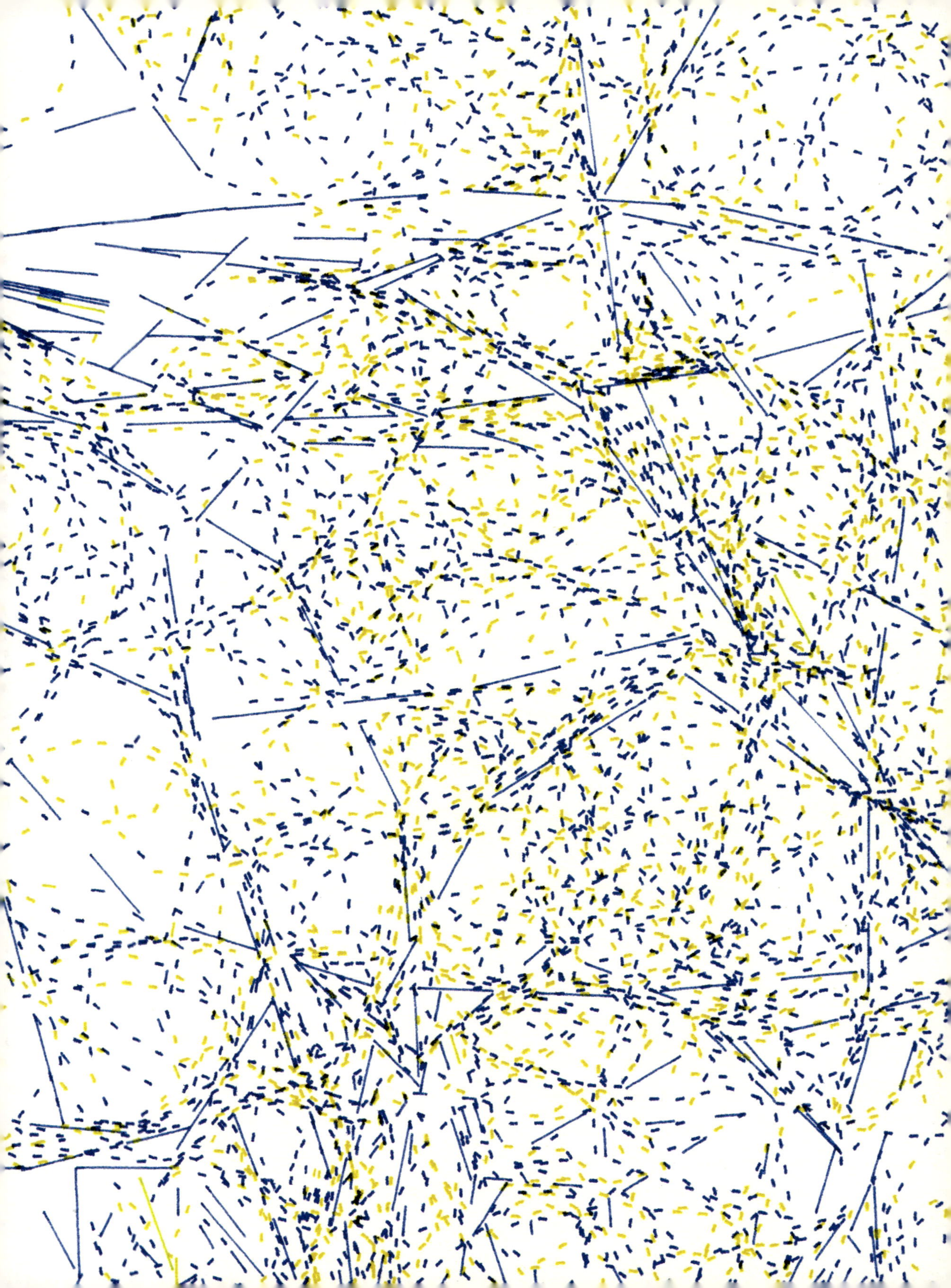

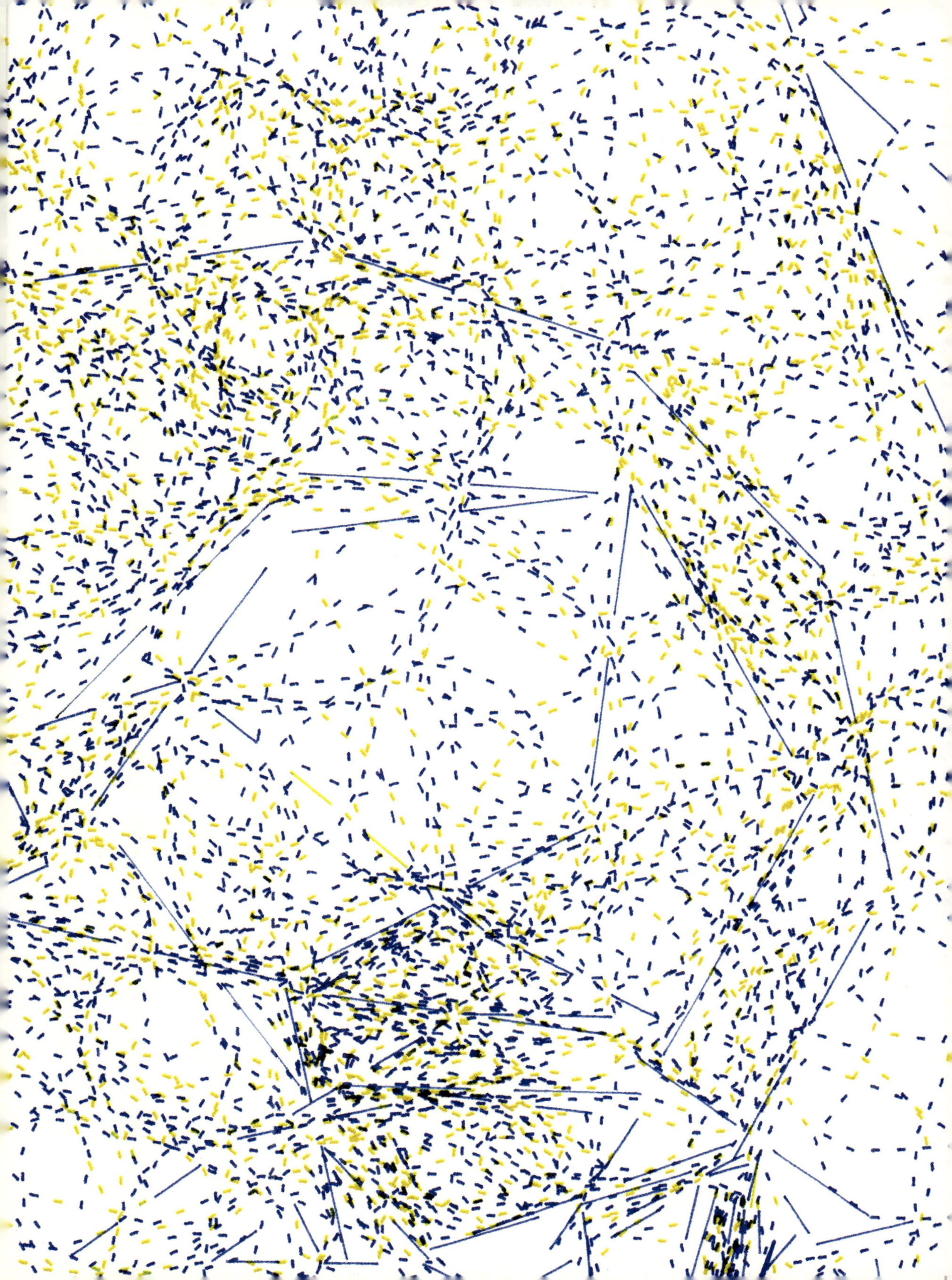

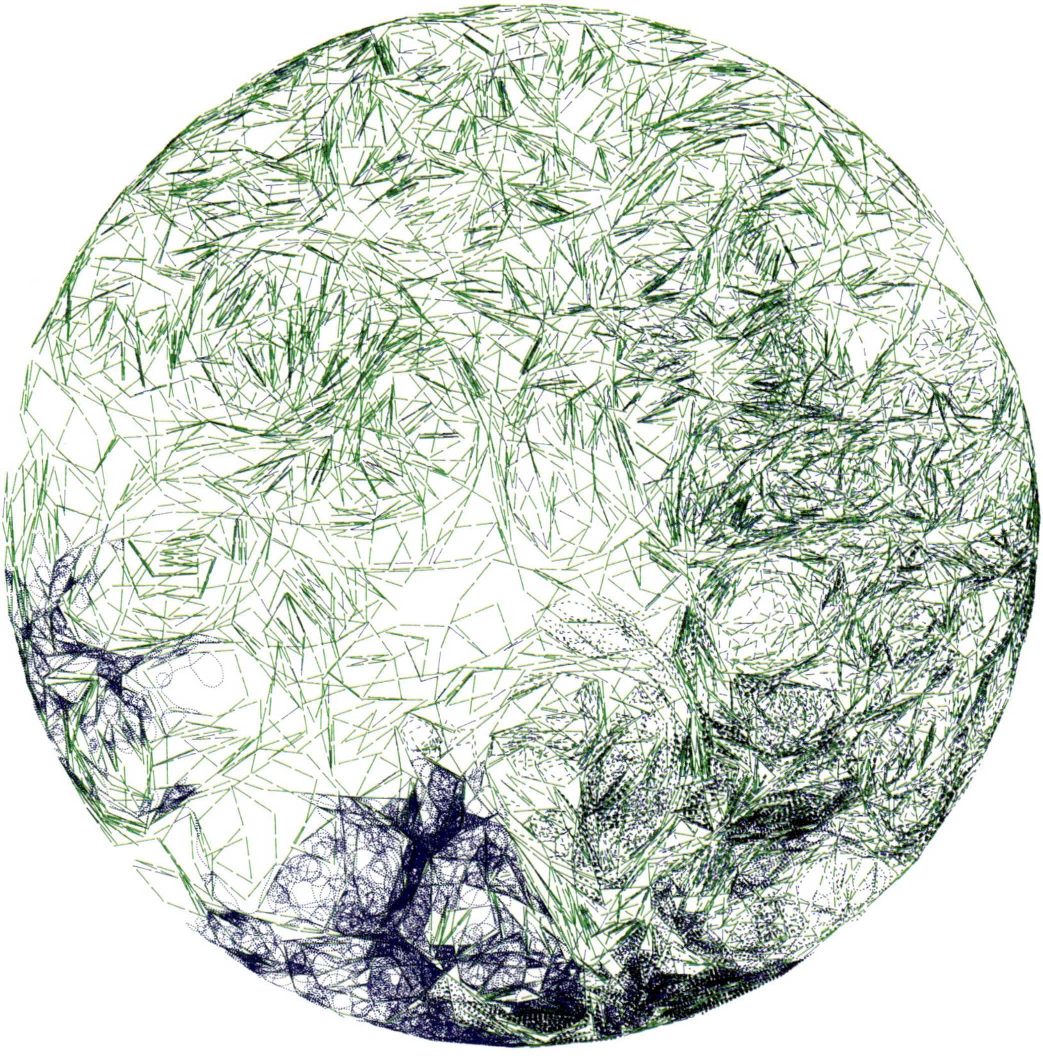

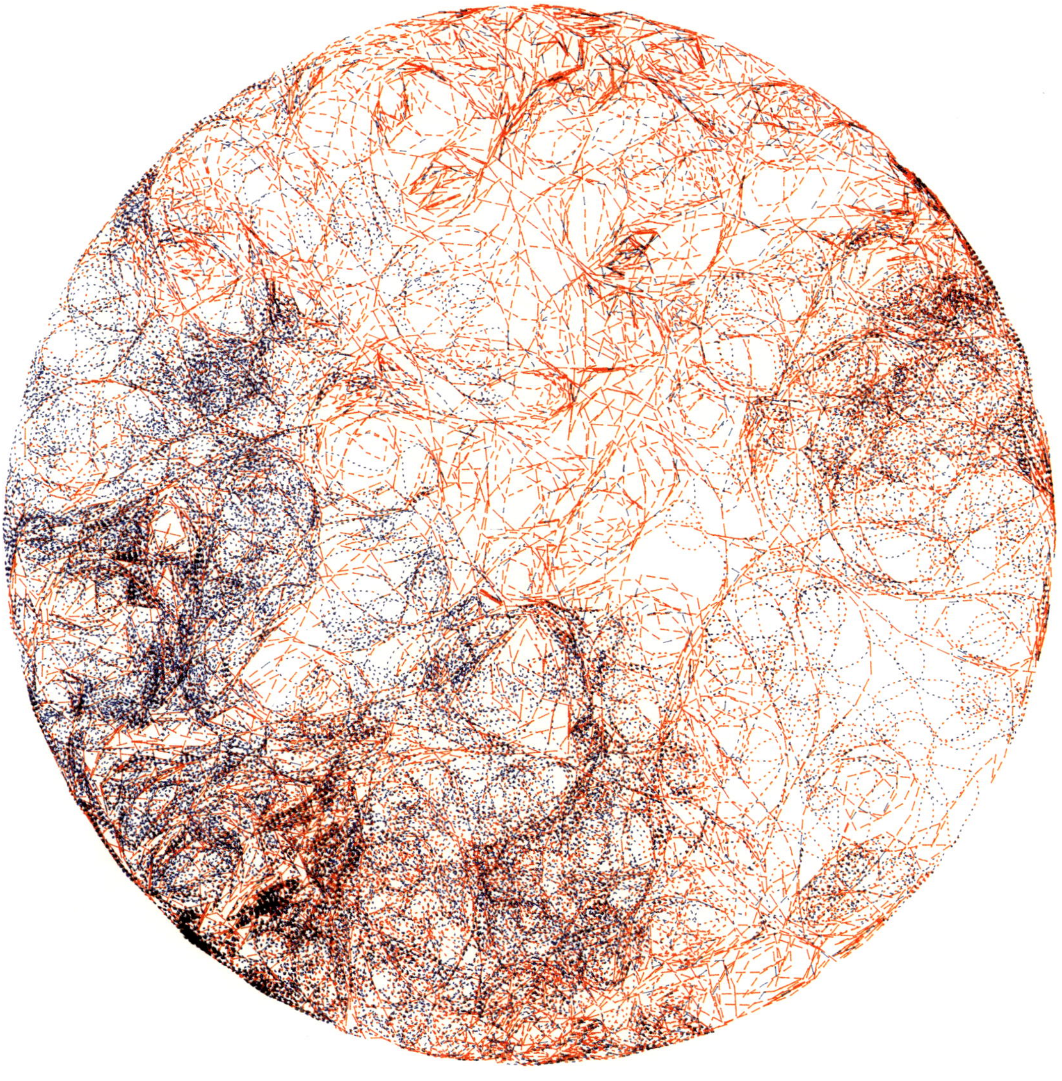

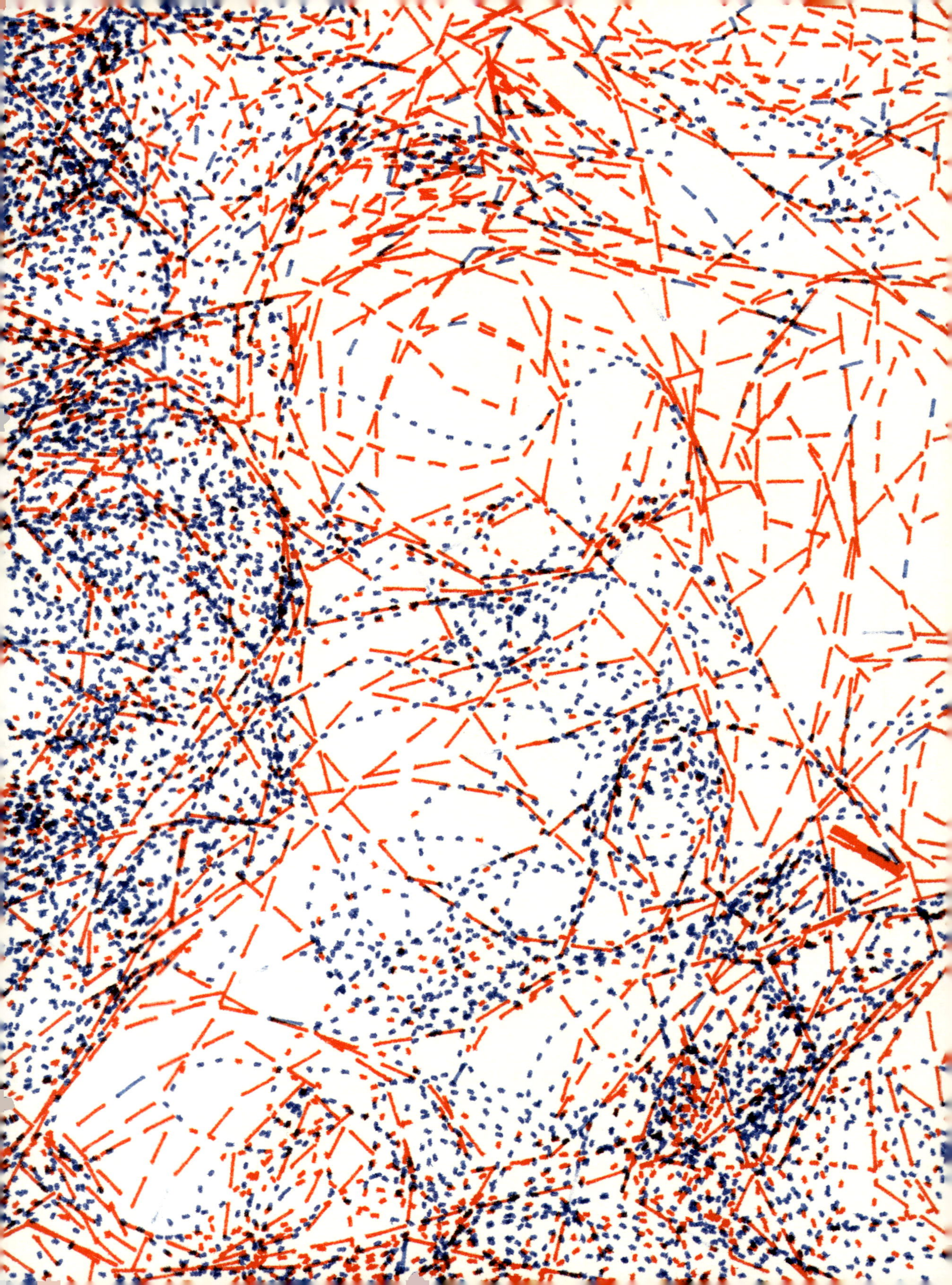

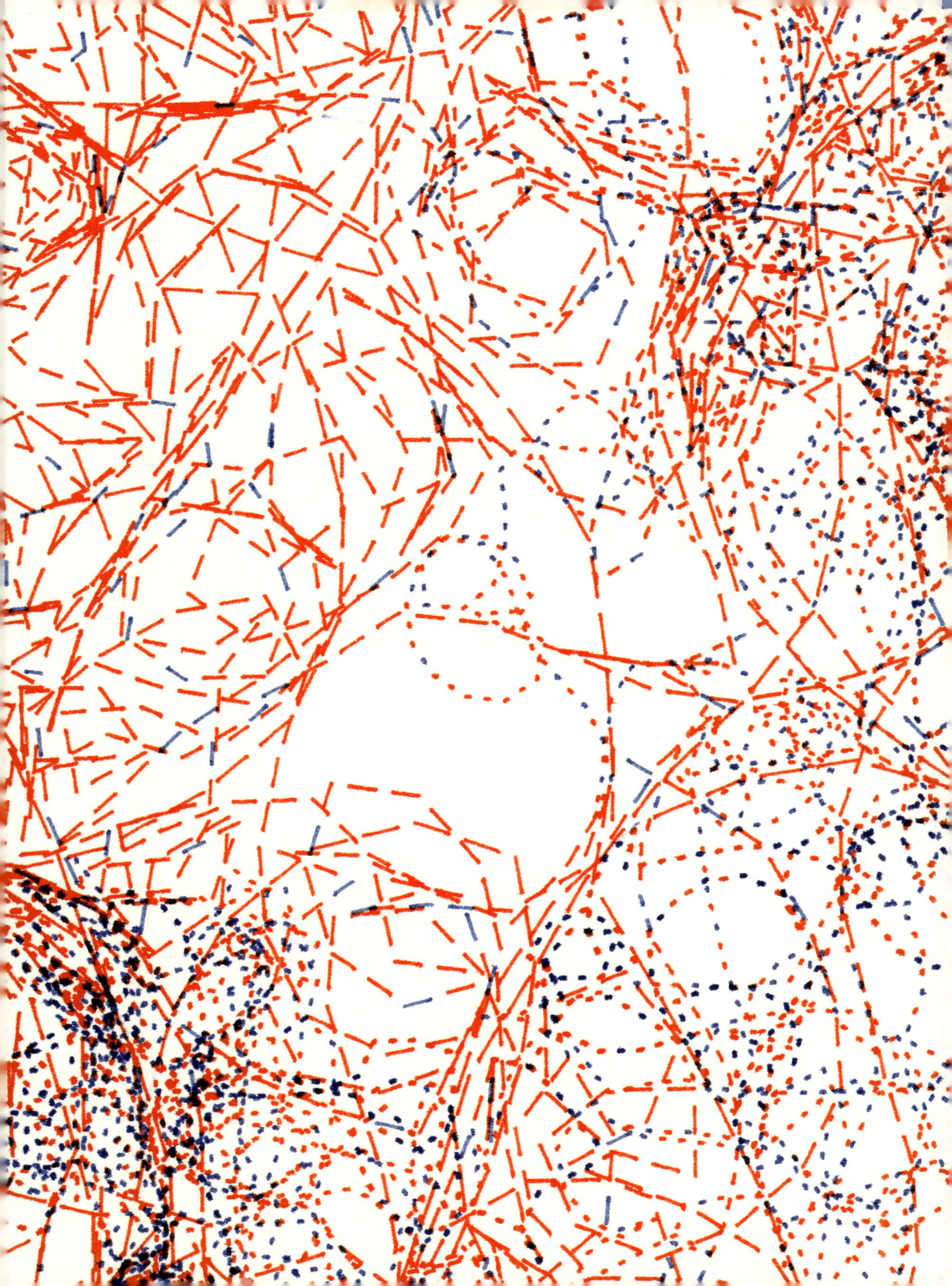

The temporal taxonomy

In this taxonomy, lines are distinguished based on their relationship to time. For example, path lines can trace a record of time, or serve as a one-dimensional temporal space. Alternatively, lines can be related to time in terms of their creation—the time it took to make the mark is represented by the line. Time-based lines can be smooth and continuous or choppy and discrete. Consider for example, a line made of a collection of segments that might represent a series of "snapshots" of a moving particle. Temporal lines can be a representation of time itself or render a range of forms over the course of time. Finally, a kind of "rubber stamped" line could attempt disassociation with time.

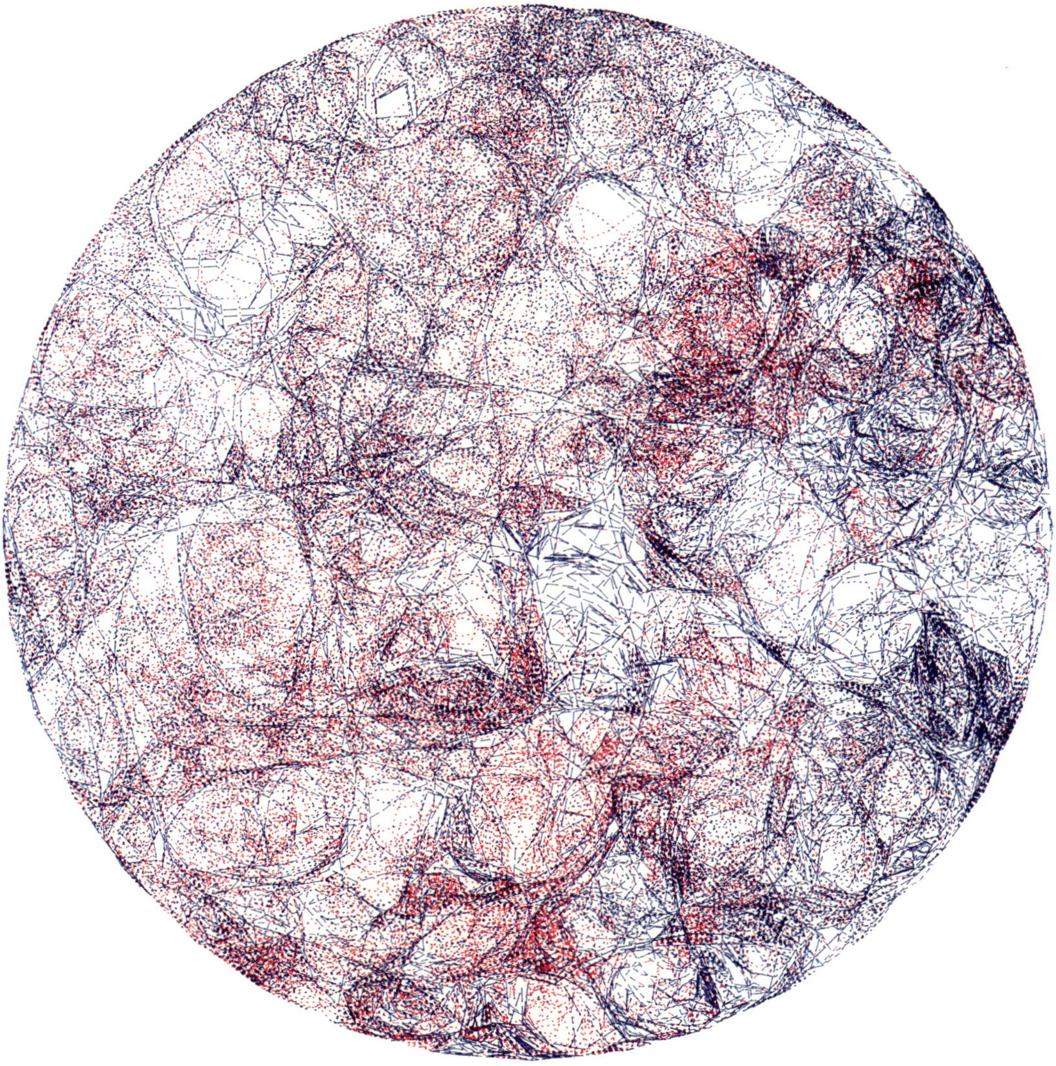

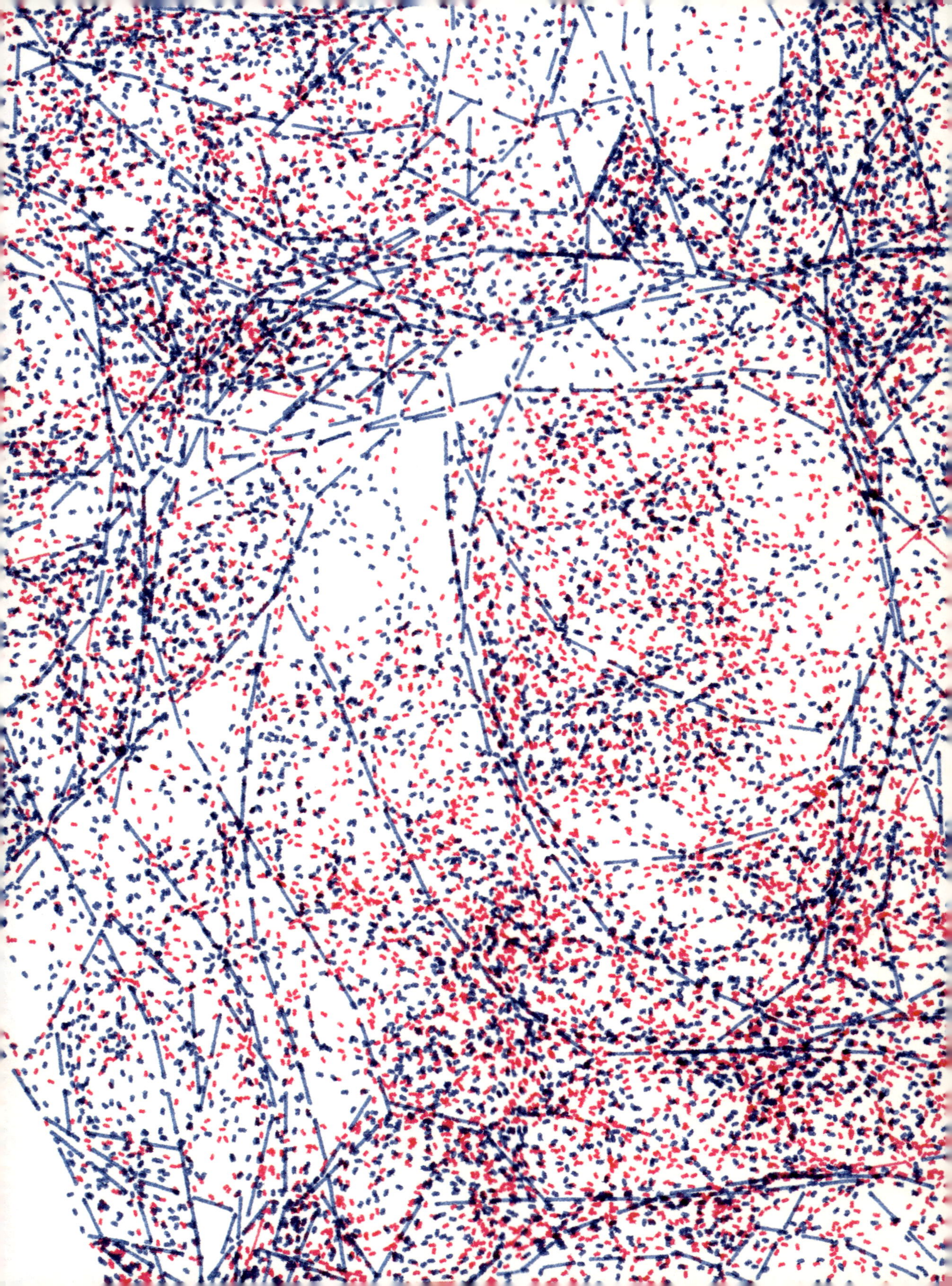

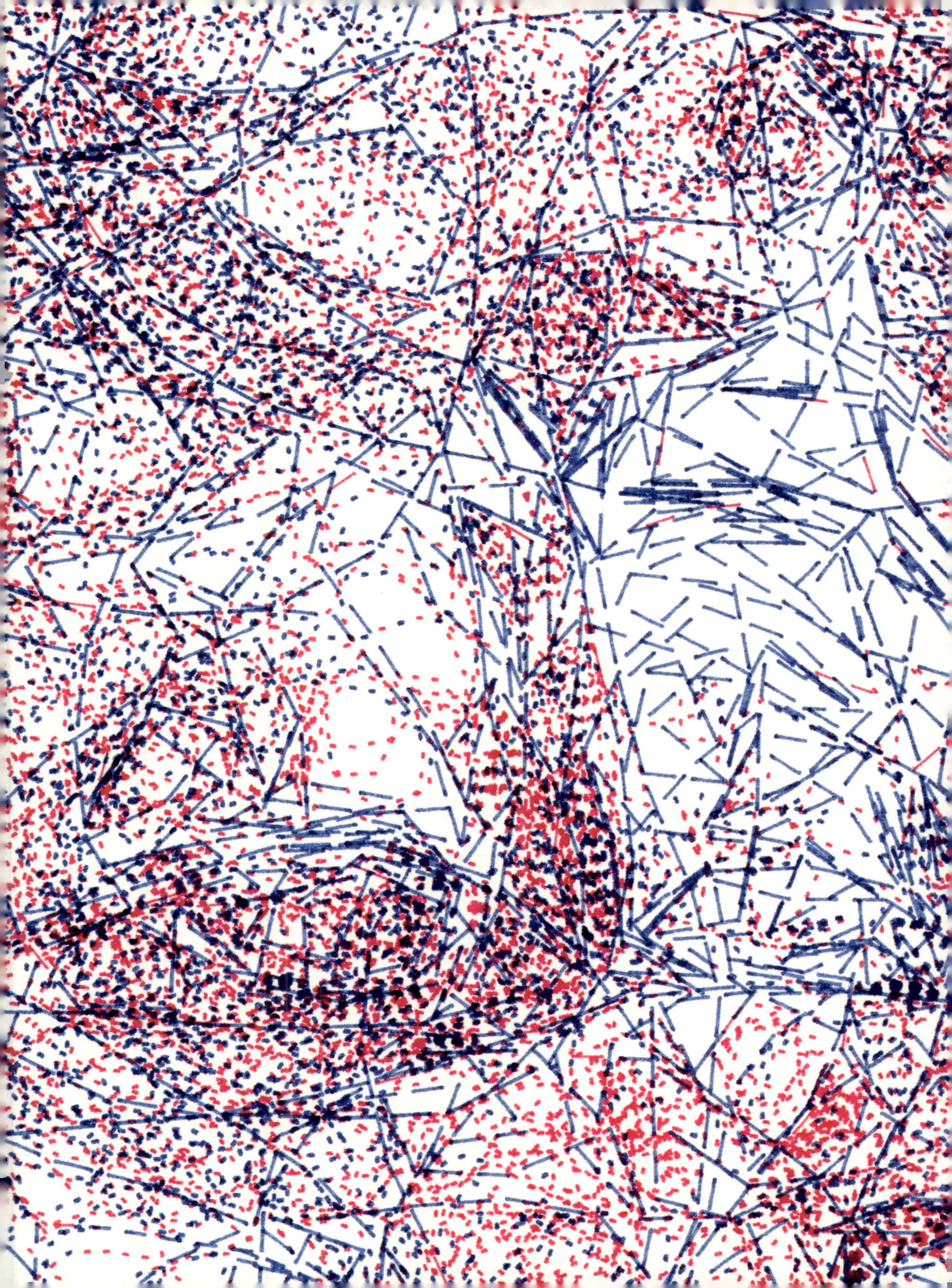

The geometry-material taxonomy

In this taxonomy, lines are categorized based on the relationship between geometry, which is understood to be the reader's mental construct of form or shape, and material, which is defined as the help by the substrate (canvas, paper, etc). Some lines exhibit a direct correlation between geometry and matter. For example, a line representing a vector might be marked from the base to the tip with a pen such that the ink at the base pools up slightly and bleeds into paper. The "base" of the vector geometry corresponds to the material base of the line. For other types of lines, the geometry and the matter of the drawing are distinct, such that the material is relegated to the domain of style. Consider for example, the use of a computer-controlled pen-plotter. The geometry of the line is independent of the color or type of pen used. In fact, a different pen could be swapped out mid plot. This would affect the appearance of the line, but would have no bearing on the geometry. If, however, the appearance of the line in a drawing was then measured and fed back into the structure of geometry such that it had a consequence on that geometry, the line would fall into another category of this taxonomy.

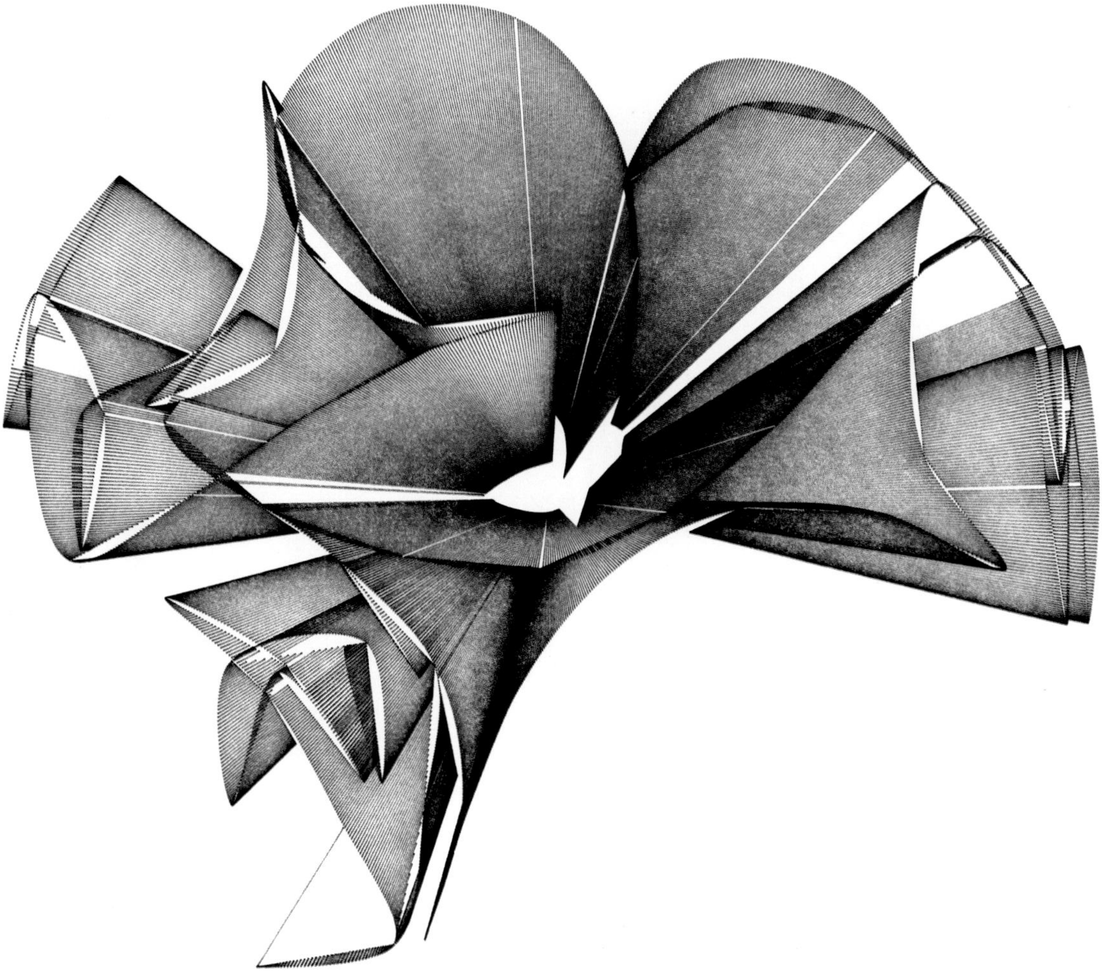

The behavior scope taxonomy

In this taxonomy, lines are organized on a spectrum relative to their local verses global behavior. Global, or compositional, behavior would be characterized by equations or logic that are defined outside of the line and imposed on the line. Local behavior is exhibited when the lines themselves are imbued with goals, rules, and traits. Local lines play out based on a vicinity or scope. Global lines are constructed systematically.

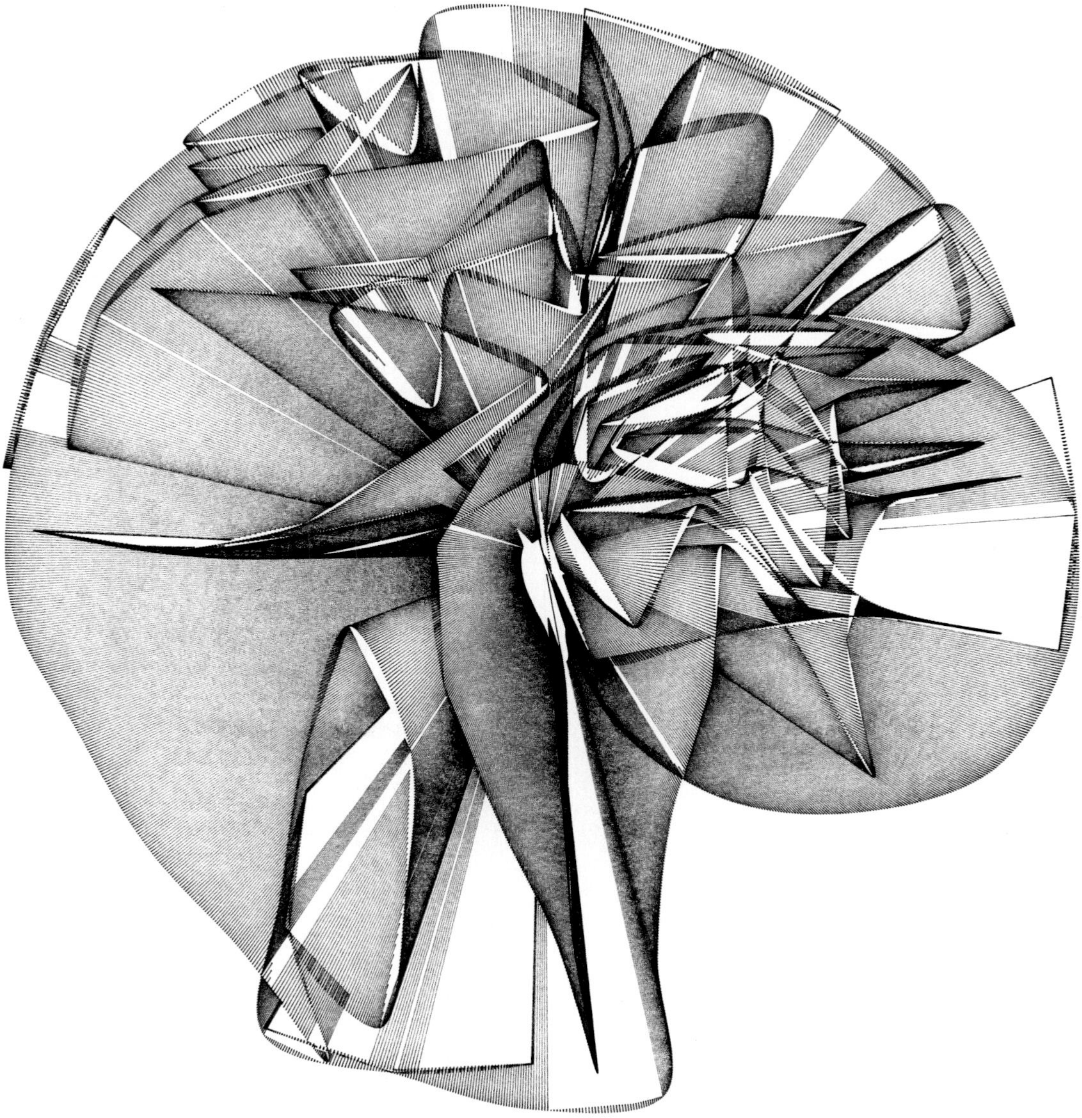

The auto-what? Taxonomy

Are lines automatic,[14] autographic, automated, or autonomous? Though these four auto-words are exact and absolute in terms of line designation, they are not mutually exclusive definitions. If deploying this taxonomy, it might be tempting to create a category, "none of the above" to classify a line that would not seem to fit under any of those categories. However, despite sharing a common root word, it may be the case that these four terms cover the complete range of all possible lines.

Exercise 2.1 *One mark, two readings*
Make a drawing with one kind of mark that can be ambiguously read based on either the taxonomies articulated, or a taxonomy of your own. Respect a notion of ambiguity that involves two or more seemingly contradictory meanings being simultaneously sustained, which is very different from what would be visible by drawing one kind of line in one area and another in a different area. It will likely be necessary to edit a mark-making function and or "wrap" it in another function.

Exercise 2.2 *Line Finder*
Write a function that finds lines in an existing drawing. Create a drawing that highlights, isolates, or otherwise materializes the found line(s).

Exercise 2.3 *Line-Maker+Line-Finder+Line-Maker*
Incorporate a "line finder" into functions already written to create lines.
Use the line finder to direct, limit, and/or bias the creation of new lines.

The final algorithm referenced in this chapter is an example well articulated by Neil Gershenfeld in his book, *The Nature of Mathematical Modeling*, in which Gershenfeld presents highly technical methods for mathematical modeling as a craft-based inquiry into the meaning of the models themselves, not merely their applications. Gershenfeld sets this up in his introduction by explaining,

"if you seek to make a mathematical model of a violin, you could use a numerical model based on a first-principles description. This lets you match your model parameters to measurements on a real instrument and change parameters between a Stradivarius and a Guarneri. However, running it in real time will require a supercomputer, and the effort to find good parameters for the model is almost as much work as building a real violin. Alternatively, you could try to use an analytical (pencil-and-paper) solution to the governing equations in return for some large approximations you may be able to find a useful explicit solution, but it might not sound very good. Finally, you could forget about the underlying governing equations entirely and experimentally try to find an effective description of how the player's actions are related to the sound made by the instrument."[15]

Later, Gershenfeld articulates the "lattice gas," a model and algorithm that very roughly simulates the diffusion of gas. The strange but elegant aspect of this algorithm is that it never quantifies or defines a diffusing particle. Instead, a lattice swaps true/false values along the lattice, which is rendered at any single moment by converting the count of True values at each lattice vertex into a pixel value (in the case of an image) or a line (in the case of a drawing).[16]

Notes

1. Frascari, Marco. *Eleven Exercises in the Art of Architectural Drawing: Slow Food for the Architects Imagination*. London: Routledge, 2011, 9–10.
2. Stiny, George. Shape: Talking about Seeing and Doing. Cambridge, MA: MIT Press, 2006, 3.
3. Ibid., 5.
4. Ibid., 5.
5. Ibid., 61.
6. Montfort, Nick, Patsy Baudoin, John Bell, Ian Bogost, Jeremy Douglas, Mark C. Marino, Michael Mateas, Casey Reas, Mark Sample, and Noah Vawter. *10 PRINT CHR$(205.5 RND(1)) GOTO 10*. Cambridge: MIT Press, 2014.
7. Taylor, Grant D. *When the Machine Made Art: The Troubled History of Computer Art*. New York: Bloomsbury Academic, 2014. 27. This book describes the critical anxiety around computer art and the first "Computer Art Contest," held in 1963 and the winning entry, "Splatter Pattern."
8. Montfort, Nick, Patsy Baudoin, John Bell, Ian Bogost, Jeremy Douglas, Mark C. Marino, Michael Mateas, Casey Reas, Mark Sample, and Noah Vawter. *10 PRINT CHR$*(205.5 RND(1)) GOTO 10. Cambridge: MIT Press, 2014, 106–118.
9. Hendrix, Grady. "Choose Your Own Adventure Books: How The Cave of Time Taught Us to Love Interactive Entertainment." Slate Magazine. February 17, 2011. Accessed February 20, 2018. http://www.slate.com/articles/arts/culturebox/2011/02/choose_your_own_adventure.single.html
10. Empson, William. *Seven Types of Ambiguity*. New York: New Direction Publ., 1980.
11. Perlman, Elliot. *Seven Types of Ambiguity*. New York: Riverhead Books, 2005.
12. Ingold, Tim. *Lines a Brief History*. London: Routledge, 2016, 41–50. In this text, a taxonomy of lines is offered: the thread, the trace, and the cut/crack/crease. Though Ingold acknowledges that many lines don't fit within this taxonomy, it is nonetheless relatively comprehensive.
13. Powell, Helen, and David Leatherbarrow. *Masterpieces of Architectural Drawing*. New York: Abbeville Press, 1983, 40.
14. Maclagan,David. *Line Let Loose: Scribbling, Doodling and Automatic Drawing*. London: Reaktion Books, 2014. In this context, automatic refers to that which is without planning, conscious control, or attention, like a scribble or doodle. This is described in detail by David Maclagan as he writes, "What are the factors that might then qualify a drawing as being "automatic"? Besides the claim to have been drawing in a dissociated state or under some compulsion, there is also a style of drawing that is more or less fluid or gestural, and that seems to bear the evidence of spontaneity. But many such drawings are called automatic not so much because they have been created spontaneously, or with a variable degree of "floating attention," but because the are laying claim to being authentic examples of unconscious form creation, or else because their impoverished and fluent appearance is simply assumed to have been the result of some kind of automatism.
15. Gershenfeld, Neil. *The Nature of Mathematical Modeling*. Cambridge: Cambridge University Press, 2000, 1.
16. Ibid., 102–104.

A nearly filled drawing with *spaceFillingLines*.

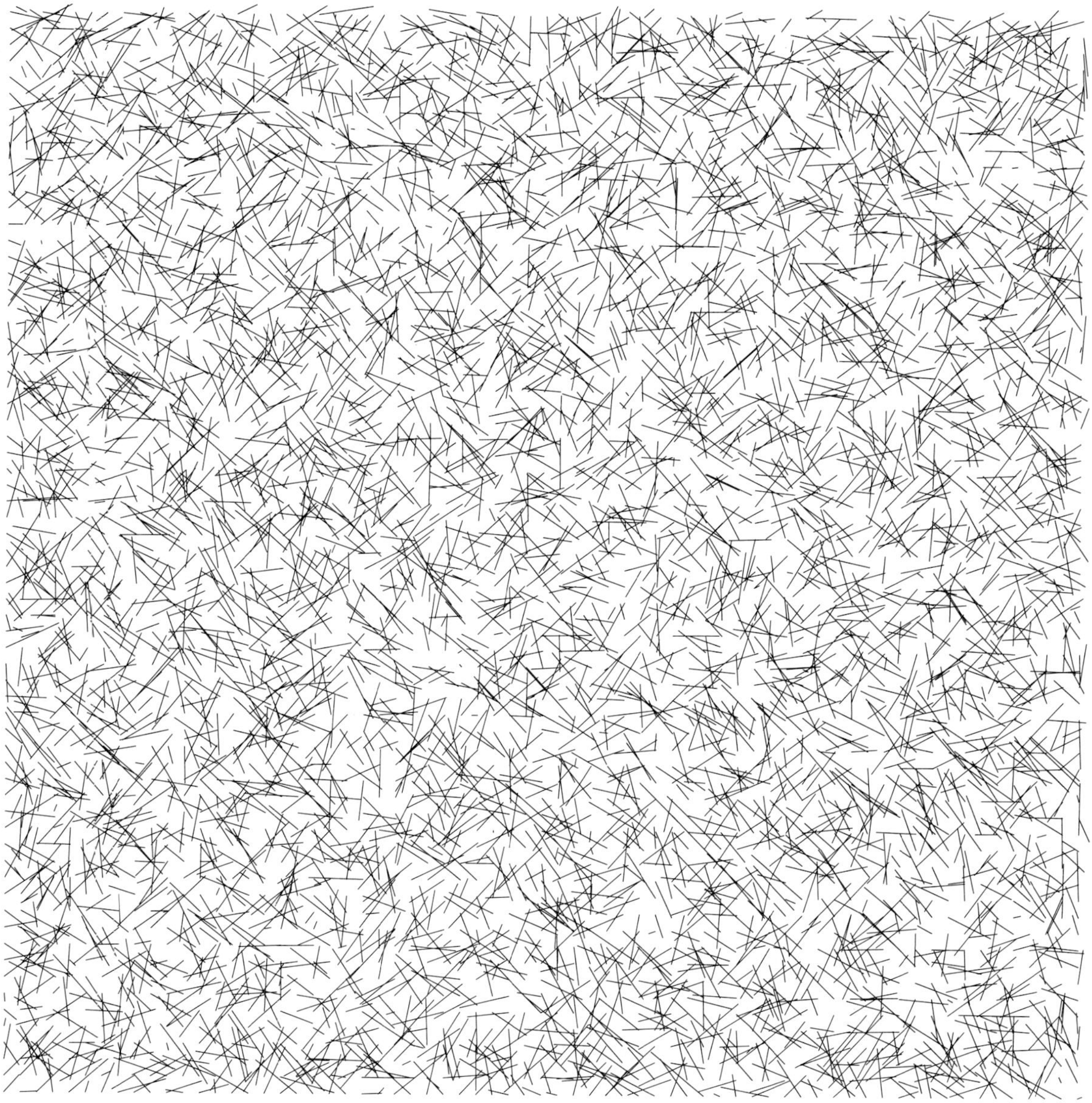

This field of segments is barely classifiable as a drawing. The algorithm provides a basic structure, but nothing is done to relate the marks to one another.

We could adjust so that the segments are trimmed based on previously marked segments, so the presence of lines has implications on future lines.

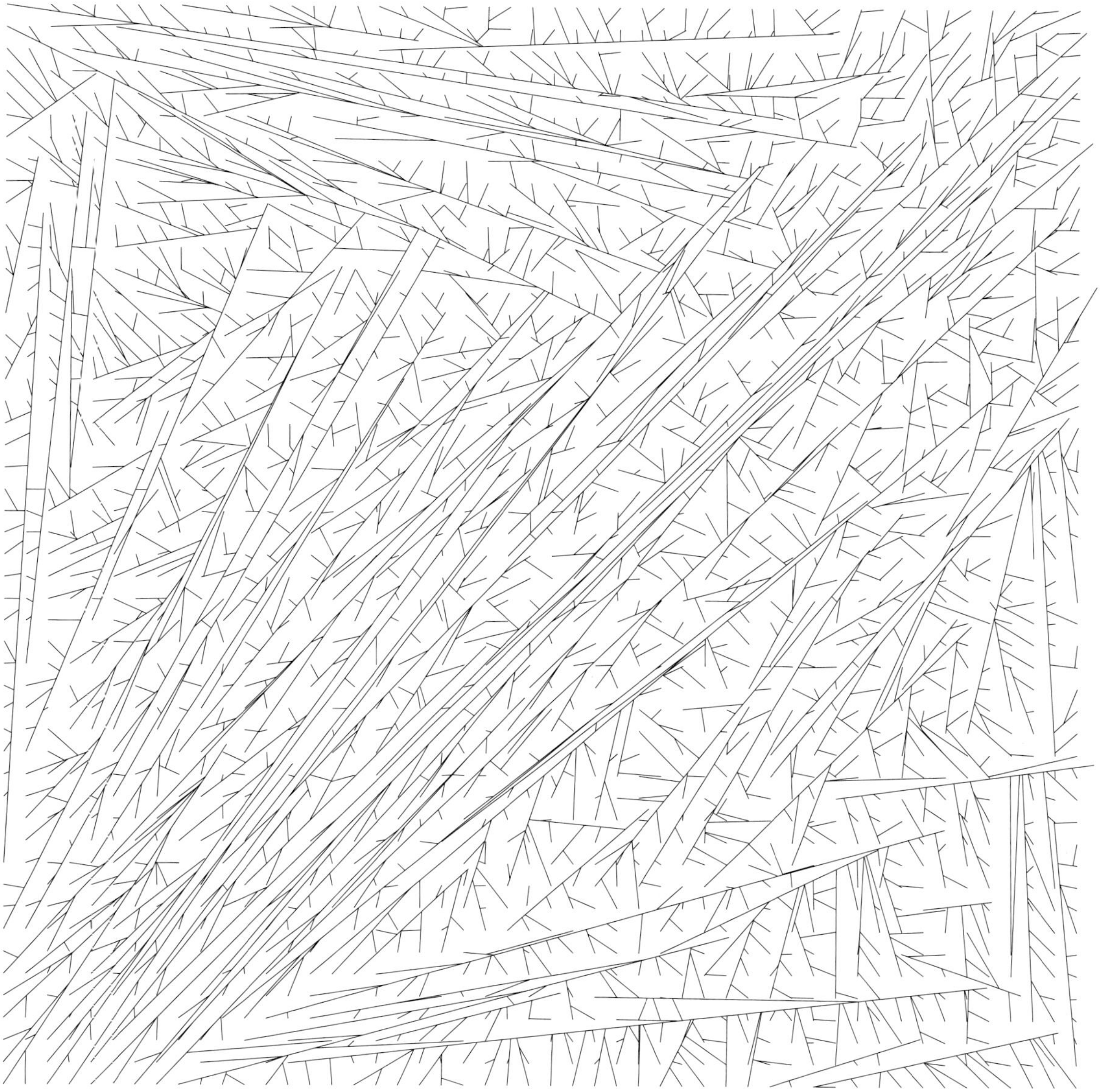

This would be even more significant if the segments were longer.

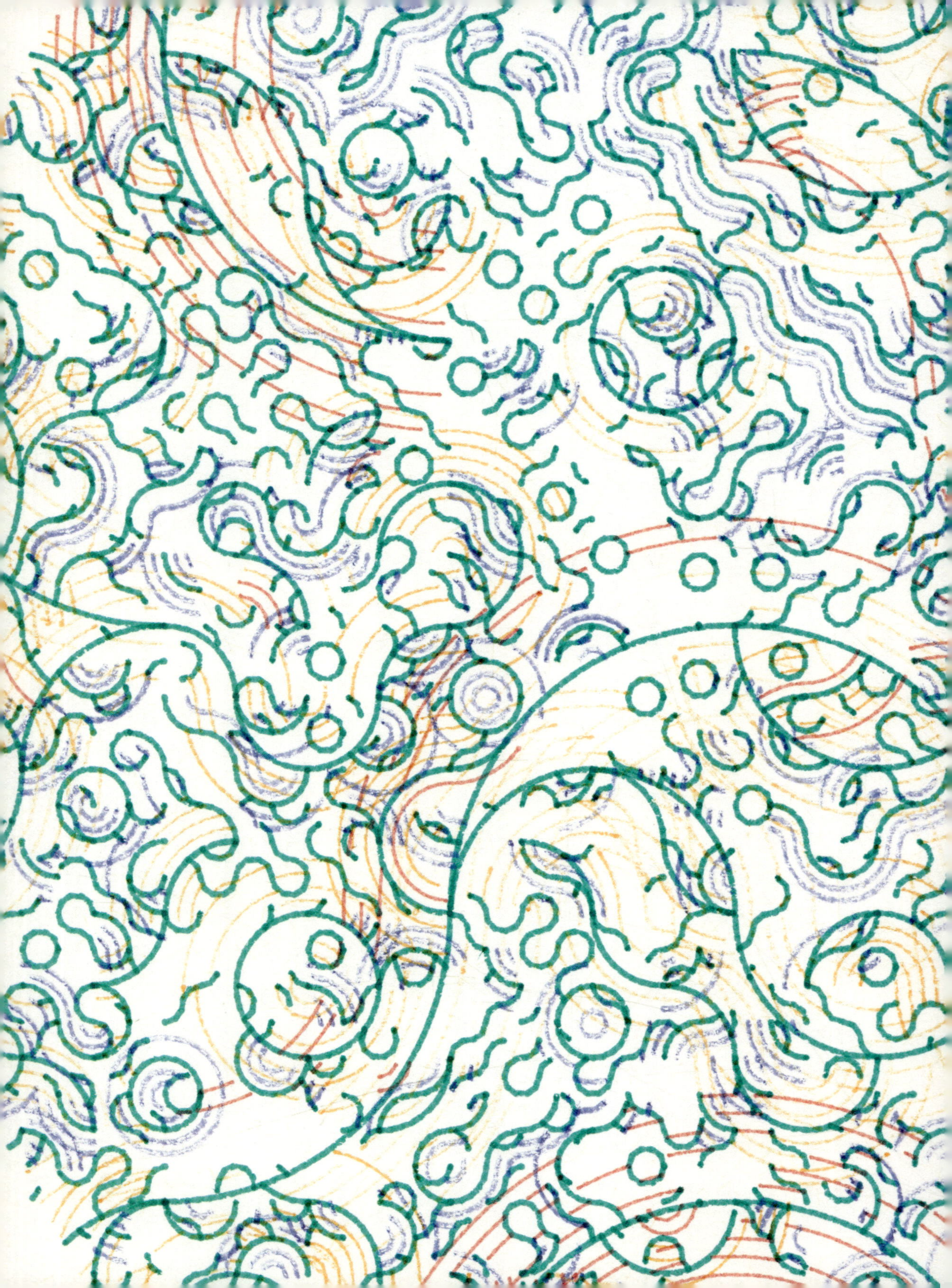

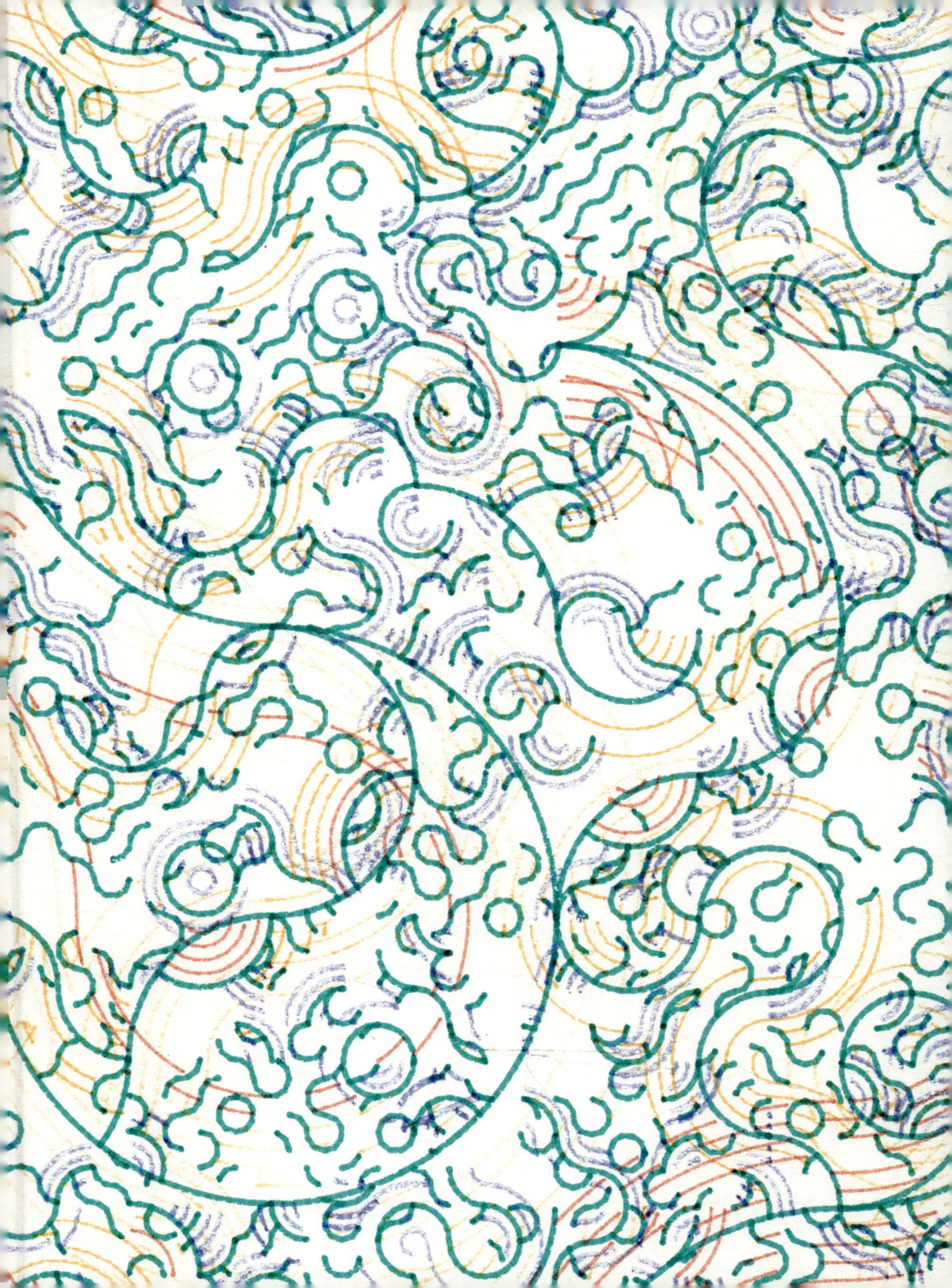

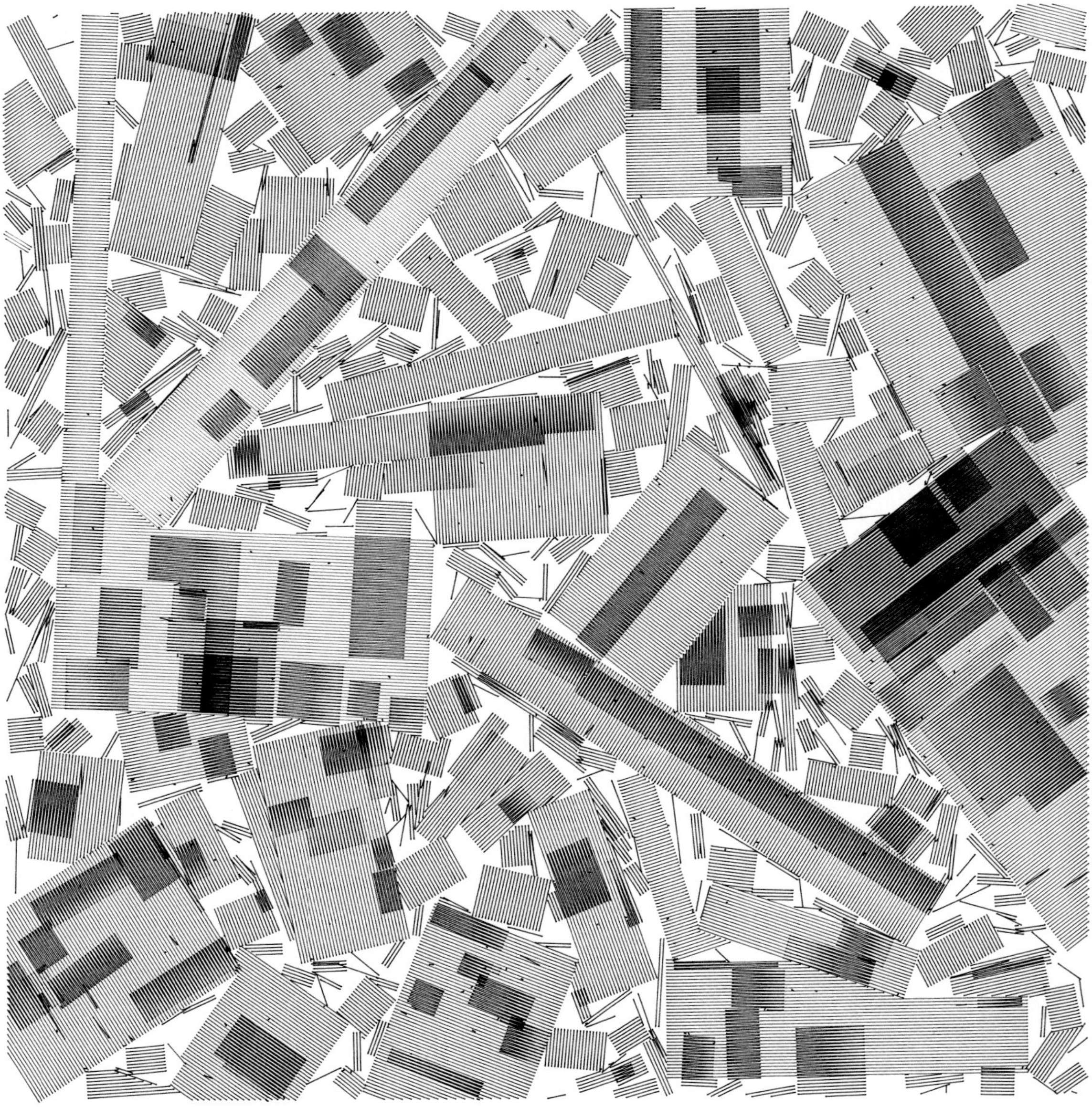

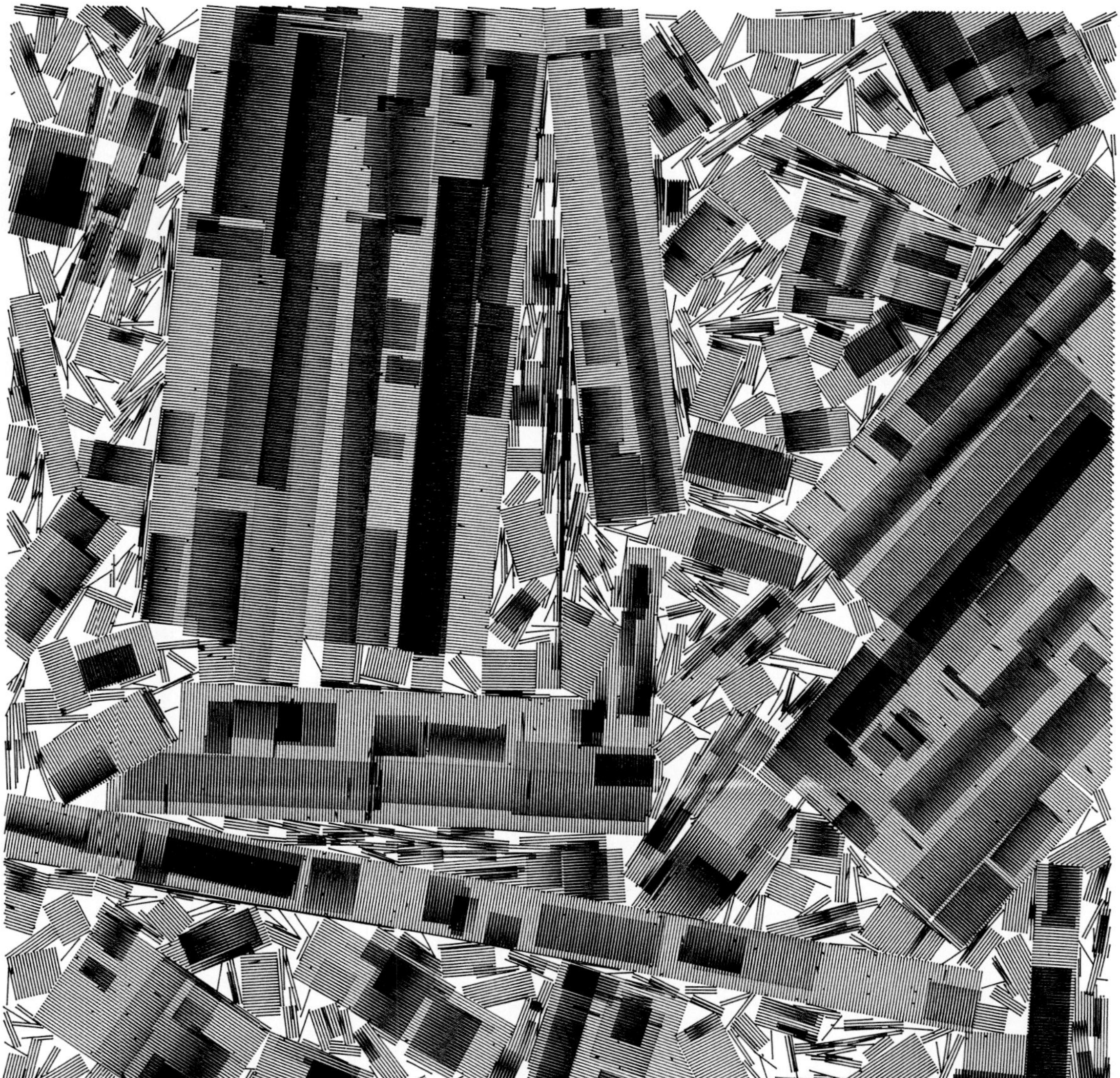

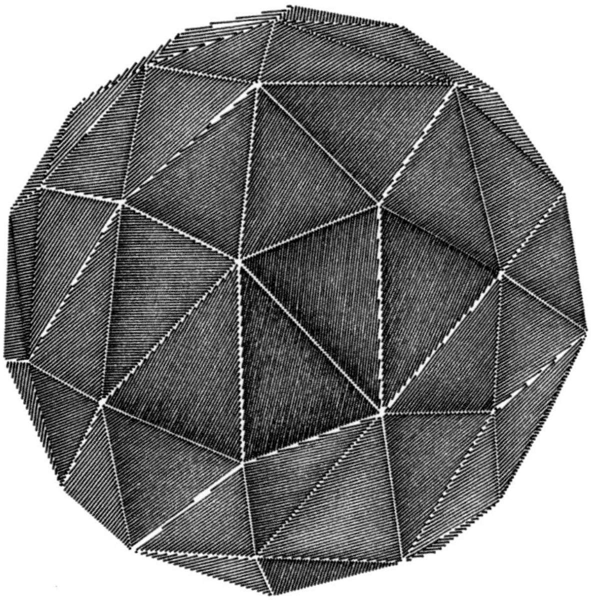

A field of lines, broken by each other and receding to a moving focal point.

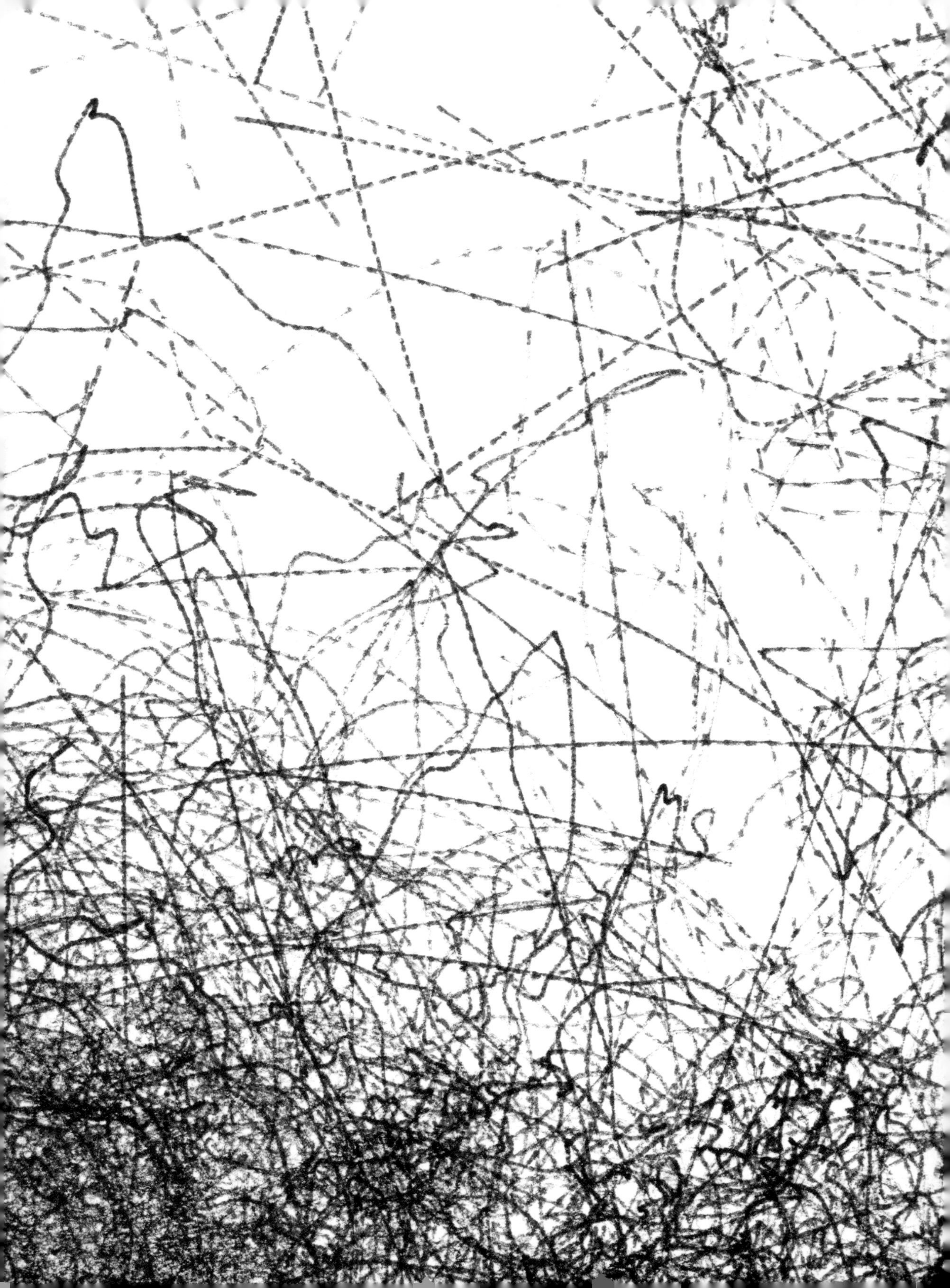

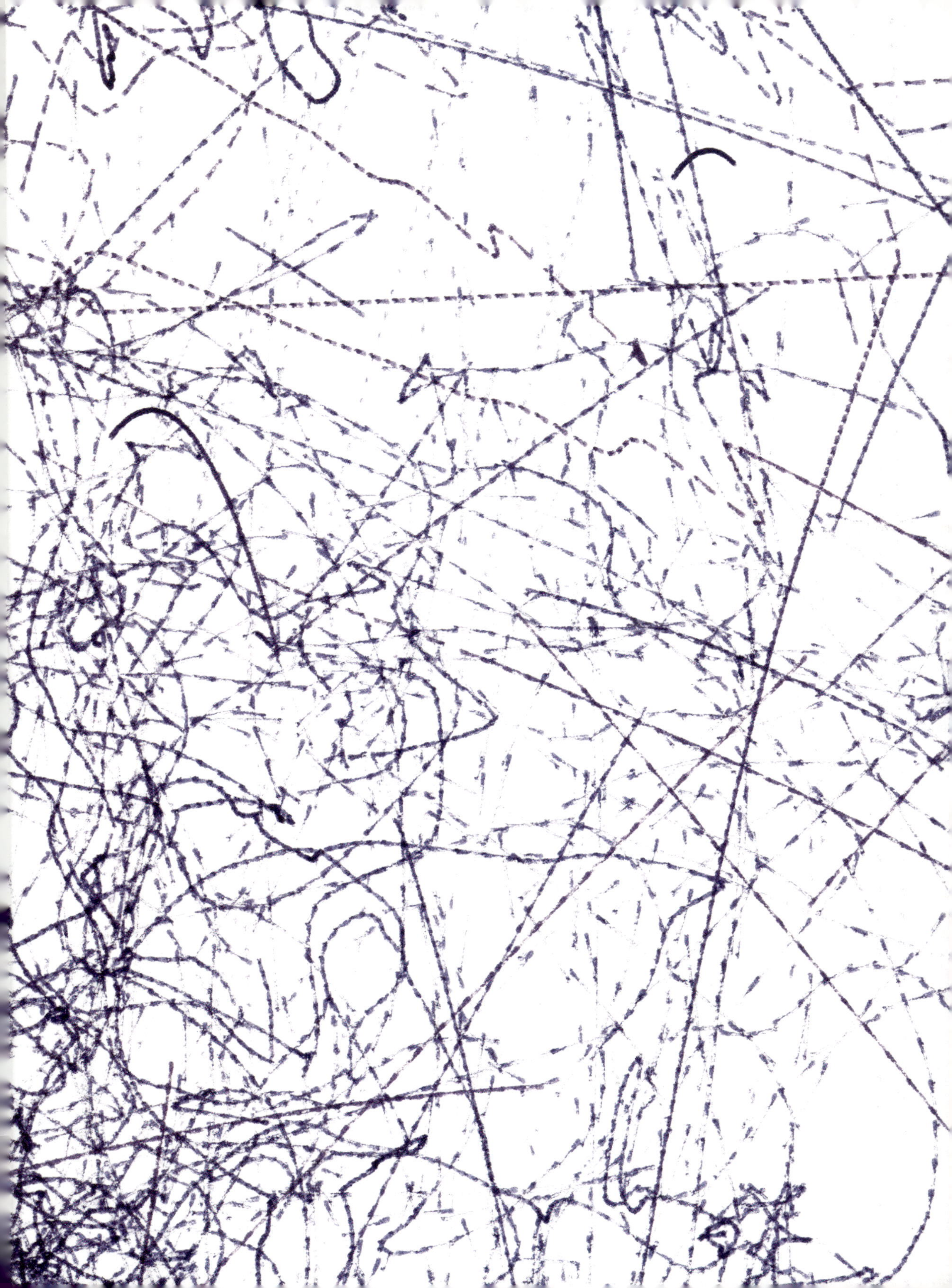

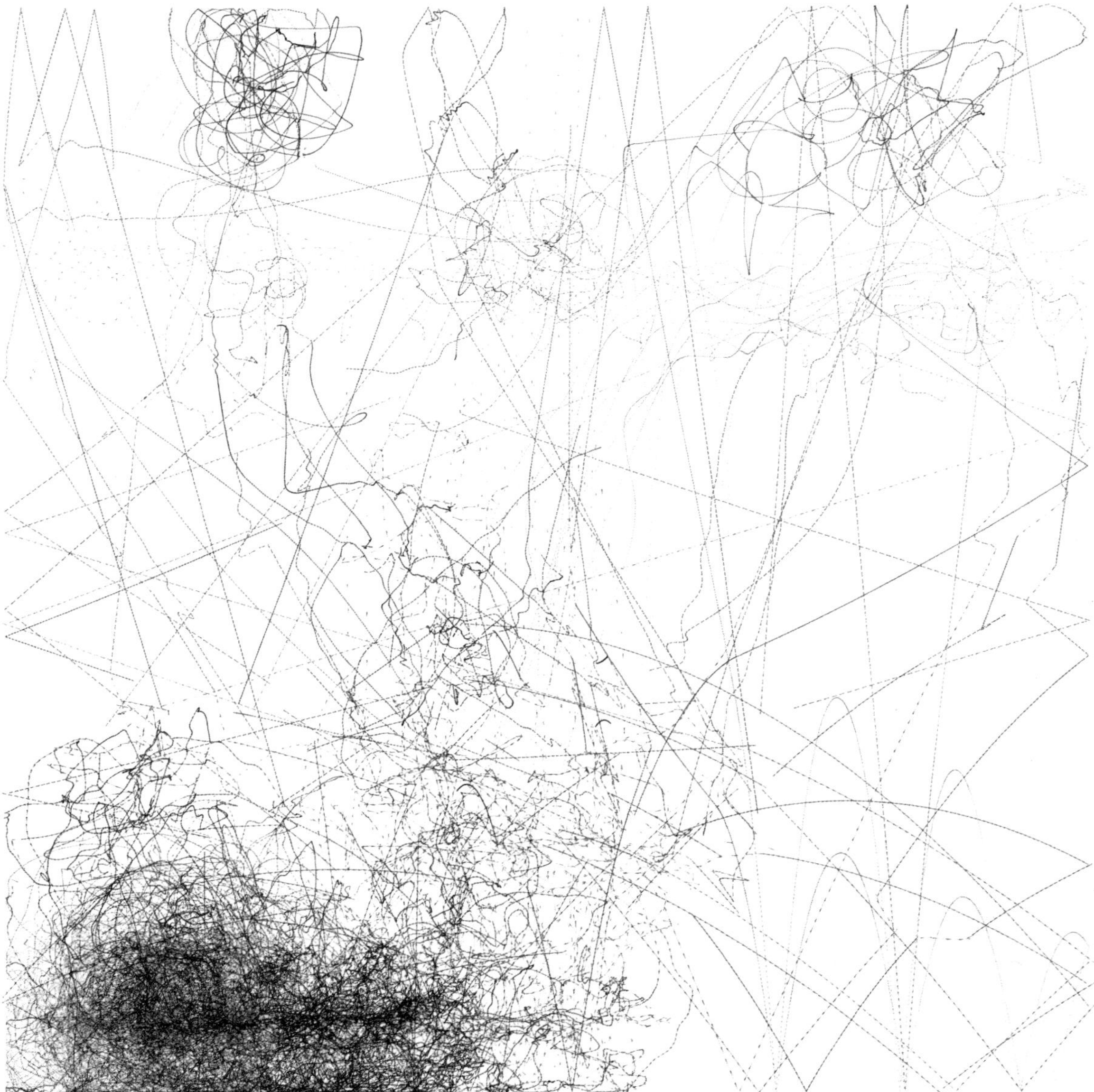

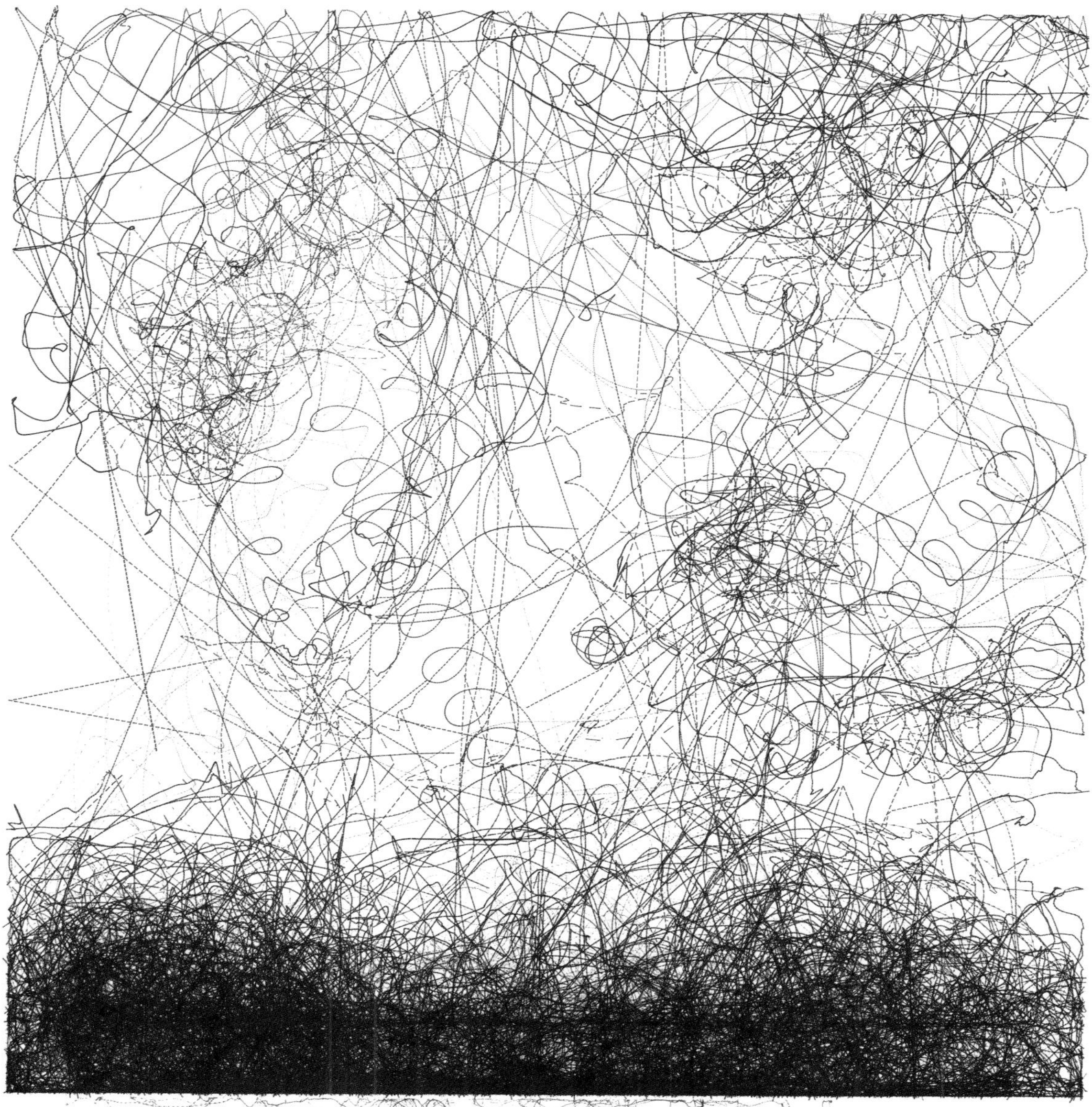

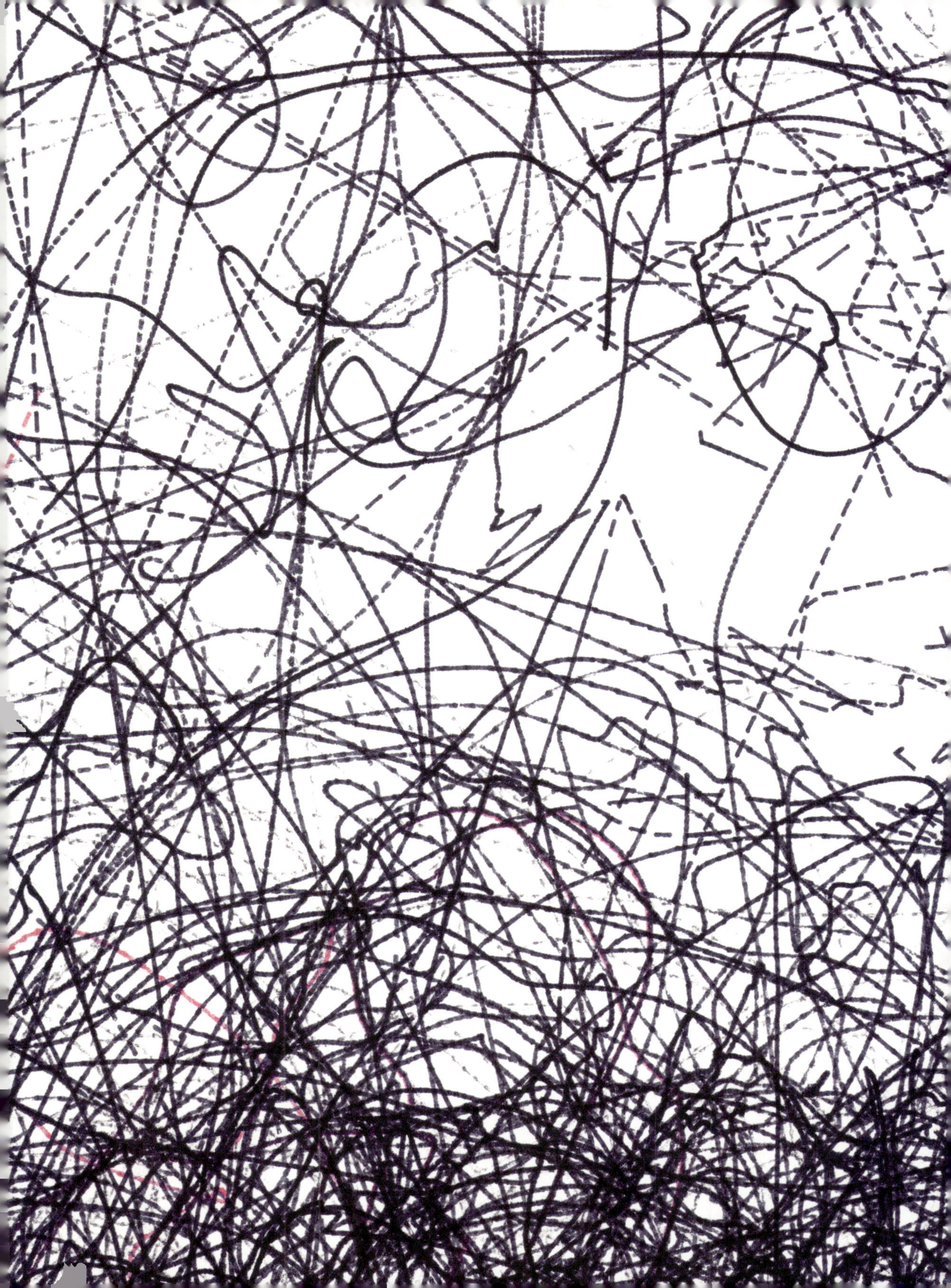

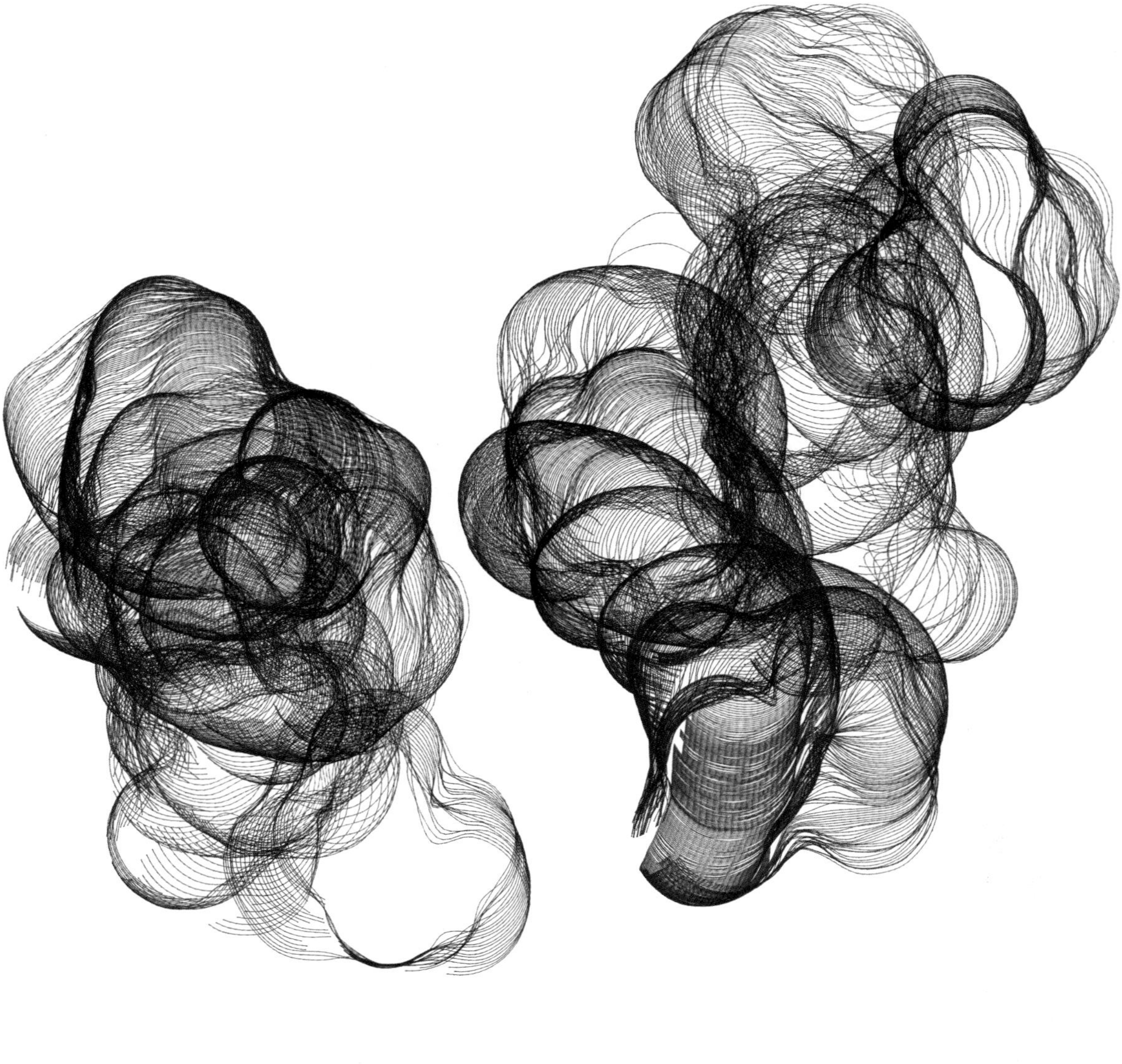

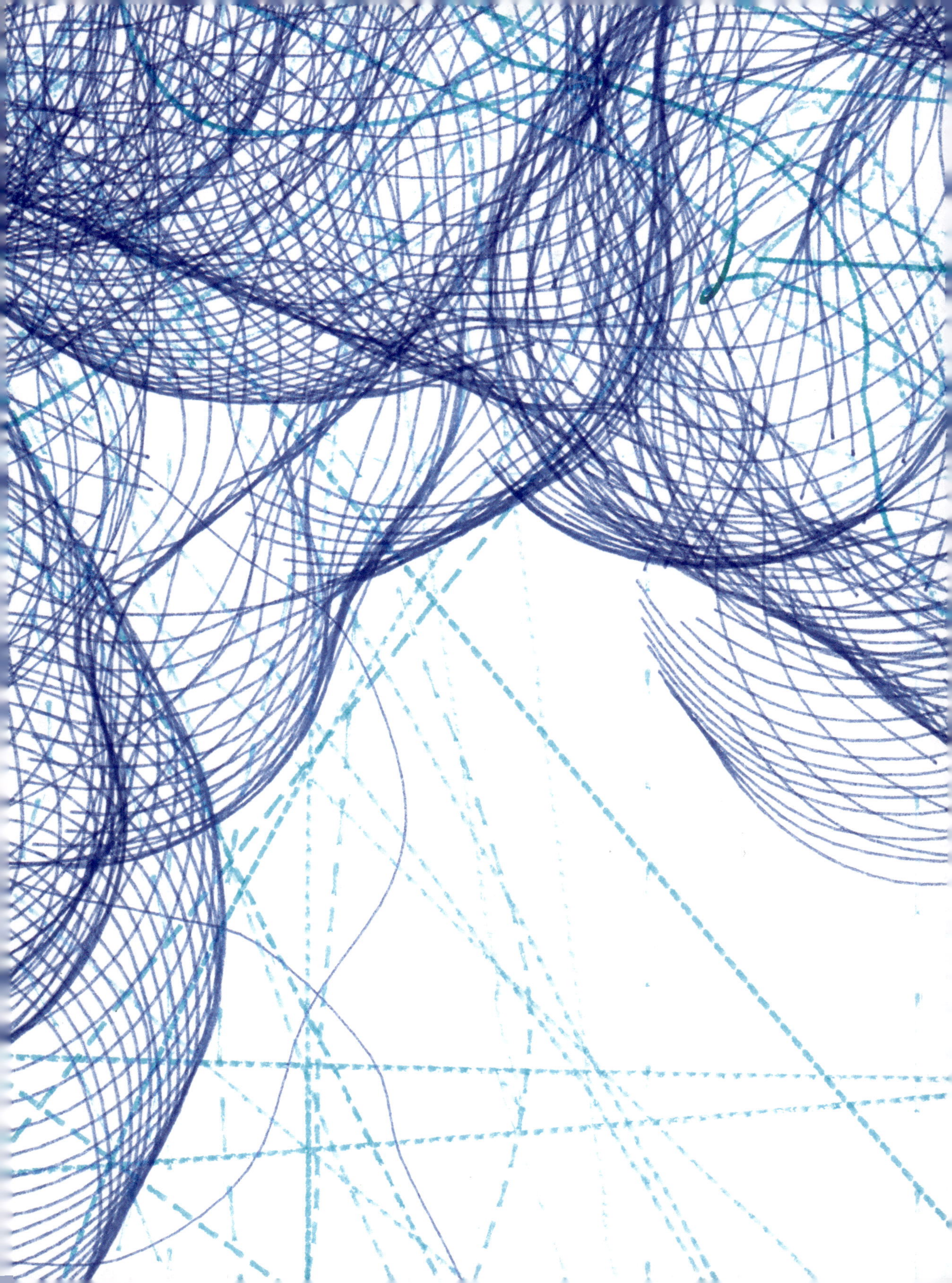

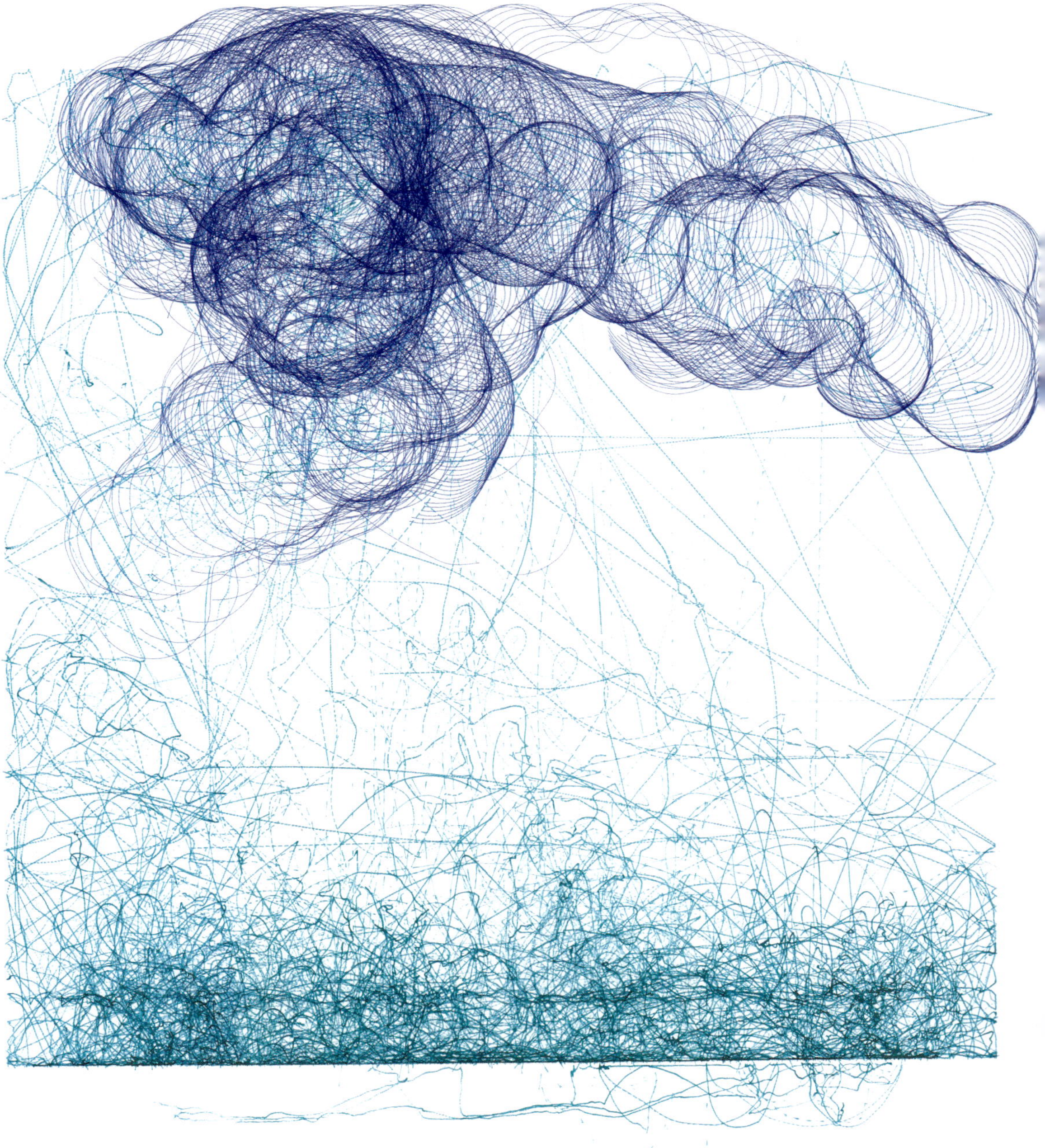

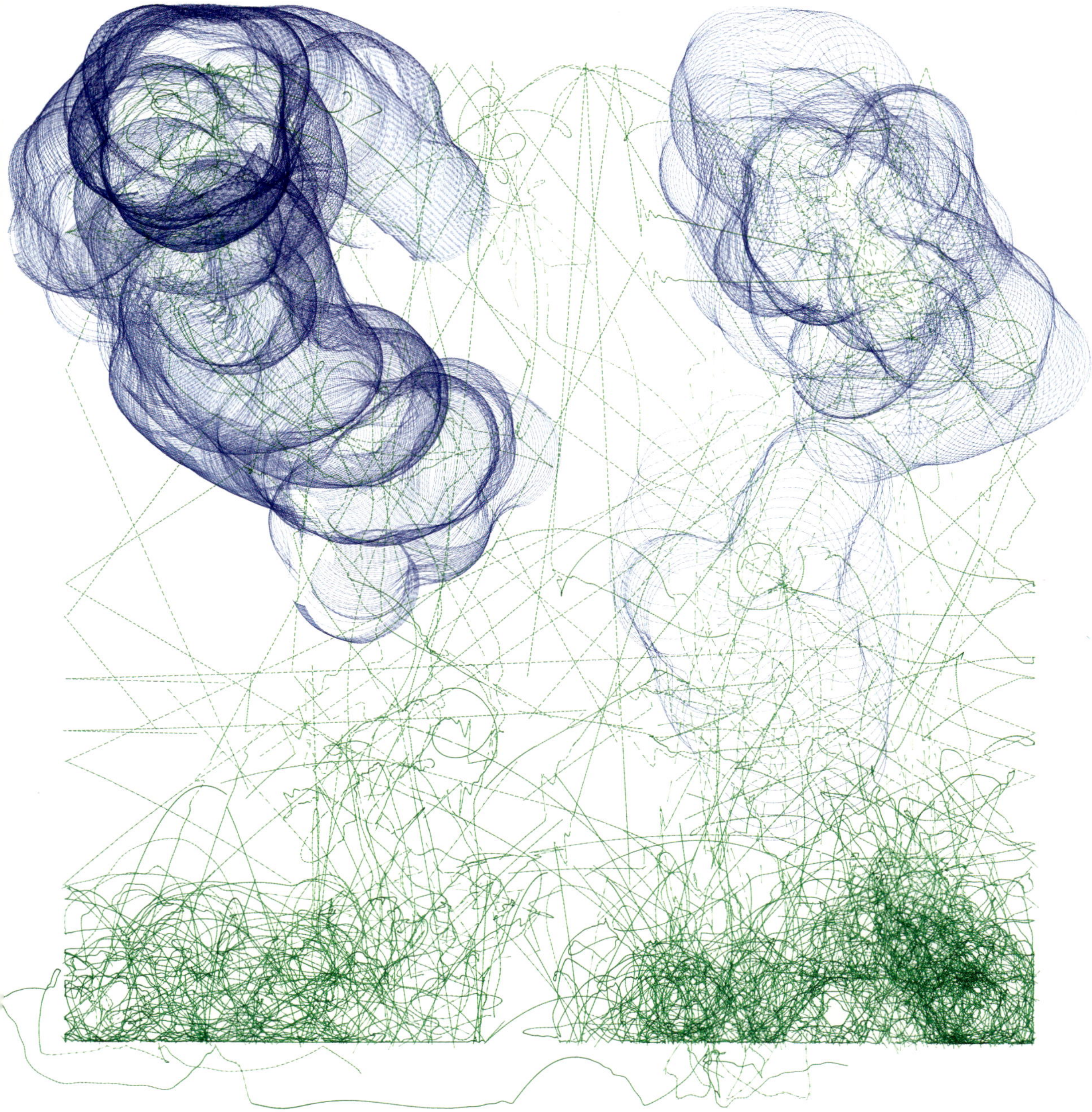

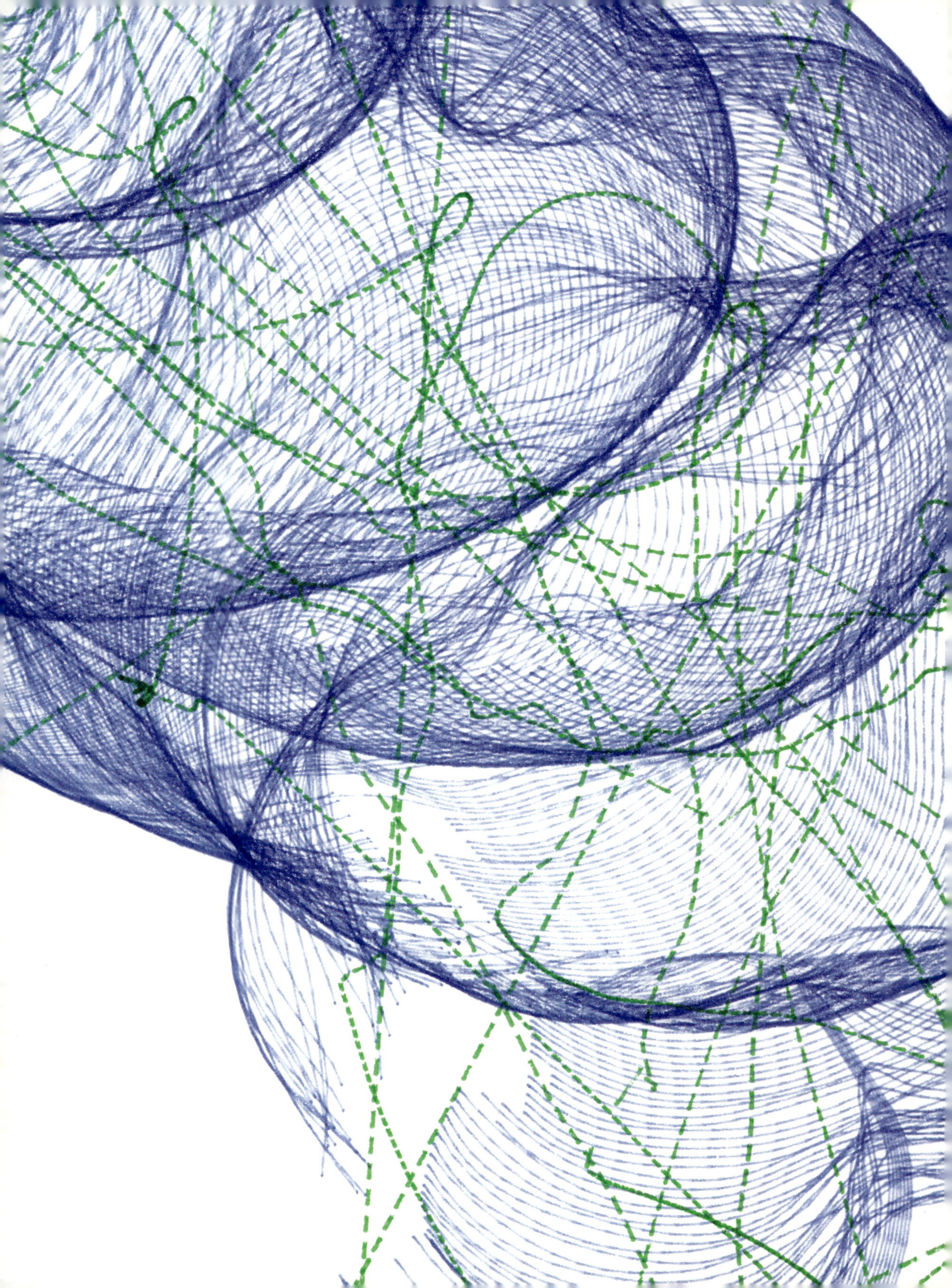

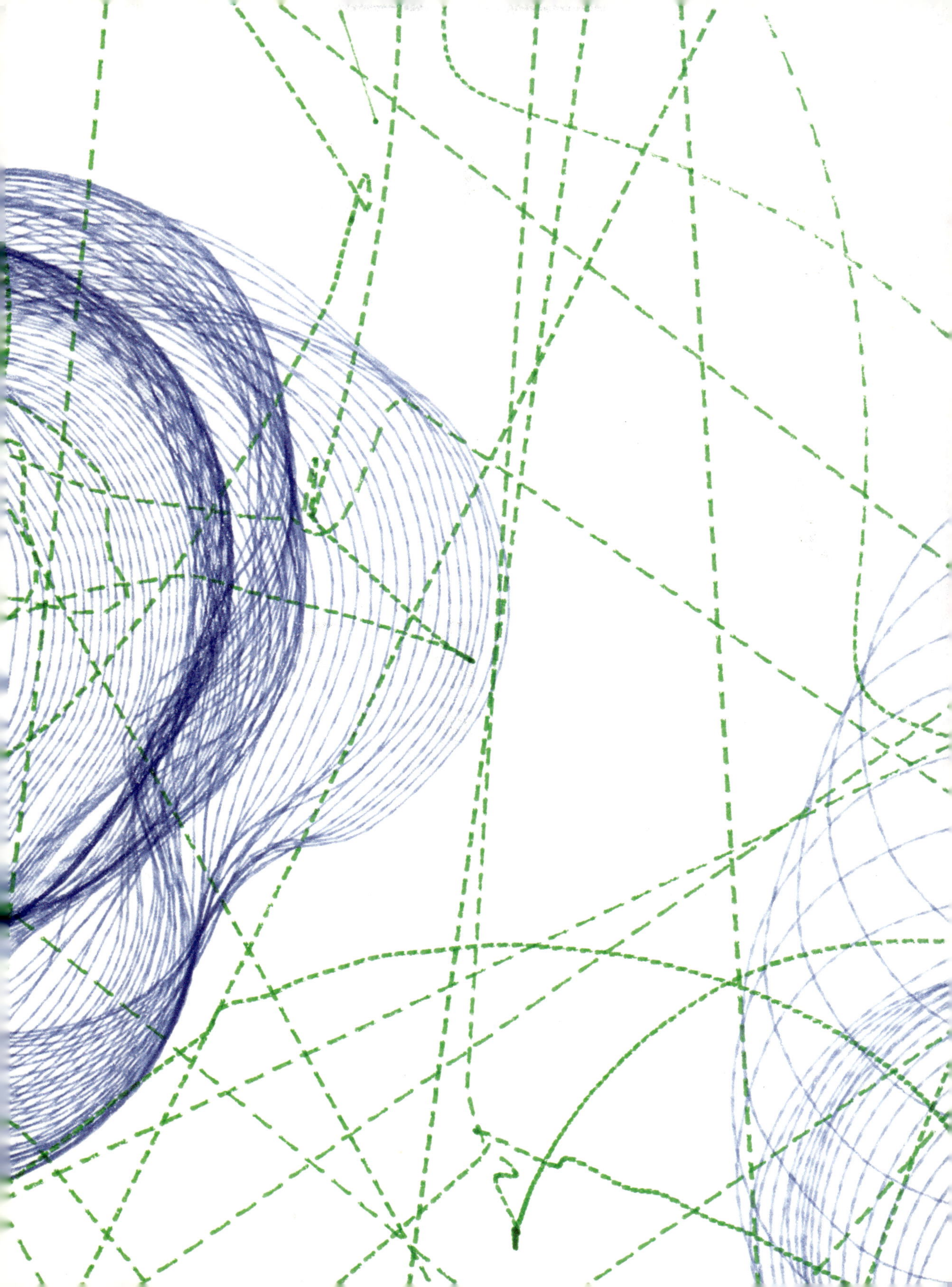

The initial state of a true/false lattice rendered as a pixel grid. If a joint and its neighbors are all true, pixels are rendered white; if all false, black. Four stages of gray in-between are based on the count of true/false at each joint.

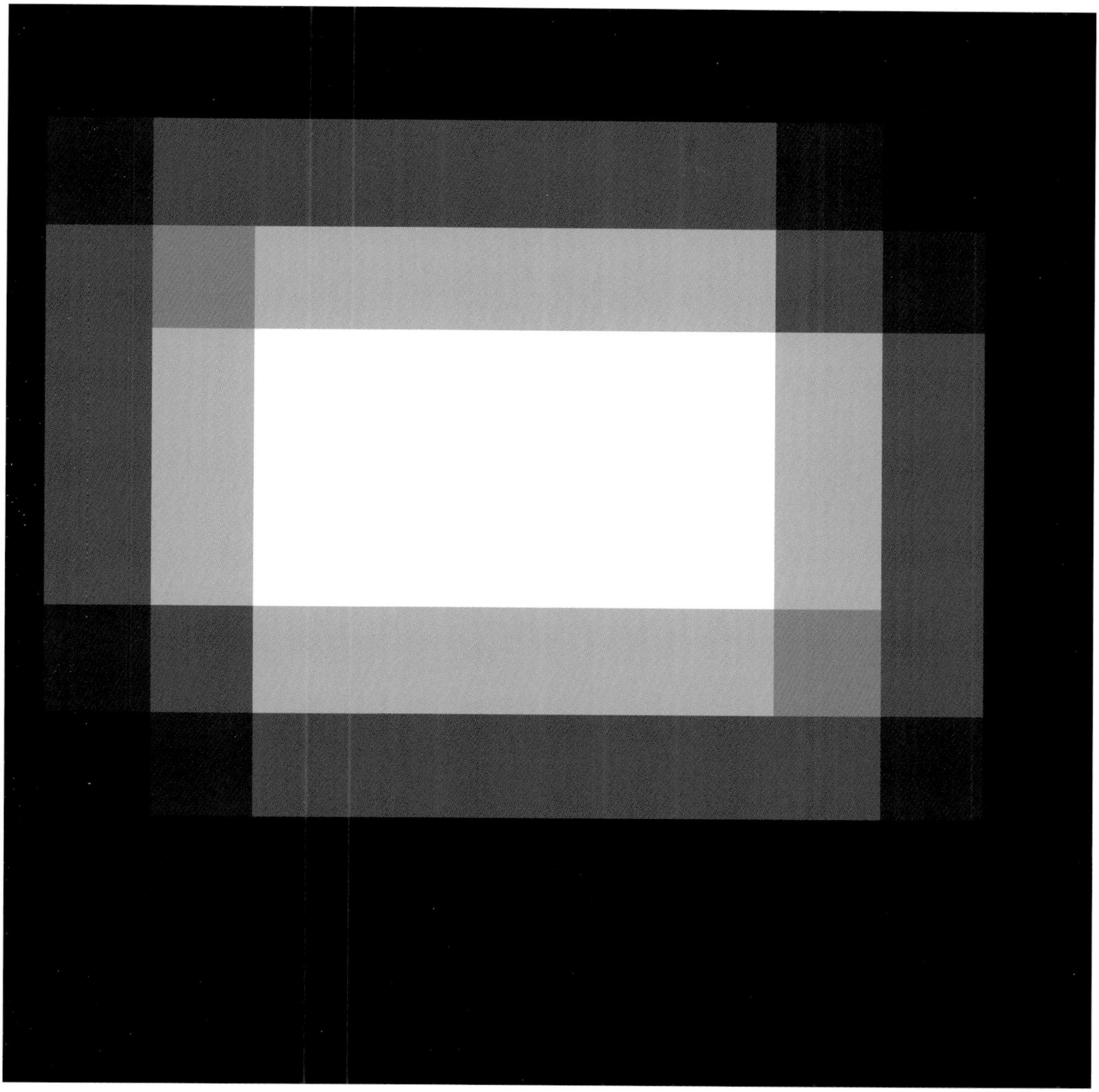

ABOVE AND FOLLOWING SPREAD After a few steps of a diffusion simulation with a true/false lattice rendered as a pixel grid. If a joint and its neighbors are all true, pixels are rendered white; if all false, black. Four stages of gray in-between are based on the count of true/false at each joint.

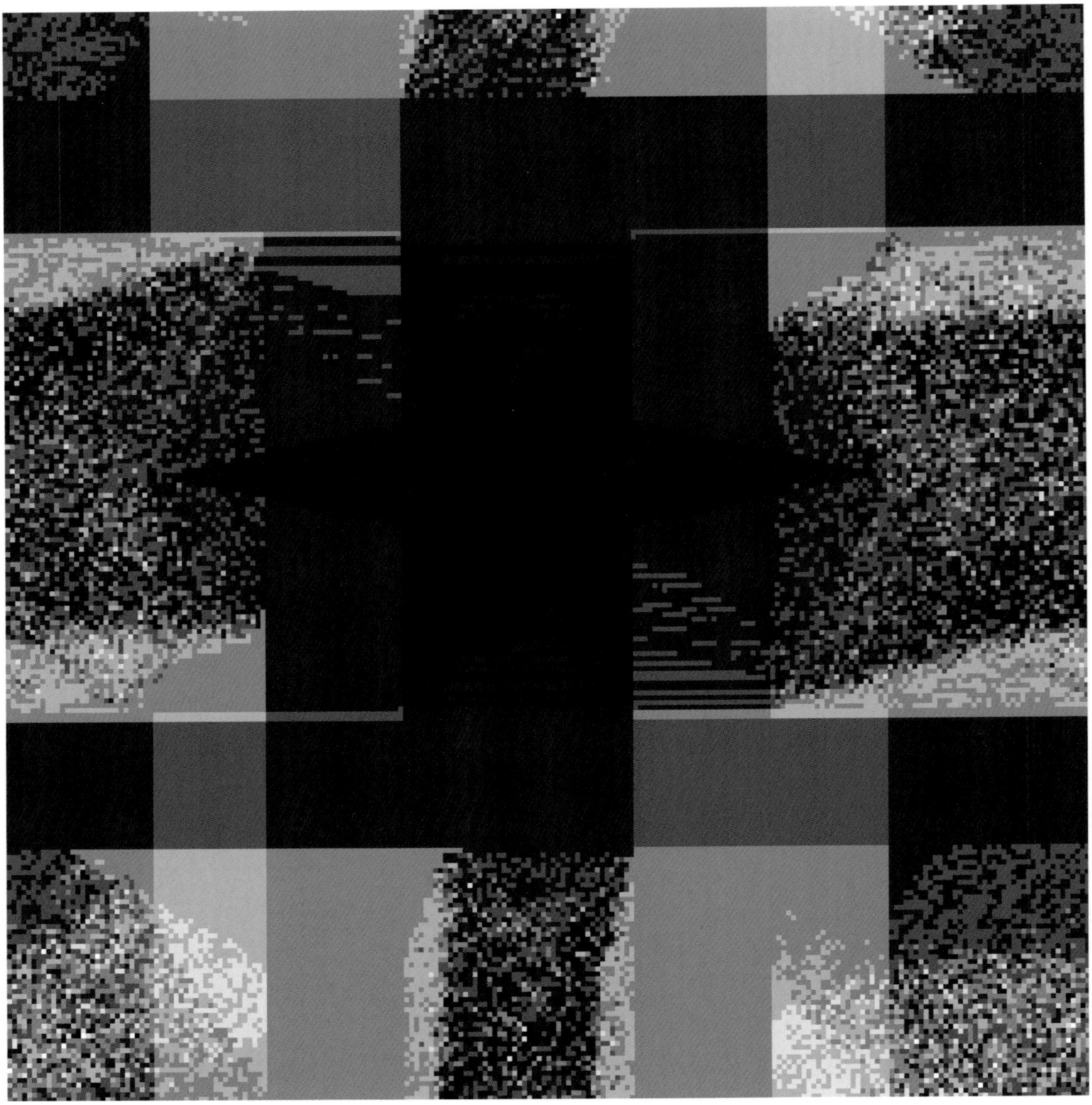

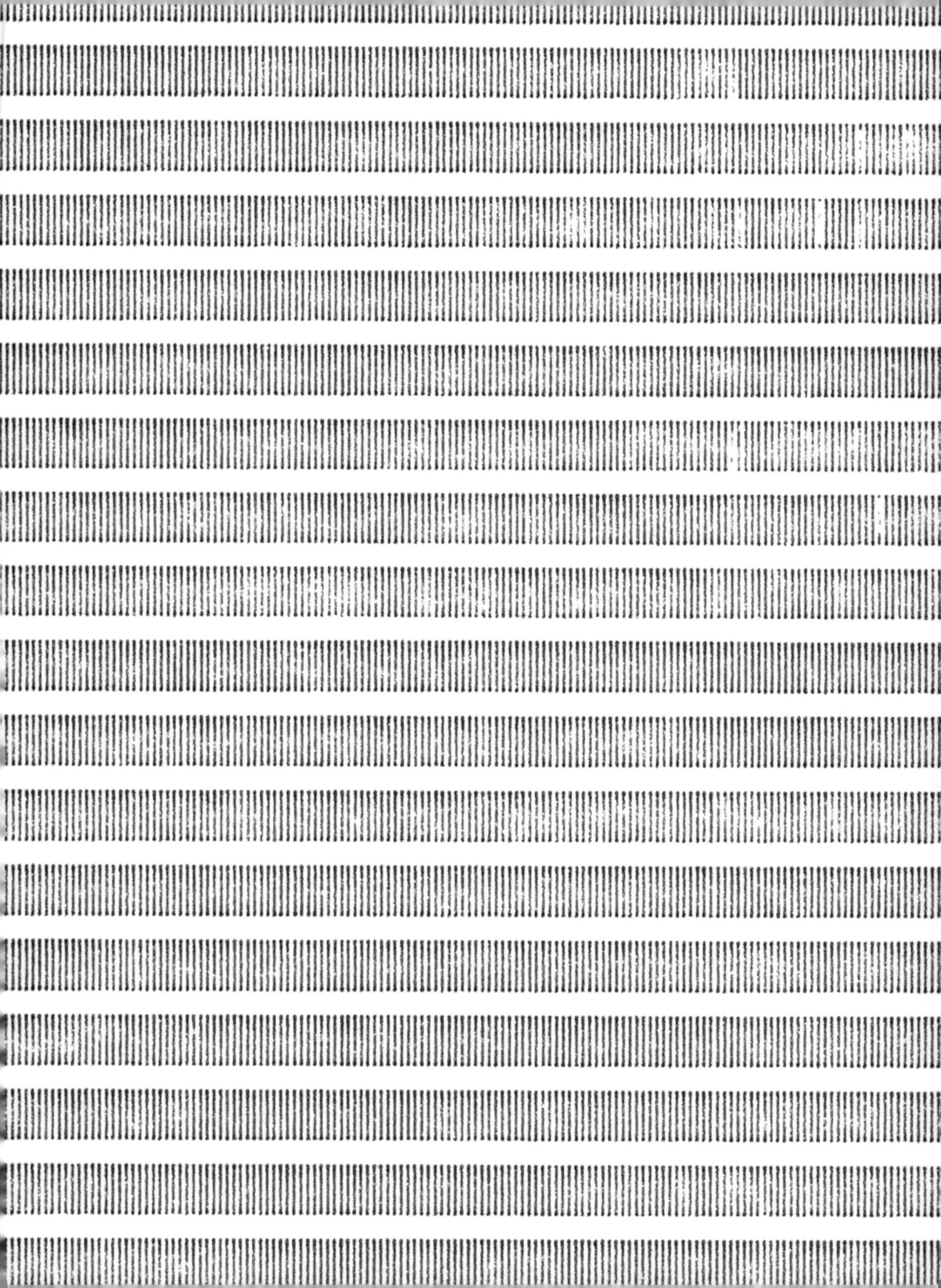

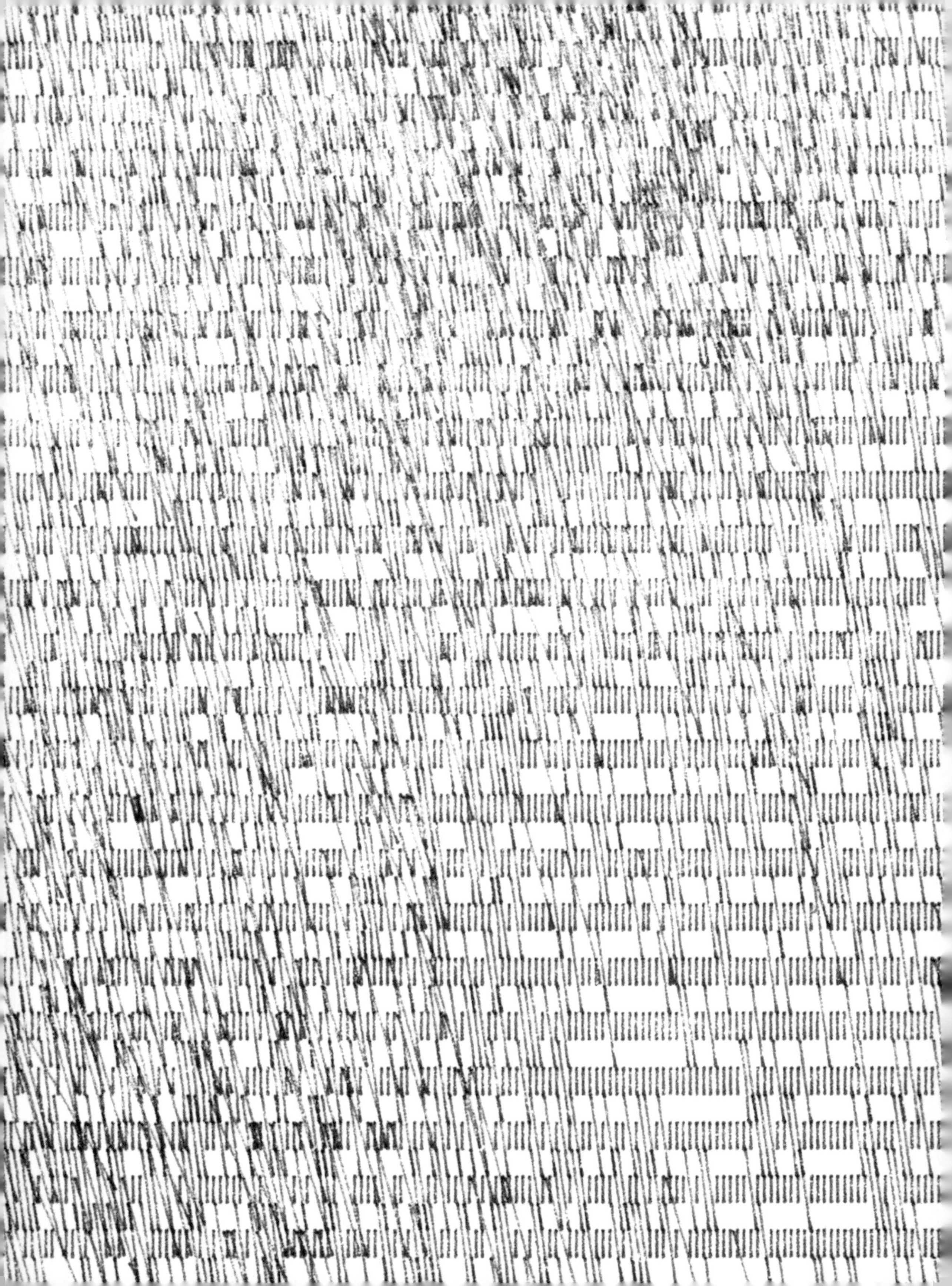

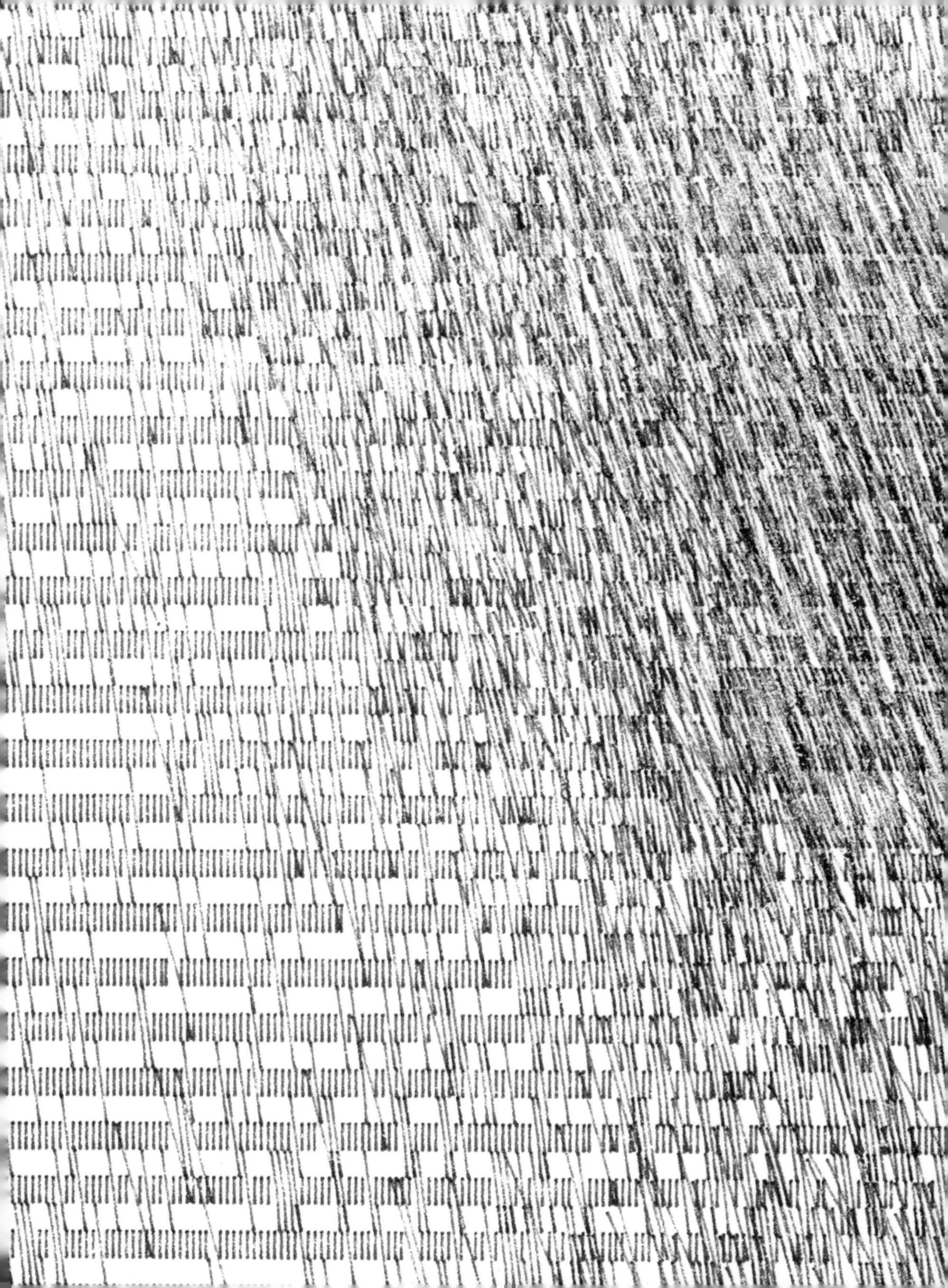

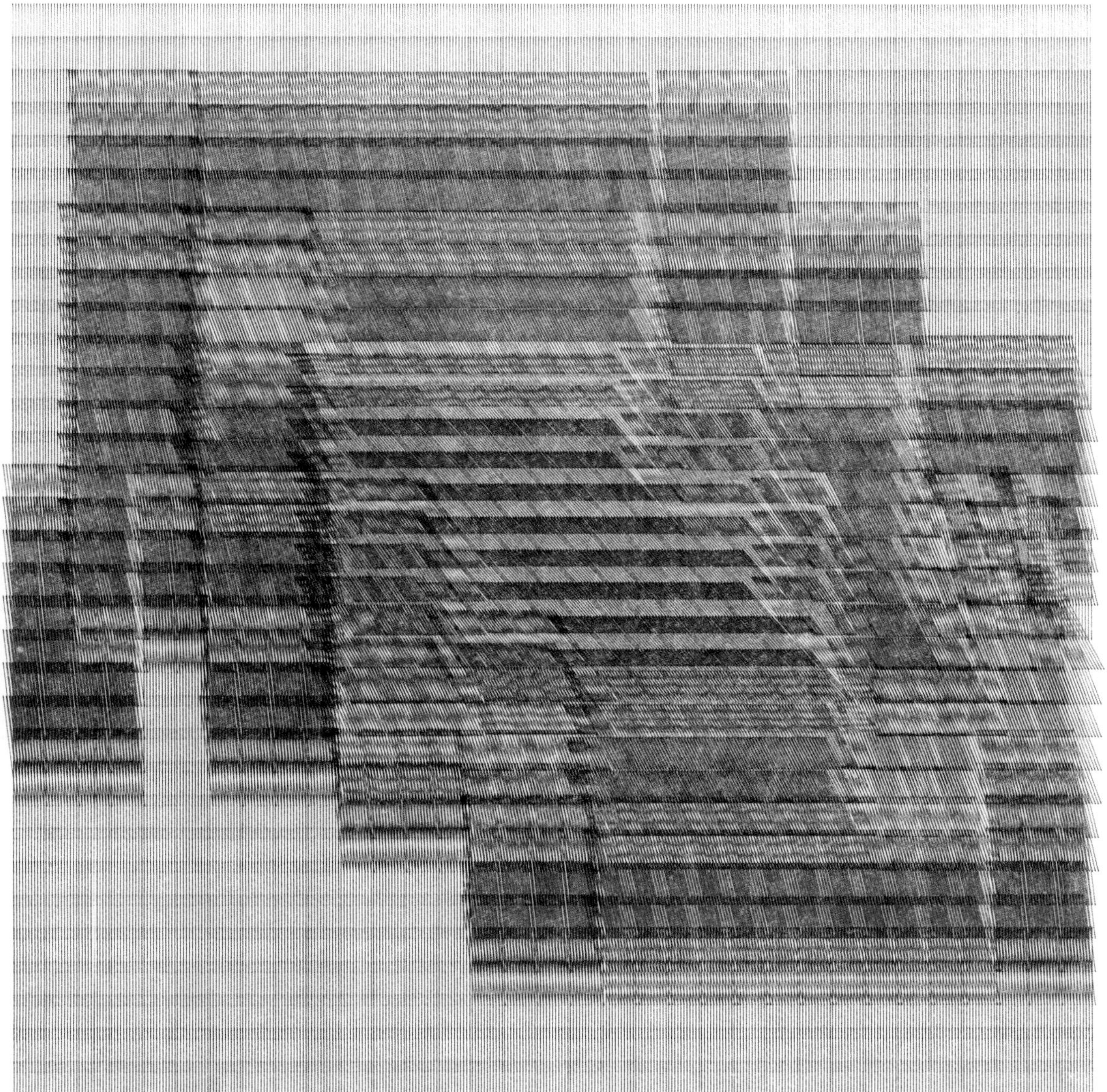

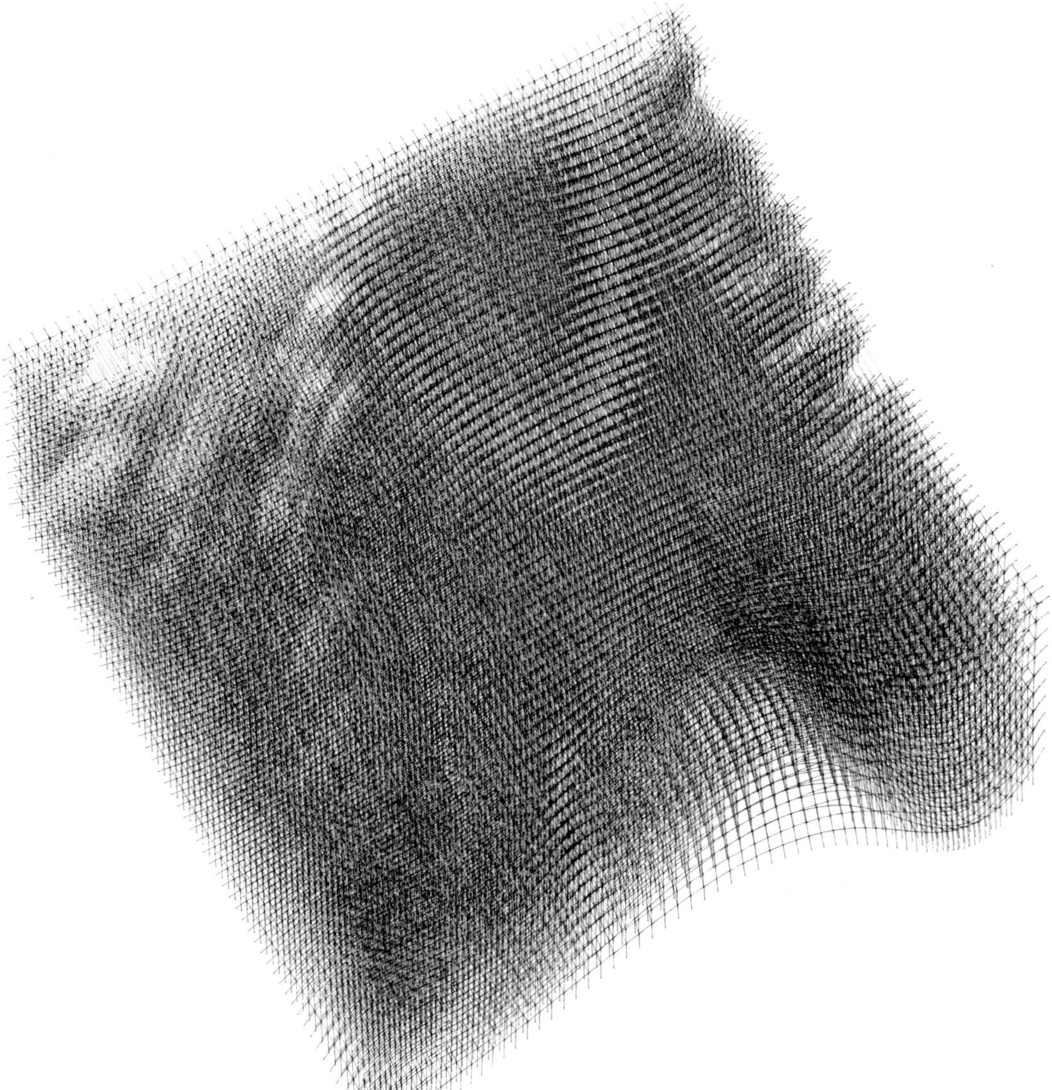

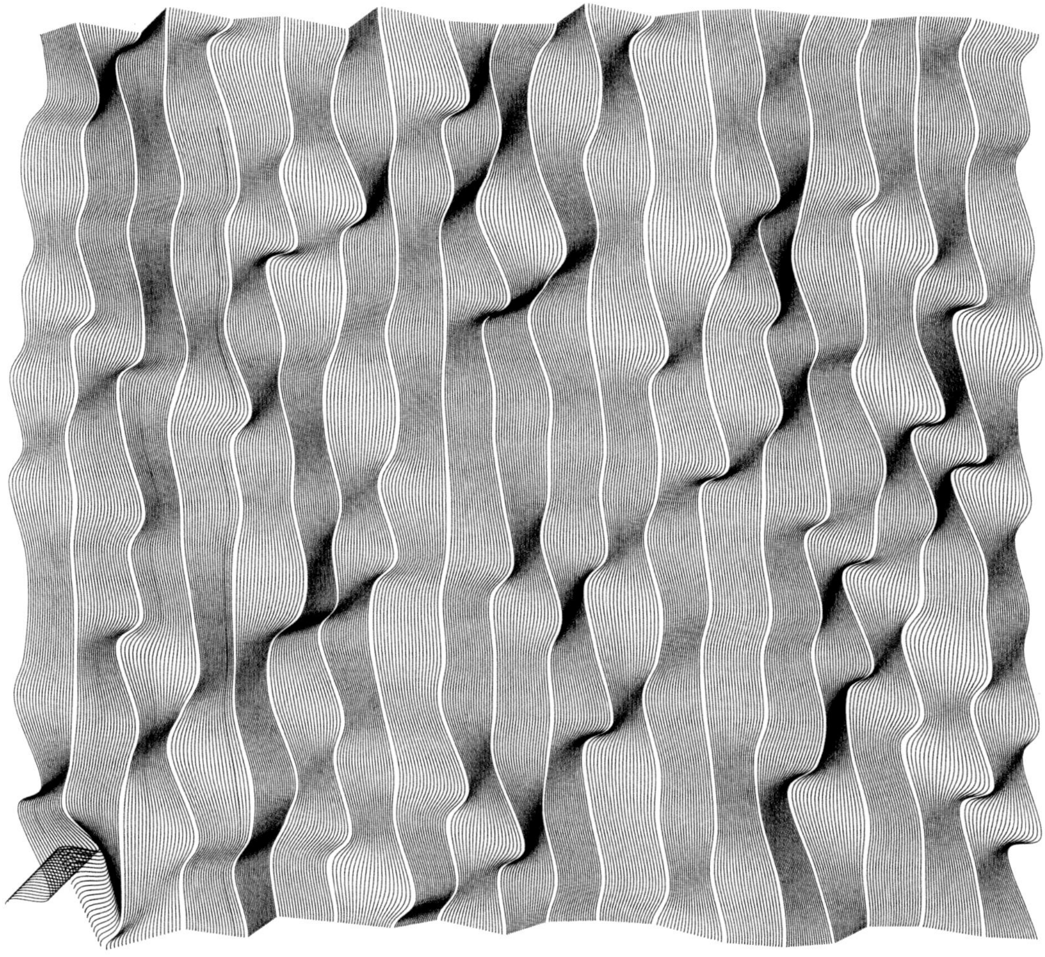

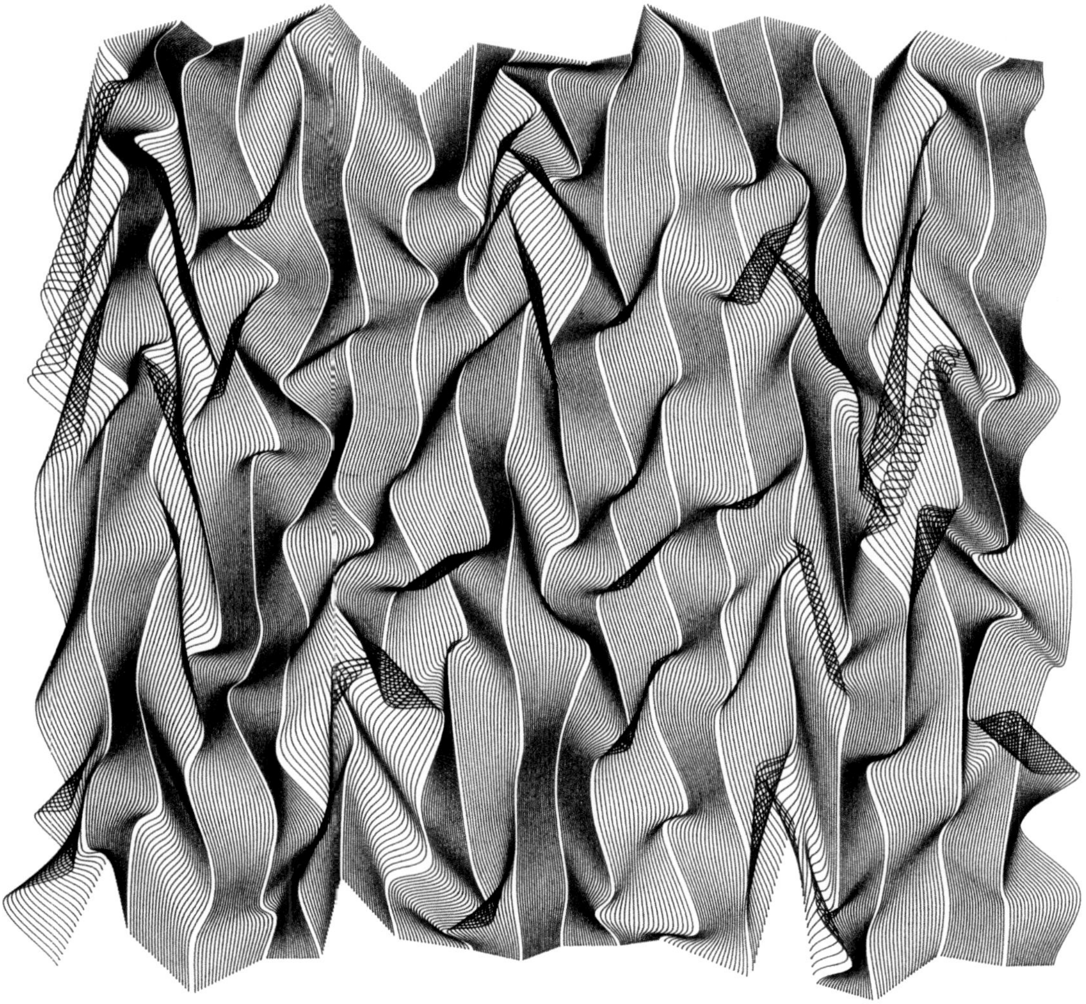

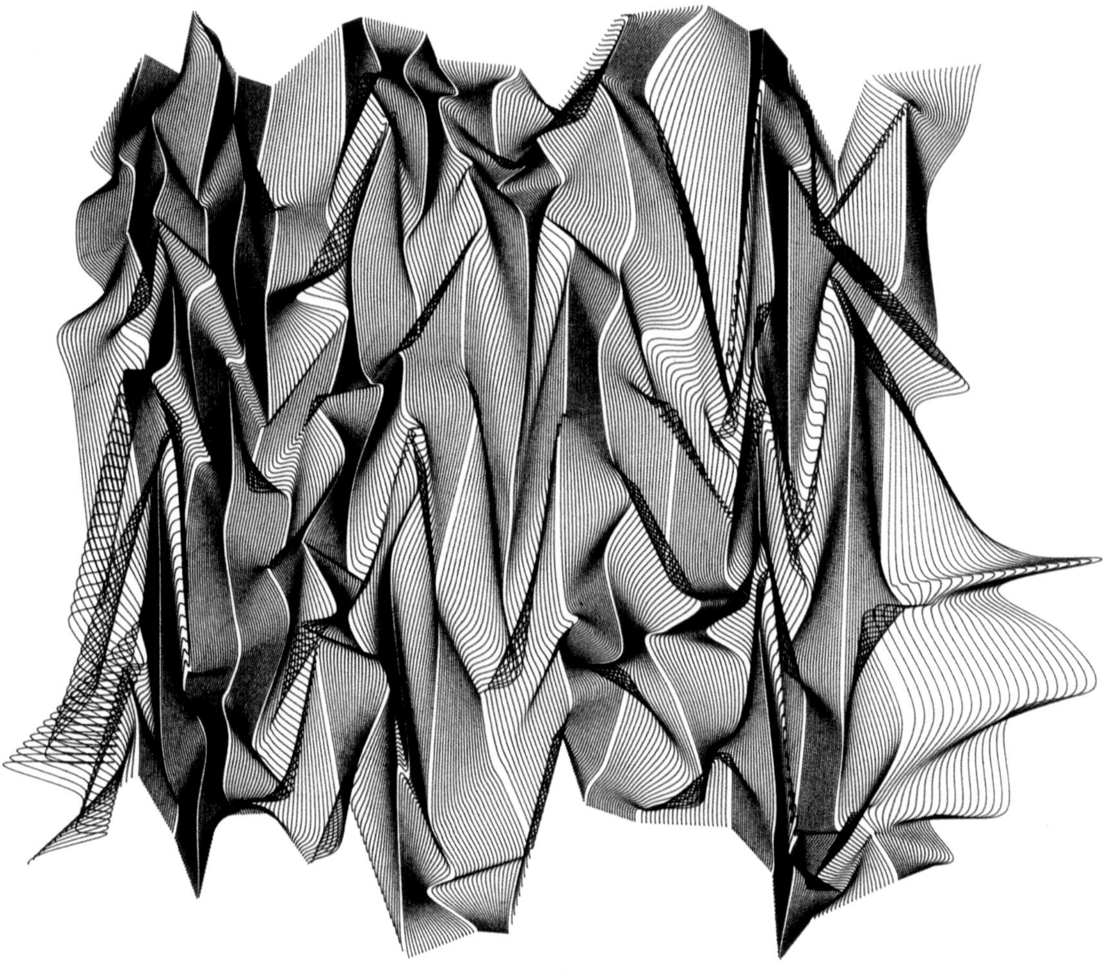

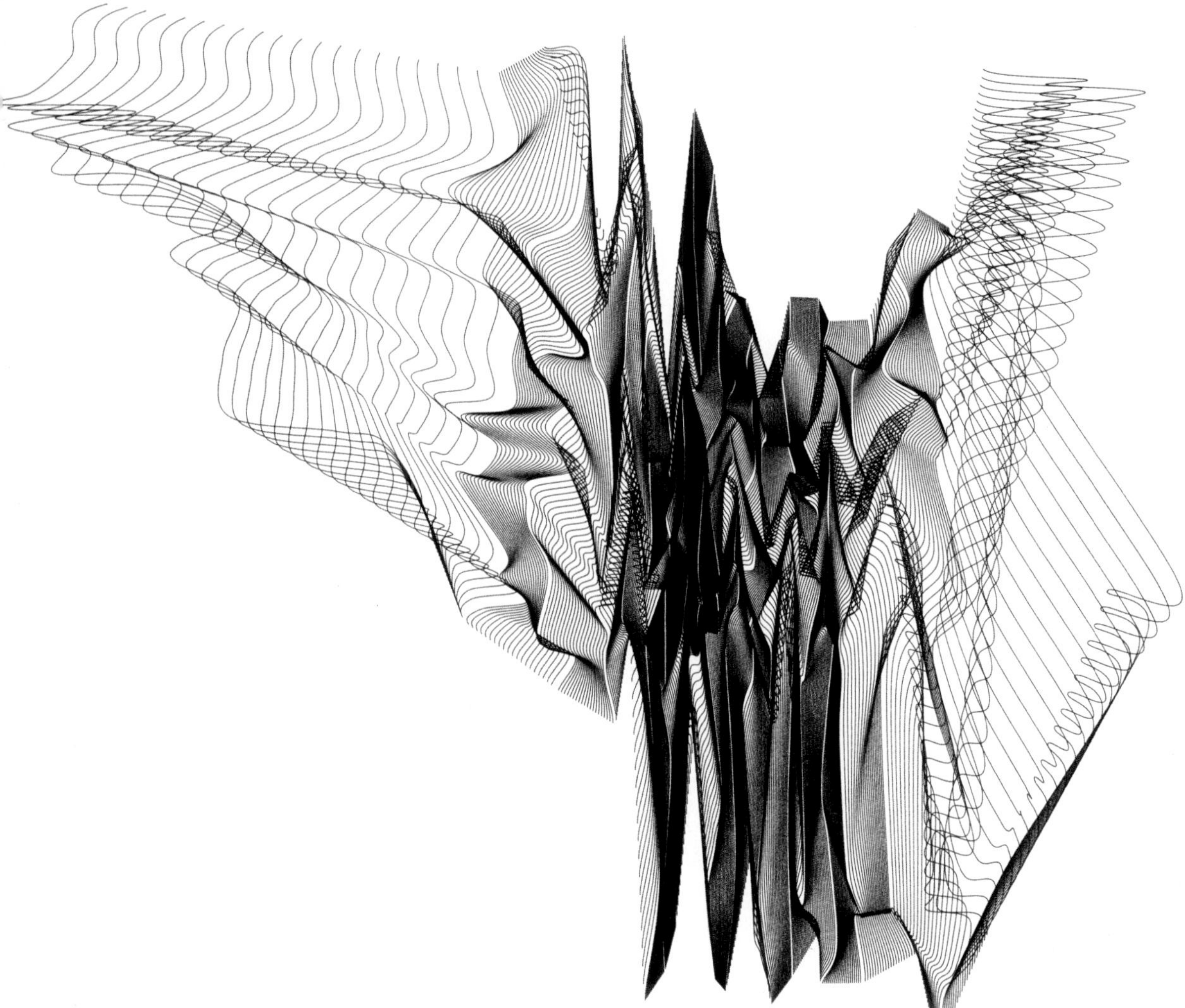

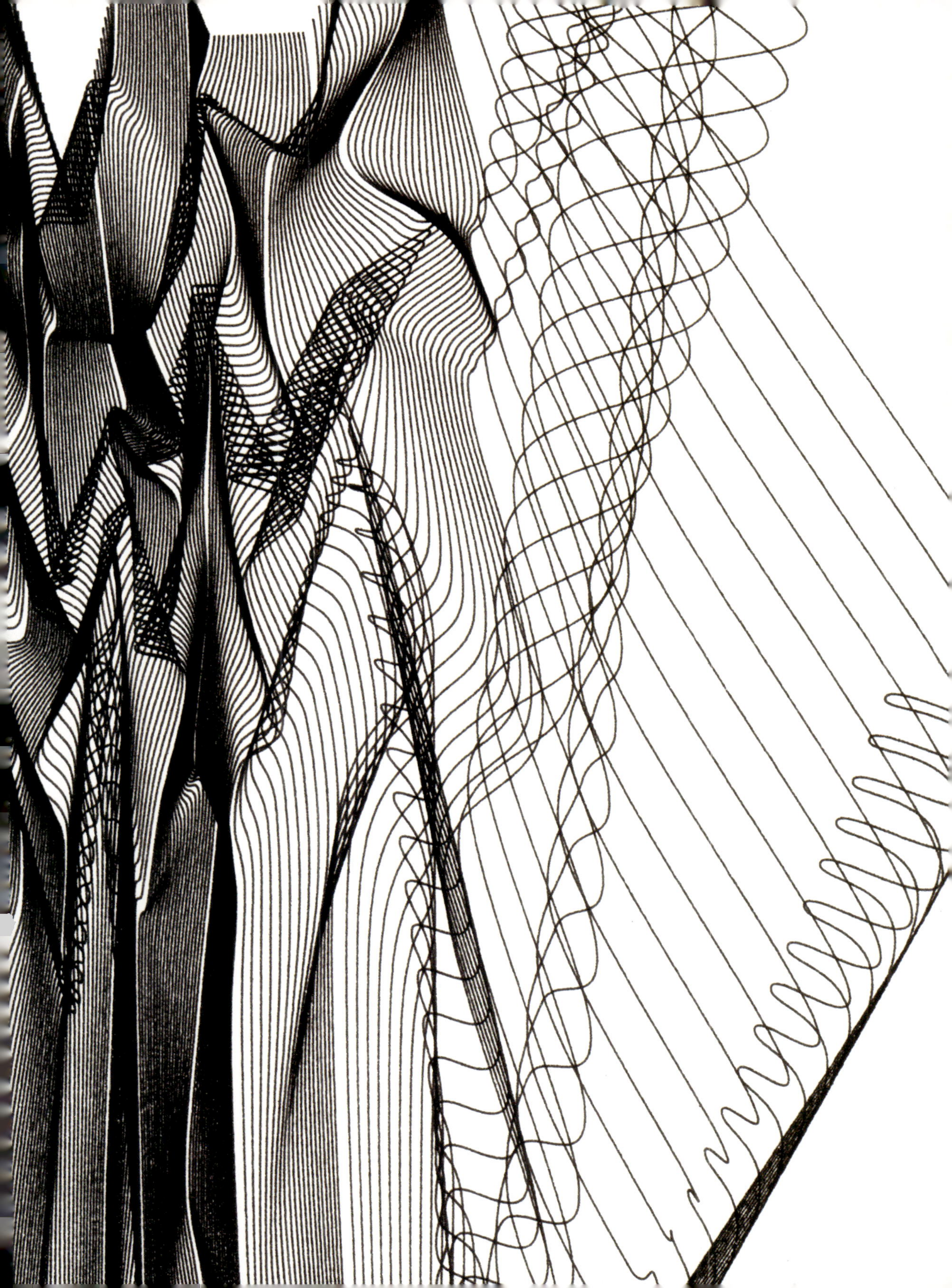

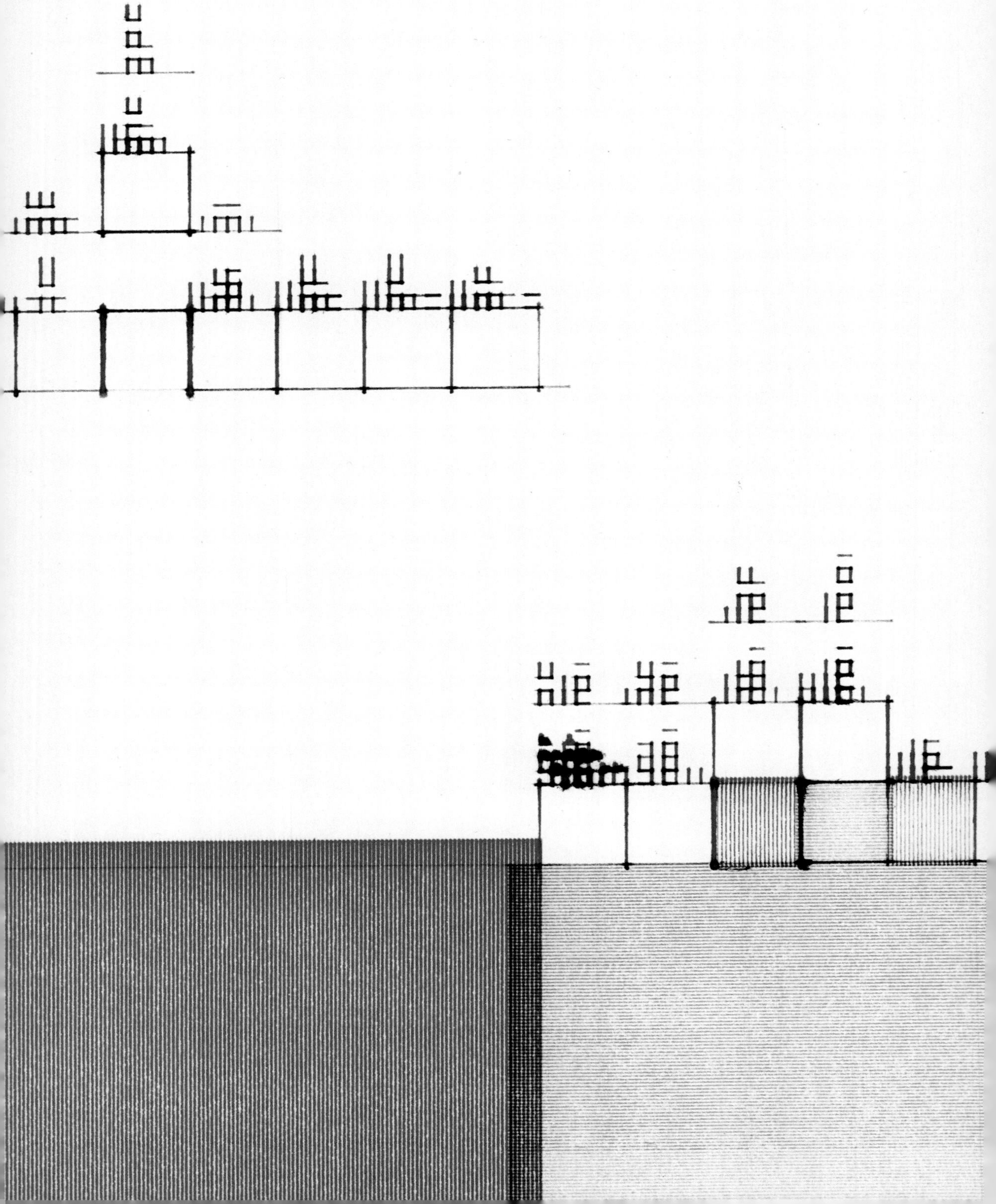

Chapter 3
Strategies

What makes a good computational drawing? What over-arching principles guide the creation of computational drawing projects? Architects have been drawing for much longer than they have been writing computer programs, and some answers to these questions can be gleaned from the traditions of the discipline. Architecture thrives within media that extend the capacity of the individual human author while simultaneously limiting, filtering, or structuring the domain of inquiry. Drawing and writing computer programs–"coding" for short–require a mastery of instruments, the deployment of knowledge, the definition of mark, and the structure of line. It is an architectural endeavor with architectural outcomes.

A good drawing project can affect our ideas in the pursuit of architecture, certainly. It can also transform conceptions, architectural actions, ordering principles, and even the nature of the world, thereby allowing us to cultivate ideas in the pursuit of new art, architecture, and design. In that context, this chapter will focus on strategies that can be narrowly applied to drawing in such a way that they will resonate beyond the scope of drawing.

From Willful Misuse to Opportunistic Surprise

Exercise 3.1. *Re-Code a Common Digital Tool*
Identify an existing tool in a piece of software you regularly use. Some examples could include the "paint bucket" tool in digital imaging software, the "blend surfaces" command in a digital modeling environment, or the "array along curve" command in digital drafting software. The tool itself is not extremely important, though it should be a tool that you understand completely in terms of its performance.

Before you start, be sure you understand what it requires to function—its inputs. You should also be able to predict the outcome before you use it. That's the one of the requisites of any tool: the ability to deploy it in a specific way to achieve some kind of desired outcome. Write code for your own version of that tool, from scratch.

That may have been the first exercise in this book that warrants the question of, was that really necessary? Beyond becoming a better programmer (certainly a laudable pursuit), what is the purpose of re-making a readily available tool? Why spend time re-inventing the wheel? In all likelihood, tool users understand tools less than is assumed. What actually happens "under the hood" may not always be apparent. It is equally unlikely that most designers will need to reach for a computer graphics textbook for the solution to this exercise. Some intuition about the tool was present in the mind of the user, but programming transforms that intuition into design knowledge. Roman philosopher Seneca is often attributed to what is now a truism, "While we teach, we learn." Programming something–even something that we know on some level already–is like teaching to a computer. It creates deeper more solid understanding.

With the value of programming to articulate knowledge that was previously tacit, incompletely formed, or latent established, it is possible to shift focus to the *creative* potential of coding a tool that already exists. The next step is to consider the new opportunities afforded to given access to the code of a programmed tool.

Exercise 3.2 *Misuse a Common Digital Tool*
Make a work of art with your code by continuing to change and evolve it. Embrace the surprising results that may emerge as you treat your code not as tool to perform a single function but a medium to explore new possibilities. What may have been considered a flaw during the first part of the exercise now may be prized as a generator of a new kind of line, form, shape, or space. Furthermore, explore the productive misuse to the code. Can the code be modified to expand the set of possible inputs beyond what would've made sense within the narrower scope of possibilities when interpreted as a mere tool?

If part one of this exercise revealed some changes to ways of thinking about tools, part two aims to make those changes salient in the kind of work that can be produced. The tool has become a medium thanks to the technology of programming.

What does this have to do with drawing, specifically? Let's return to a fundamental feature of drawing: the inherent connection between process and product. A drawn line carries with it evidence of its making. By writing code to perform a function the author controls the process and the product. This is the difference between a computational user and a computational maker. But it's not just about control. Perhaps a bug[1] eliminated during the coding process might be purposefully re-inserted later (or even cultivated and exaggerated) when nature of the task shifts from using to making.

The blank page does not contain structure or bias about what can be created in the subsequent drawing. The possibilities are completely open. The same is true when writing code. As many artists report epiphanies from the accidental blot of ink as creative writers stumble upon new meanings only after writing or speaking. Likewise, computational designers discover projects, agendas and opportunities in what, at first, might have been a logical flaw, or even a typo in the code.[2] Many critics of computational design egregiously assume that coding is an unforgiving medium, and that expression is replaced with an engineering mindset. One such example, and perhaps that which exhibits the most genuine expertise possible on the subject, is well articulated by David Ross Scheer:

> "unlike human beings who have considerable ability to interpret (and make creative use of) faulty or ambiguous utterances, computers have no tolerance for errors in parsing a program. Imprecise computer code does not produce evocative images as an impressive sketch might; it simply doesn't work. A high degree of precision is required in a computational design process from the outset. This contrasts strongly with a drawing-based design process in which vagueness and ambiguity are essential. They allow the designer to explore and develop partially formed ideas, or even give rise to new ones."[3]

First, an acknowledgment is in order. If we read Scheer's comment in the context of the norm of computer applications in architectural design and the kind of algorithmic optimization that he cites in his text, he certainly has identified a troublesome rift between drawing and computing. However, if we dig a little deeper there are some problems with his characterization of computation. Computers actually have almost limitless tolerance for errors (as opposed to humans, who are error averse). Encountering an error, as opposed to, say, a computer crashing, is welcome when computer programming. Of course, repeated errors can be frustrating, just as teaching while students seem to be missing the lesson. Just as an unformed idea sometimes becomes obviously flawed only as it is spoken out loud, the discovery of errors is fuel for, not an impediment to, creativity. More to the point, it is very common for an error-free program to do something unexpected. Just as likely is a scenario in which one sits down envisioning a program that does one thing, and the agenda completely changes as discoveries are made. Still, Shceer's impulse is correct: if we treat the computer as a solving machine or simulator, we fundamentally change the nature of creativity. However, if we can articulate vagueness or ambiguity, computational media can advance, not kill, drawing.

Identifying a happy accident when coding can be exciting. Unlike a drop of ink or the smudge of a mark, computational accidents can be at profound scale. They tend to illicit utterances like "oh damn" rather then "hmmm." It's also important to note that computational accidents can result without any mistake whatsoever. It may be that the sheer scope, scale, or range of variation was outside the bounds of what was predicted. Even still, it is important to scrutinize the results and their relationship to process. Although many conditions, orders, forms, and shapes may arise serendipitously, without an understanding of how and why they appeared, control over the rationality of code can easily slip away. Falling into a "guess and check" method of coding is never productive. When in doubt, pause and trace through the code manually, or deploy more advanced "debugging" techniques.[4]

The value of process also explains why some computational artists and designers are rationally nostalgic for eras of slower computing. Take for example an algorithm for filling contiguous areas of similarly called the "Flood Fill."[5] Today this algorithm is virtually instantaneous, but in early computer graphics software it was possible to see the algorithm in process as something like a paint bucket tool literally flooded a few pixels at a time until contrast boundaries were reached.

```
Define floodFill in terms of a coordinate lookAt, and a fillColor
  create lookFor and set it to be the color at lookAt
  create a list called floodQueue
  add lookAt to floodQueue
  while floodQueue has any items in it
    remove an item from floodQueue and call it newLookingAt[6]
    set x to be the x-coordinate value of newLookingAt
    set y to be the y-coordinate value of newLookingAt
    set west to be a coordinate value at (x-1, y)[7]
    set west to be a coordinate value at (x+1, y)
    set north to be a coordinate value at (x, y-1)
    set south to be a coordinate value at (x, y+1)
    create a new list called newDirections
    if west is within the bounds of the image and the color at west equals lookFor
      set the color at west to fillColor[8]
      add west to newDirections
    if east is within the bounds of the image and the color at east equals lookFor
      set the color at east to fillColor
      add east to newDirections
    if north is within the bounds of the image and the color at north equals lookFor
      set the color at north to fillColor
      add north to newDirections
    if south is within the bounds of the image and the color at south equals lookFor
      set the color at south to fillColor
      add south to newDirections
    add each item in newDirections to fillQueue[9]
```

```
A frankensteinRebuild is defined in terms of a referenceLine
  create 40 samplePoints randomly distributed along referenceLine
  sort the samplePoints base on their position on the line
  take between 2 and 5 samplePoints at a time to form a subset
    if a random integer between 1 and 3 is 1
      swap two of the points in subset
    based on a random value, create an arc, a curve or a straight poly-line through subset
```

Misplacing Intelligence

When shown the inner workings of artificial intelligence systems–the algorithms that make computers perform intelligently–many are surprised at how little those systems mimic the human brain. Humans do not play chess the same way a computer plays chess. Arguably a chess-playing computer might not actually know anything about chess. Because intelligence is a complex label that humanity has ascribed to itself, a real definition can be tricky. For this reason intelligence is often measured in terms of performance and autonomy rather than knowledge, understanding, or awareness. In art and design, we can classify algorithms in terms of their capacity to operate in place of a human. For lack of a better term, let's call the autonomous human-replacement algorithms "smart" and algorithms that do almost nothing while depending heavily on human input as "dumb." Smart algorithms might seem to be more valuable, but this is not always the case. Taking an opportunity to explore the role purposefully dumb algorithms keeps the burden of intelligence on the human author.

Exercise 3.3 *Dumb Algorithm*

Create a computational drawing instrument that requires regular human input. The form of this input can be anything. It might be something minimal like pressing a single button on a keyboard or more complex like the acceleration vector of a mouse cursor. This is an opportunity to employ gaming input devices like joysticks or to explore input via microphone or camera (see appendix for some Python Programming resources for input). The most obvious design necessary here will involve the conversion of human impulse into usable data for your algorithmic instrument. If using some kind of visual or auditory stream as input, some kind of processing may be necessary to distill it down to a quantity of data that is manageable. However, even if the input comes from a keyboard, decisions will need to be made. For example, will the state of the button be regularly sampled to determine if it's pressed? Or, will you keep a record of times certain keys are pressed and address them in due course? Which moment matters more, the moment the key is pressed or the moment it is depressed? Does it matter how long the user holds the key down?

Consider feedback to the human user, or, if we're using the term "instrument," maybe it's more appropriate to use the term "player," or even "performer." Regardless of the label, will the human see the drawing as it's being made? Will that be enough feedback for him or her to refine the input? Explore other ways that the human may receive feedback other than by viewing the drawing. Think about meters and gauges in a car, or the way a violinist adjusts to the feel of the bow hitting the string. Finally, take on the role of the performer and create a work of art with the instrument. Work with and against the instrument. Remember, despite the time and energy invested in the design of the instrument, it still requires human input–and human intention–to create substantive work.

Despite its label, making a dumb algorithm, or an instrument, as the exercise above begins to refer to it, requires consideration and design. As is the aim with every exercise in this book, technical insights are coupled with conceptual provocations. Although there is a place for both kind of algorithms–smart and dumb–it is useful to begin with the observation that smart and dumb, as defined in the exercise, reside on a spectrum. They are not binary classifiers. Even the smartest—most autonomous–algorithms in use today pose no risk to the primacy of the human in design, even when setting aside the completely fair argument that most code is written by humans. Most experienced designers acknowledge the necessity of indeterminacy in their process. Rarely do we have an initial flash of brilliance and then spend the rest of our design process realizing that initial idea. This underlines the reason drawing is a mainstay of architectural process: the act of drawing provides feedback to the author.

Some point to the pencil and, specifically, its relationship to the hand as key to this process.[10] Drawing, according to architect Juhani Pallasmaa, must always involve bodily engagement and haptic knowledge. Often this discourse suggests or implies a criticism of digital technology as though it where conflated with an entirely digital virtual world. Indeed the hand and the body are hyper-present when operating digitally. The methods and implications for abstracting craft are unavoidable, and when analogously constructed tell us much about the human body.[11] However, without discounting the role of the hand and body in design–of course typing and programming also involves the hands quite extensively–we can also, much more productively, study the role of the eyes, or more acutely, visual perception, when drawing.[12] A focus on seeing does not position the computer and the drawing in opposition to each other. Drawings play out over time, and our ability to see them as we make them helps us develop and generate knowledge. It is not about imagining a line and then producing that line, but rather conceiving of an impulse for a line (even before it is imagined) and then forming an idea about that line as it is drawn. Computational drawing does not disrupt this. Computational drawing extends the duration of this process.

If drawing with pencil and paper is about the moment, computational drawing is about many thousands of moments, many of which are discontinuous. That resulting knowledge may be more intellectual, more logical and perhaps even more cerebral, but the focus on process and the act of drawing is still paramount. Slowing down and stretching out the drawing process has some added benefit. It helps us analyze the drawing author. A traditional difficulty in drawing discourse has been the deeply personal nature of drawing. Research depends on measurement and analysis. However, it is difficult to "step outside" ourselves, to evaluate our intentions and articulate our moment to moment thinking. It becomes even more difficult if that thinking is intuitive or subconscious. We are all experts when it comes to our own experiences despite the fact that we know very little about how our brain works. Computing drawing externalizes and records the thinking of the author. Coding drawing means writing the story of the drawing in explicitly textual language.

Opportunities also arise to distance the author of the tool from the user of the tool. Asking someone else to spend some time using the tool may provide valuable insight. Can you relinquish control over the tool while retaining authorship over the drawing made by that tool? What is the difference between tool user, human agent and artist?

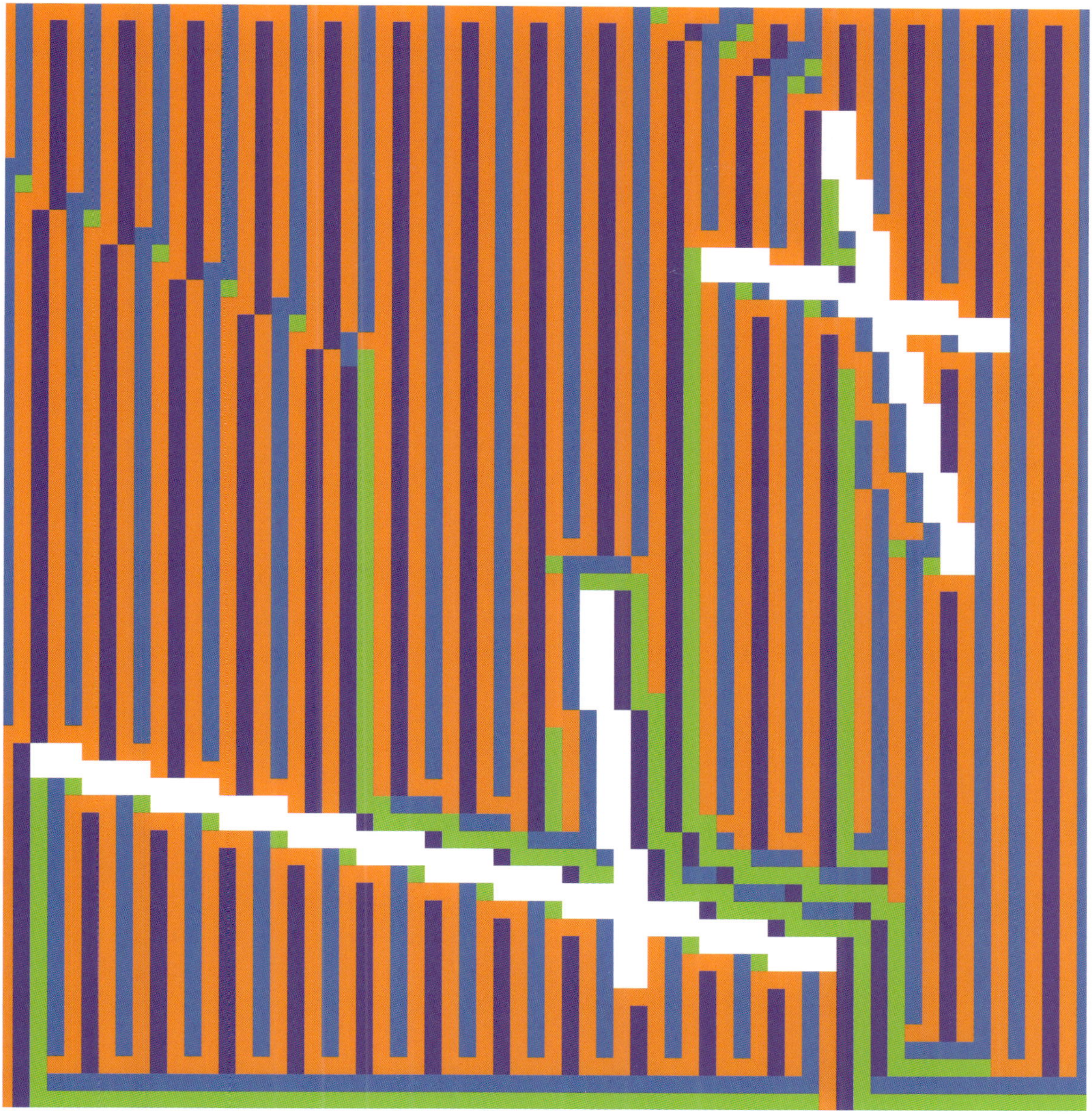

A low resolution result of a flawed *floodFill* in which the fill color is dependent on the direction of movement taken to arrive at each pixel.

The Computational Underlay

Bridget Riley, Op-Art painter, famously drew on gridded paper—the same kind that is used for charts, scatterplots, and graphs. Often in early experimental works that were used to prepare for final drawings, this paper was undoubtedly chosen purposefully and even if the paper lines did not transfer directly into the final work, they certainly were influential.

Though the role of the surface will be explored as both the subject of drawing and the topological structure of drawing model later, we should consider here the way that the drawing surface, as in the paper or whatever we draw on, can be the territory of design. This is not so much a strategy as a recognition that strategy can be productively applied to the environment that holds lines in addition to the lines themselves. Anthropologist Tim Ingold comes to a similar conclusion,

> "Evidently it is not enough to regard the surface as a taken-for-granted backdrop for the lines that are inscribed upon it. For just as the history of writing belongs within the history of notation, and the history of notation within the history of the line, so there can be no history of the line that is not also about the changing relations between lines and surfaces."[13]

Exercise 3.4. *Non-Grid Graph Paper.*
Underlay grids are not neutral; they influence the way images are created and edited. Define a new kind of graph paper to serve as an underlay for an improvisational or automatic drawing that is characterized by geometry other than a two dimensional grid. As a starting point one might consider other coordinate systems including those that are polar or hexagonal in nature. Hybrid systems such as a one-dimensional series wrapped, spiraled or folded into a grid system might be of interest. It can be productive to think about three-dimensional coordinates within a two-dimensional space. Create a pad of paper and then move on to a different project for a while. Come back to this paper after some time and only then, draw on it.

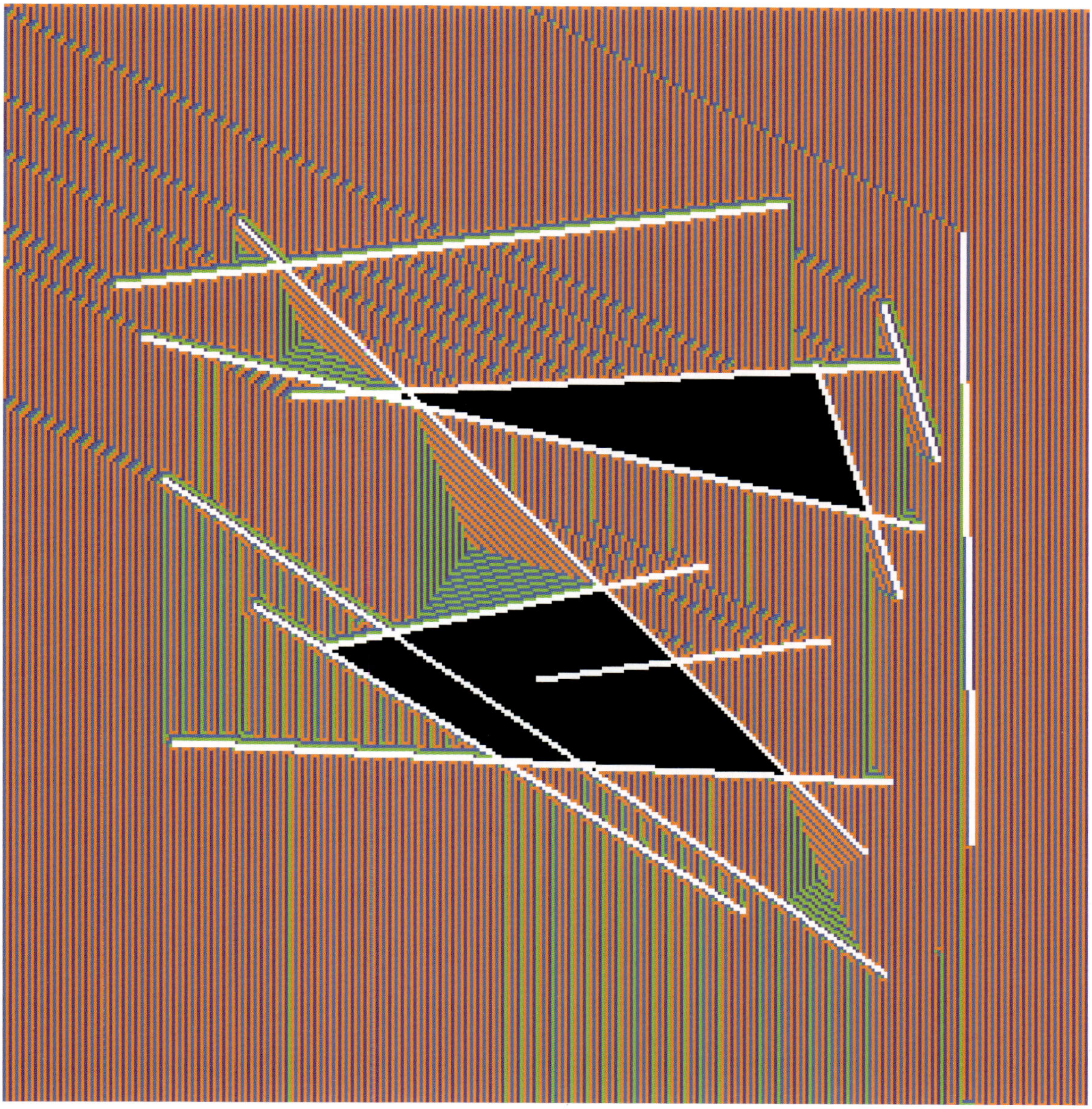

A medium resolution result of a flawed *floodFill* in which the fill color is dependent on the direction of movement taken to arrive at each pixel.

Drawing is as much about the paper as it is about the line. The characteristics of paper affect the kind of drawing that can be made and the process of its making. Historically, the transparency, materiality, weight, value, and durability of paper have affected drawing paradigms.[14] Programming drawings computationally by thinking exclusively about the line as the object and subject ignores an opportunity. The structure of the world that these lines live in is equally important, if often overlooked. Whether a digital image or a three-dimensional virtual environment, linkages between things, hierarchies, discrete vs. continuous values and systems for locating things all affect the content of what is formed in that world. The exercise above reminds us that all computational worlds–especially the digital image–are inherently limiting. These limitations provide a creative possibility.

A higher resolution result of a flawed *floodFill* in which the fill color is dependent on the direction of movement taken to arrive at each pixel.

Notes

1. In the parlance of computer programming, the "bug" is a metaphor for an error, flaw or fault of a computer program. "Bugs" are so common that "debugging," is likewise a cultural mainstay. The term existed in engineering long before computer programming. Thomas Edison Wrote, "It has been just so in all of my inventions. The first step is an intuition, and comes with a burst, then difficulties arise — this thing gives out and [it is] then that "Bugs" — as such little faults and difficulties are called — show themselves and months of intense watching, study and labor are requisite before commercial success or failure is certainly reached." Edison to Puskas, 13 November 1878, *Edison papers*, Edison National Laboratory, U.S. National Park Service, West Orange, N.J., cited in Thomas P. Hughes, *American Genesis: A History of the American Genius for Invention*, Penguin Books, 1989. 75.
2. Productive errors abound throughout the history of art and design. One such example is Duchamp's The Bride Stripped Bare by Her Bachelors, Even. In which shipping damage was repaired by the artist in such a way as to assimilate the marks of that damage into the work. Disturbed by the connotations of "error" and "accident." In a radio interview conducted in 1950, Jackson Pollock made a clear distinction between lack of "classical" order and random accident in his work. The interviewer may have been implying that his work lacked any order by positing that it must me impossible to control the paint when using a stick instead of a brush. Pollock replied, "No, I don't think so... With experience–it seems to be possible to control the flow of the paint, to a great extend, and I don't use–I don't use the accident–'cause I deny the accident."
3. Scheer, David Ross. *The Death of Drawing: Architecture in the Age of Simulation*. London: Routledge, 2014. 152
4. Aside from the many engineering resources available regarding the "best practices" for debugging and analyzing the performance of code, a particularly salient and entertainingly narrative resource on the culture associated with the craft of computer programming can be found in Jon Bentley's *More Programming Pearls, Confessions of a Coder*. AT&T Bell Laboratories. 1988
5. "Lode's Computer Graphics Tutorial." Flood Fill. Accessed June 20, 2016. http://lodev.org/cgtutor/floodfill.html.
6. This is an opportunity to introduce a flaw: what if the fillColor was adjusted slightly here so that at each step in the algorithm, the fill color changed?
7. This is an opportunity to introduce a flaw: what if instead of checking one pixel over to arrive at north, south, east and west coordinates, the algorithm checked a few pixels over so that some pixels were skipped over?
8. This is an opportunity to introduce a flaw: what if the color set was not the fill color but a custom color based on the direction being checked?
9. This is an opportunity to introduce a flaw: what if not every item in the list was added to the queue? What if the list as shuffled first?
10. Pallasmaa, Juhani. *The Thinking Hand: Existential and Embodied Wisdom in Architecture*. Chichester, U.K.: Wiley, 2010.
11. McCullough, Malcolm. *Abstracting Craft: The Practiced Digital Hand*. Cambridge, MA: MIT Press, 1996
12. Lettvin, J., H. Maturana, W. Mcculloch, and W. Pitts. "What the Frog's Eye Tells the Frog's Brain." *Proceedings of the IRE Proc. IRE* 47, no. 11 (1959): 1940-951. doi:10.1109/jrproc.1959.287207.
13. Ingold, Tim. *Lines a Brief History*. London: Routledge, 2016. 39
14. Frascari, Marco, Jonathan Hale, and Bradley Starkey. *From Models to Drawings: Imagination and Representation in Architecture*. London: Routledge, 2007. Especially of interest is Frascari's Chapter, "A reflection on paper and its virtues within the material and invisible factures of architecture"

A low resolution result of a flawed *floodFill* in which the fill color gradually changes and eventually resets as the fill incrementally colors one pixel at a time.

A medium resolution result of a flawed *floodFill* in which the fill color gradually changes and eventually resets as the fill incrementally colors one pixel at a time.

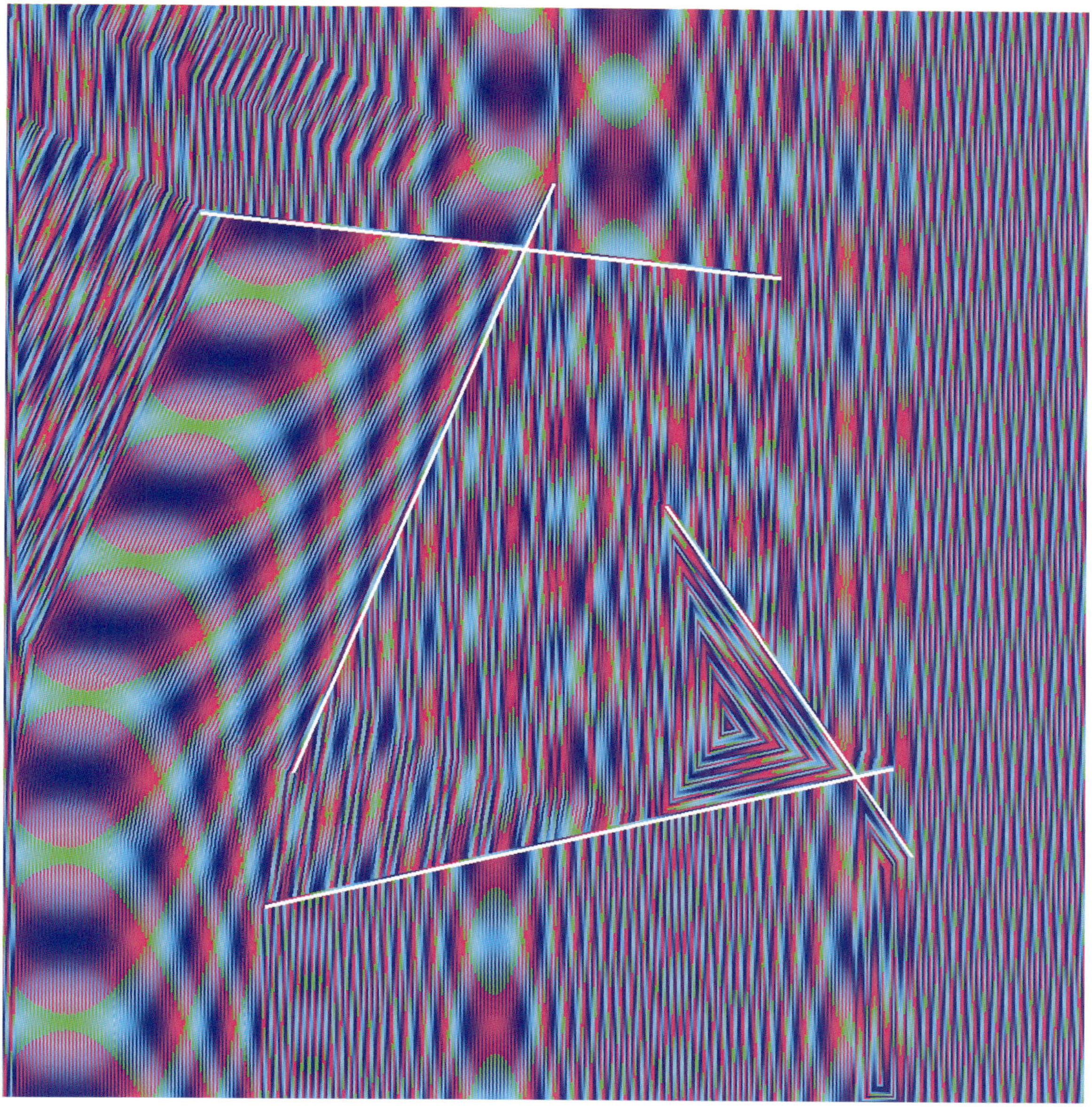

A higher resolution result of a flawed *floodFill* in which the fill color gradually changes and eventually resets as the fill incrementally colors one pixel at a time.

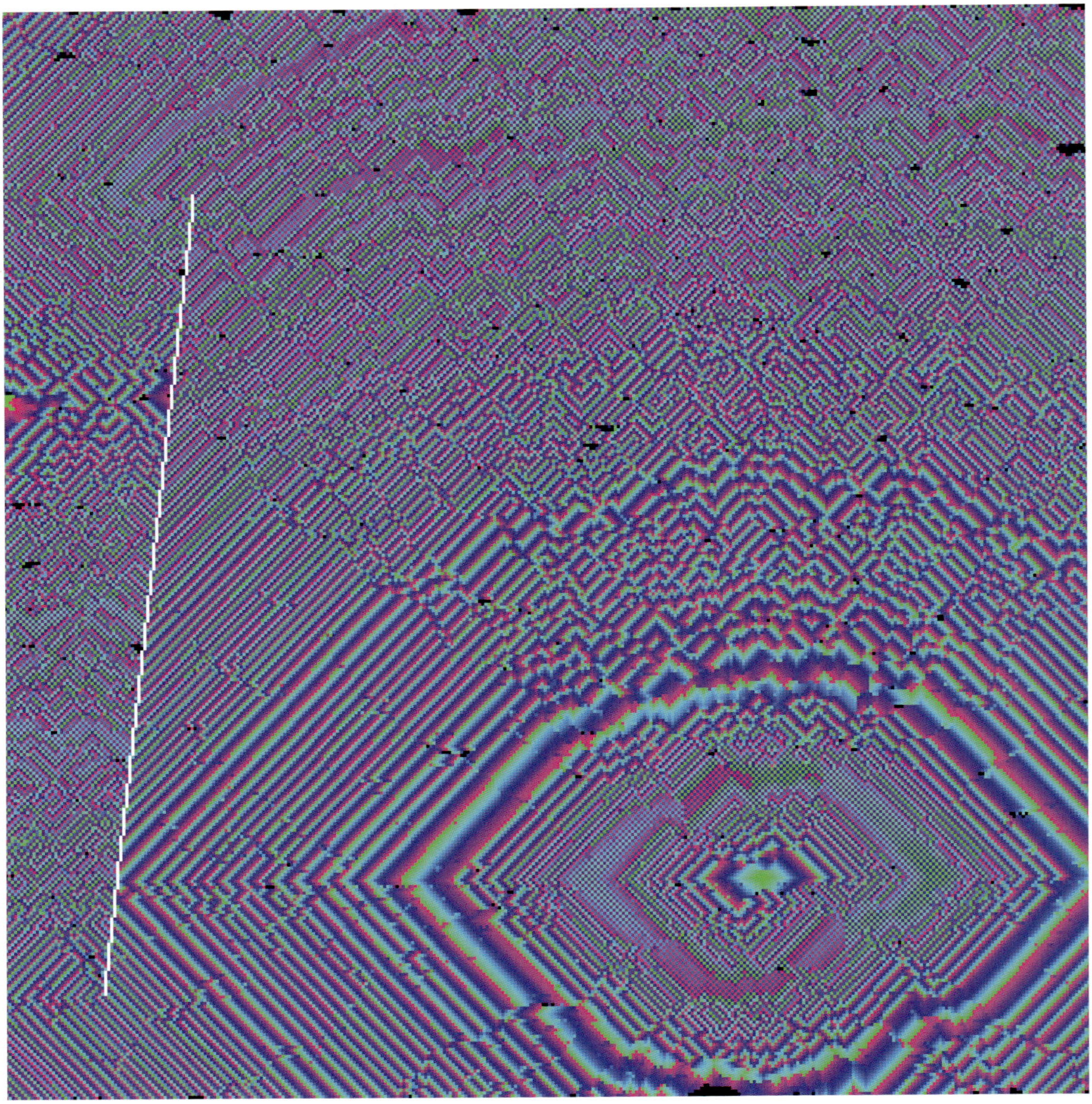

A medium resolution result of a flawed *floodFill* in which the fill color changes gradually over the course of the life of the fill, but the queue is leaky, loosing one item per step.

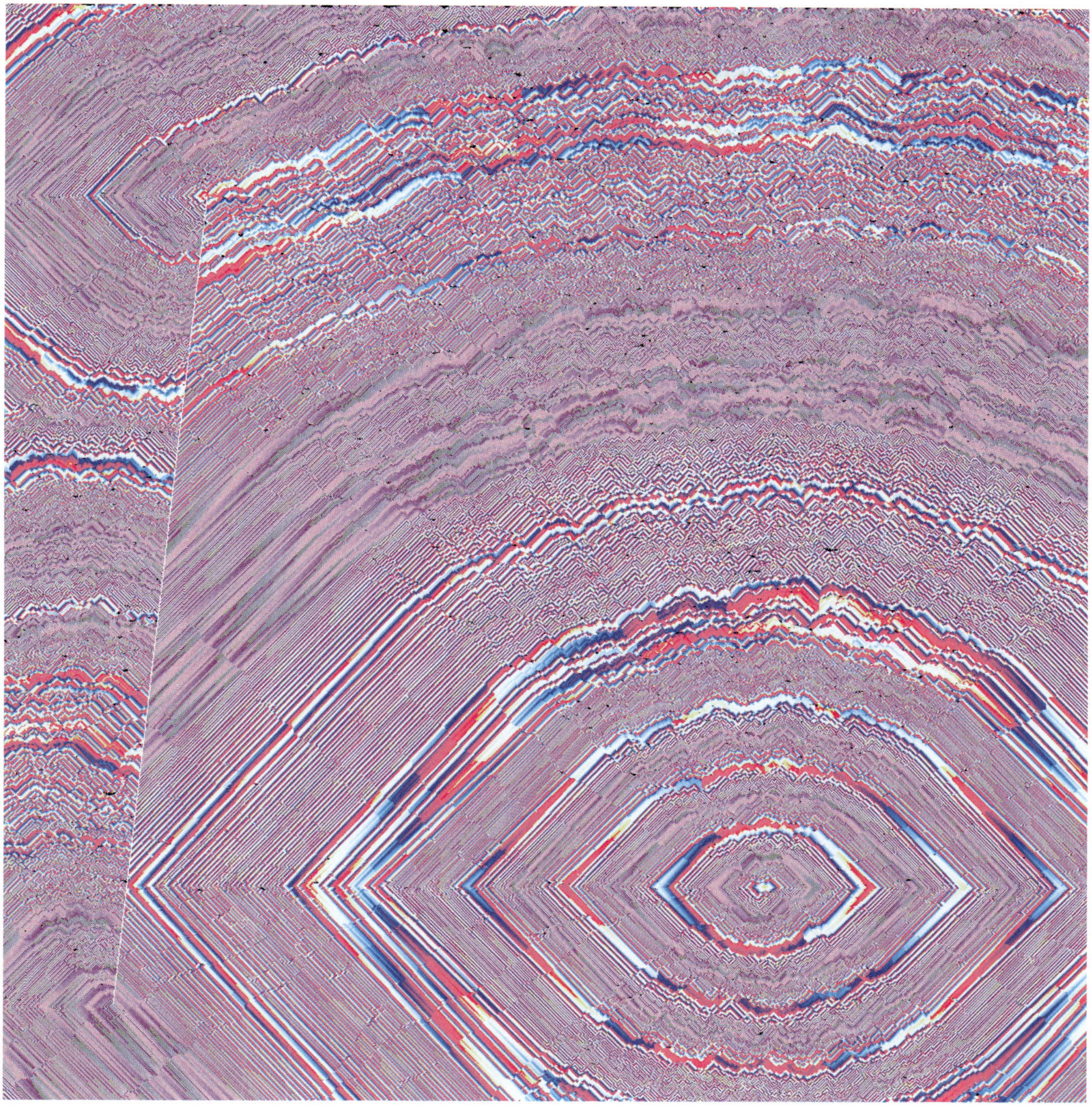

A higher resolution result of a leaky *floodFill*.

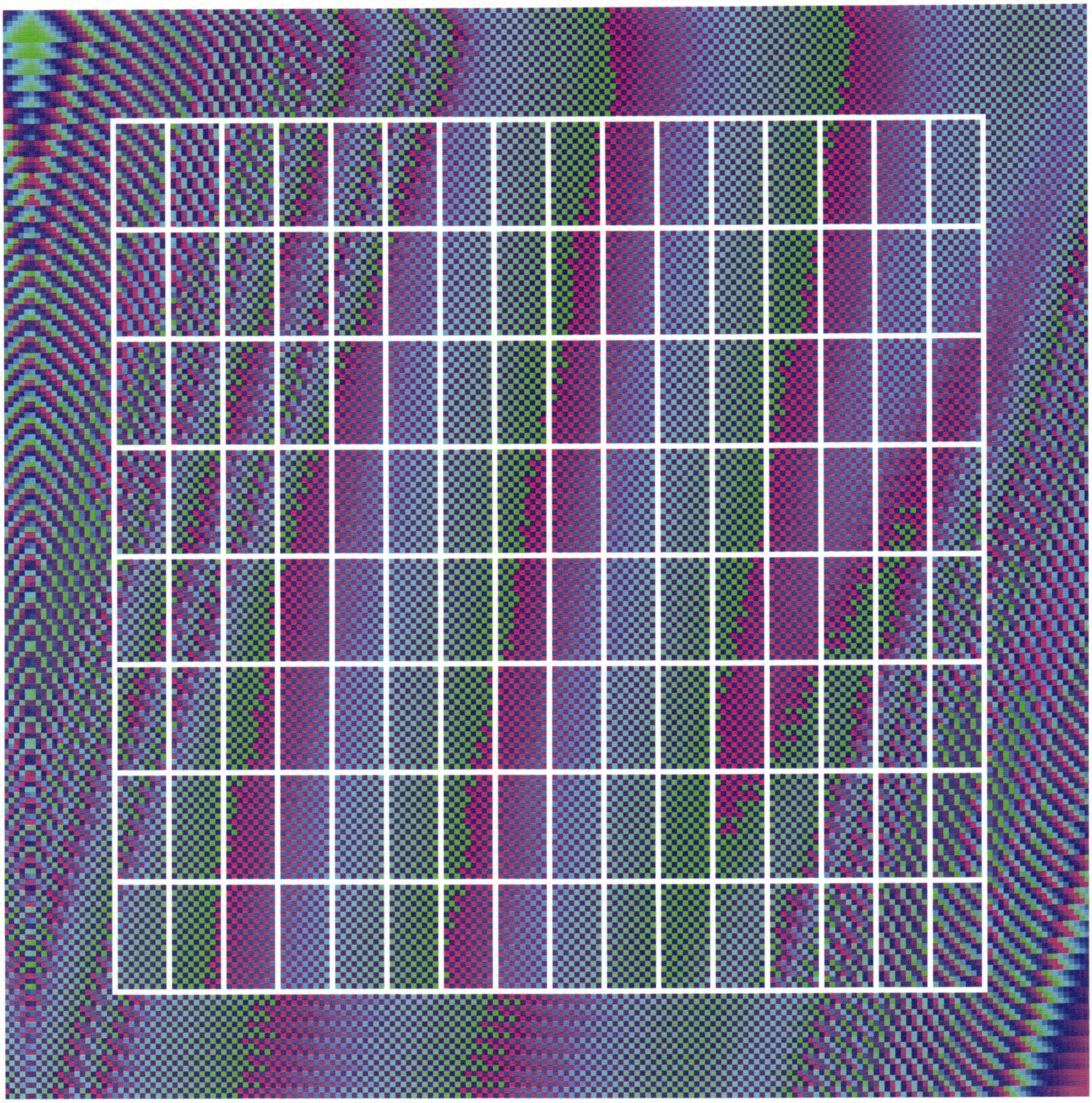

A low resolution result of a flawed *floodFill* in which the fill color gradually changes and eventually resets and the directional shift skips two pixel allowing the fill to cross over, but still be influenced by barrier pixels.

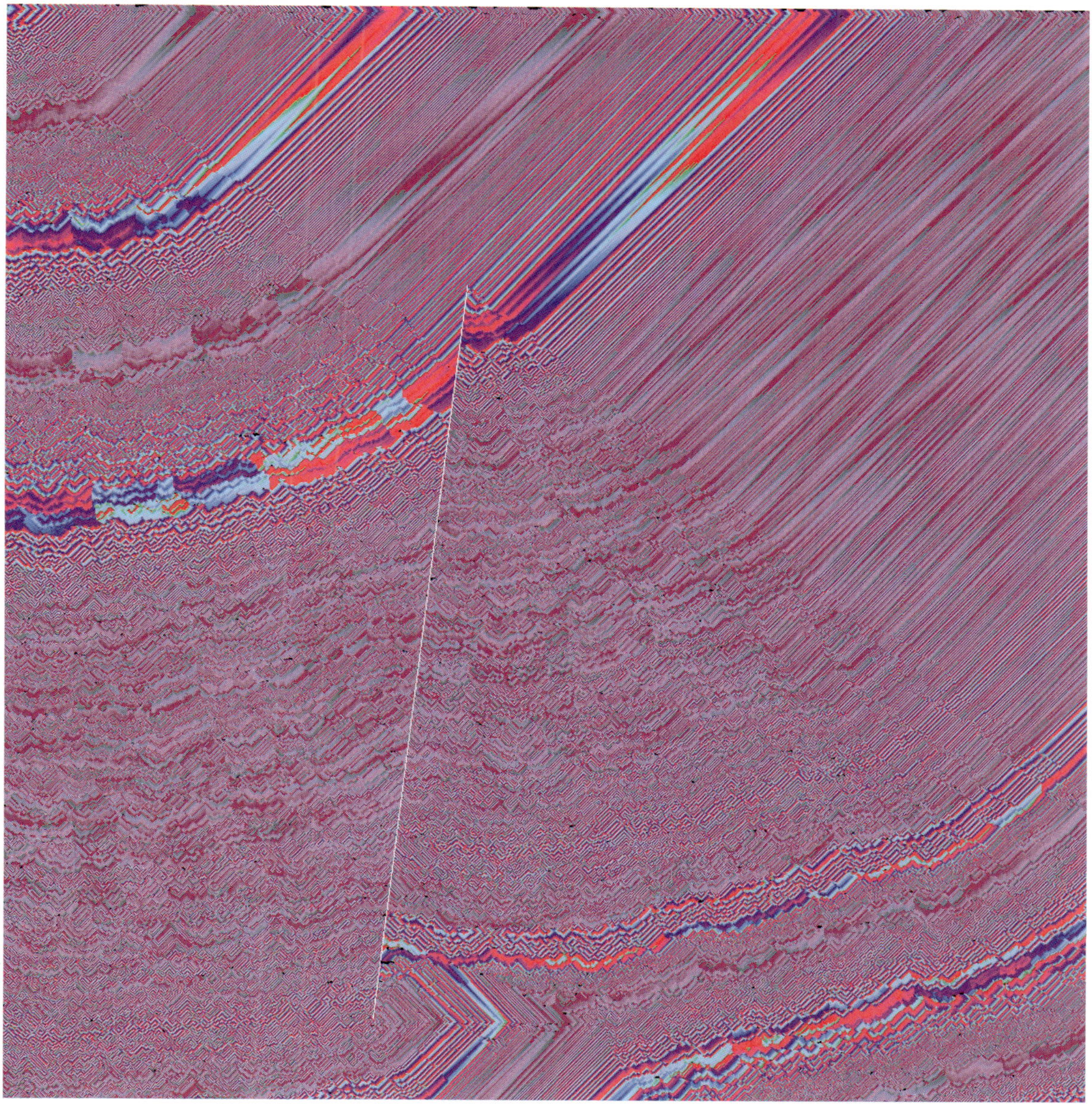

ABOVE AND FOLLOWING SPREADS A higher resolution pixel-skipping *floodFill*.

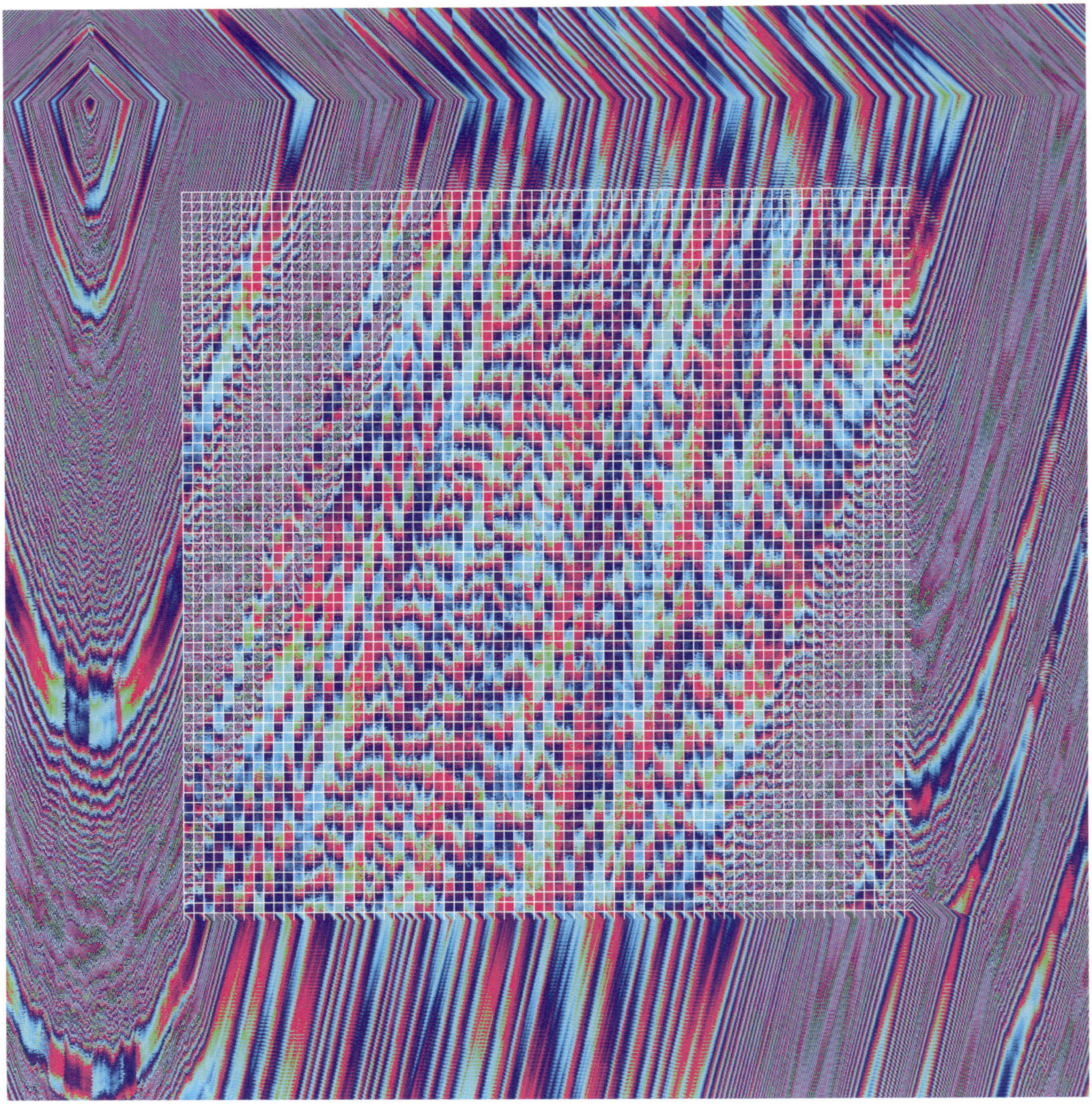

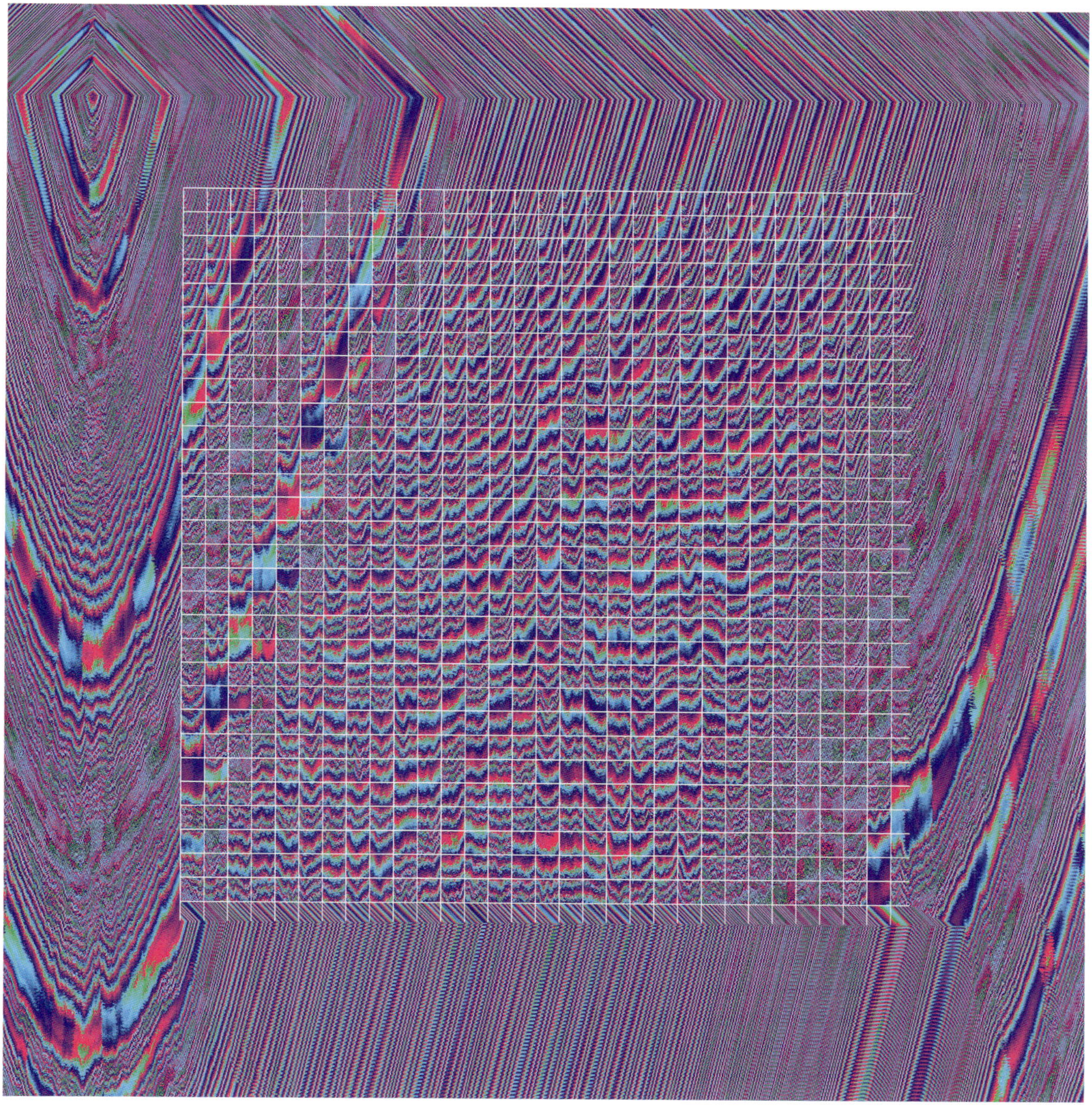

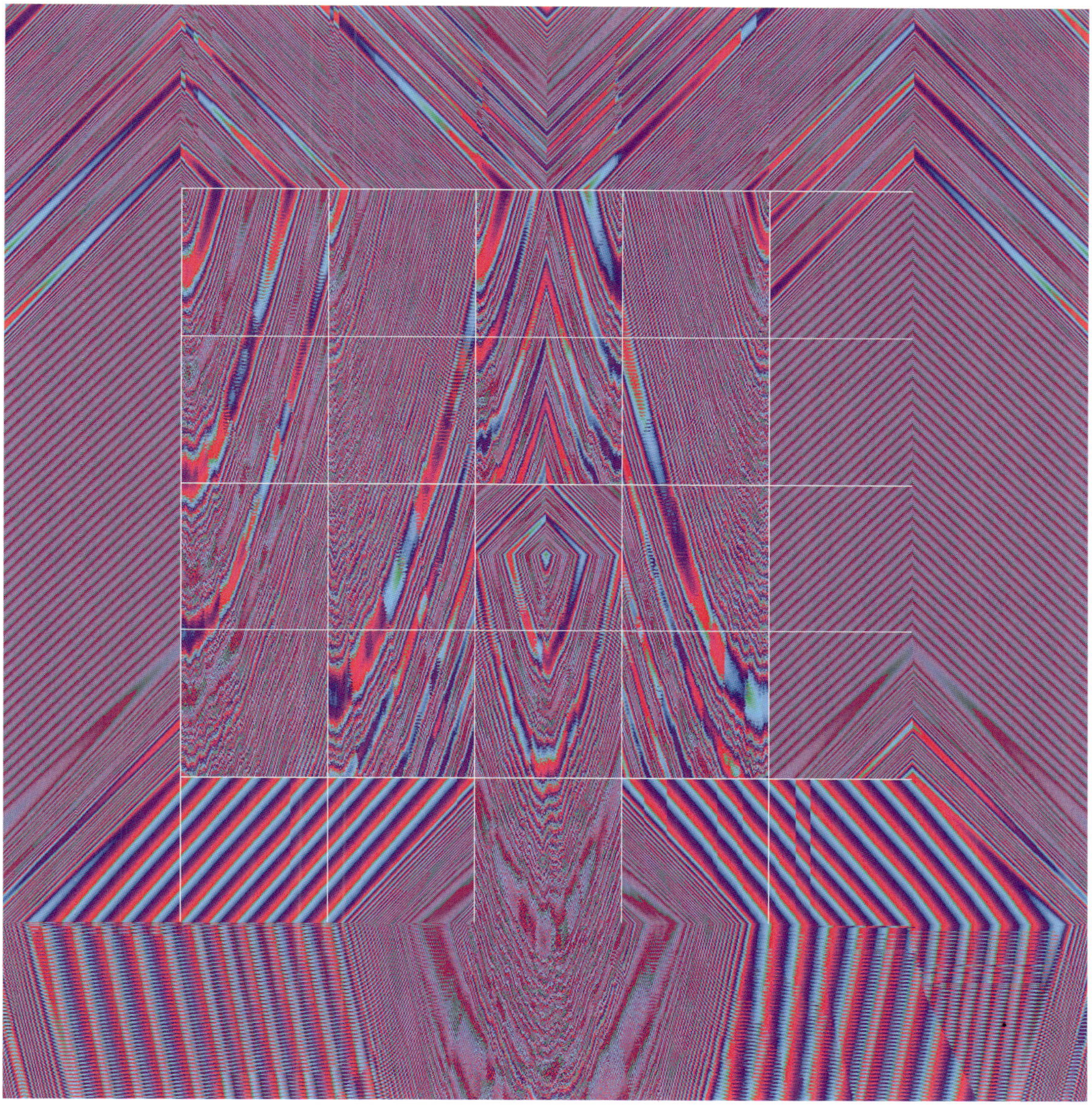

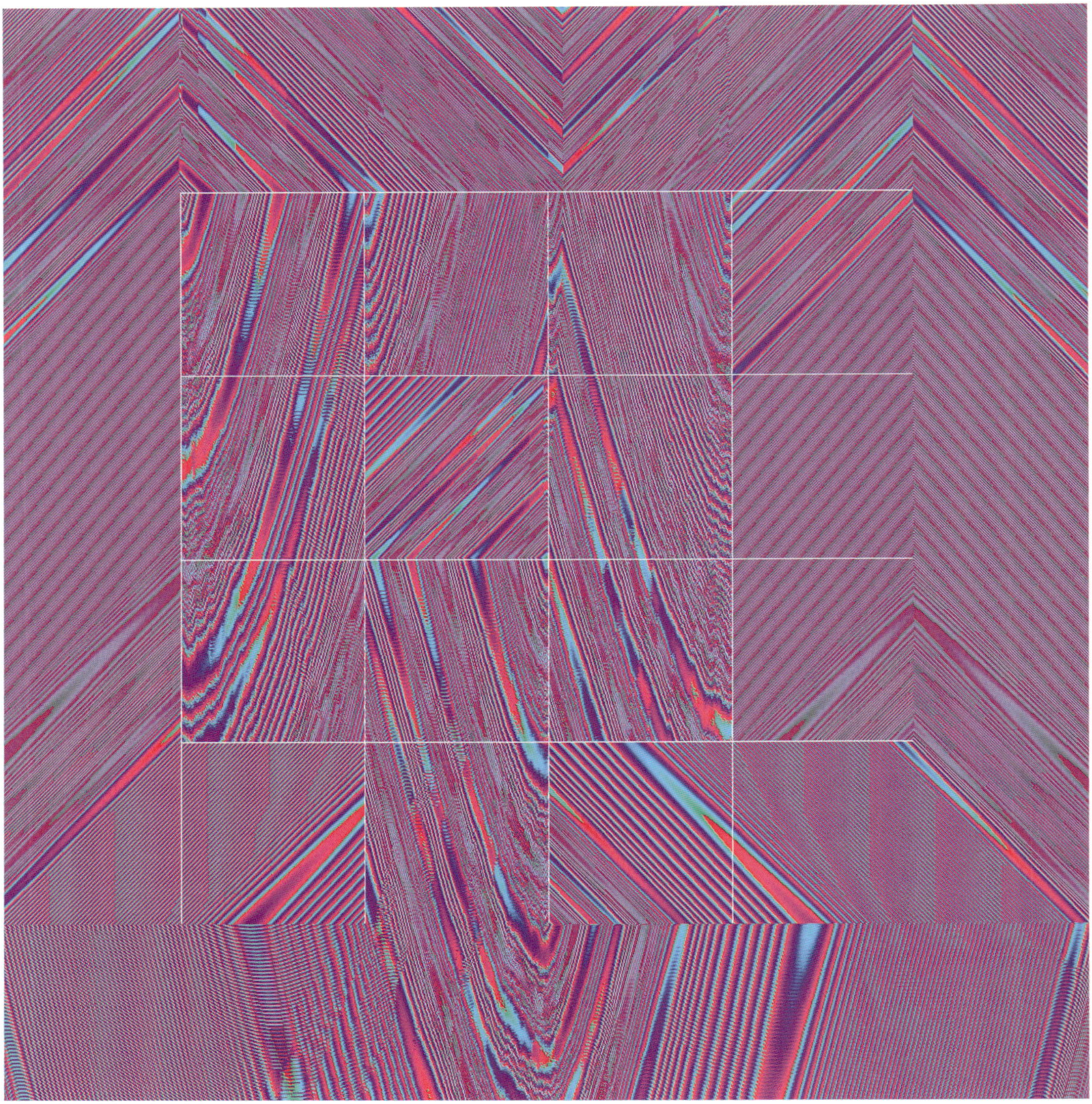

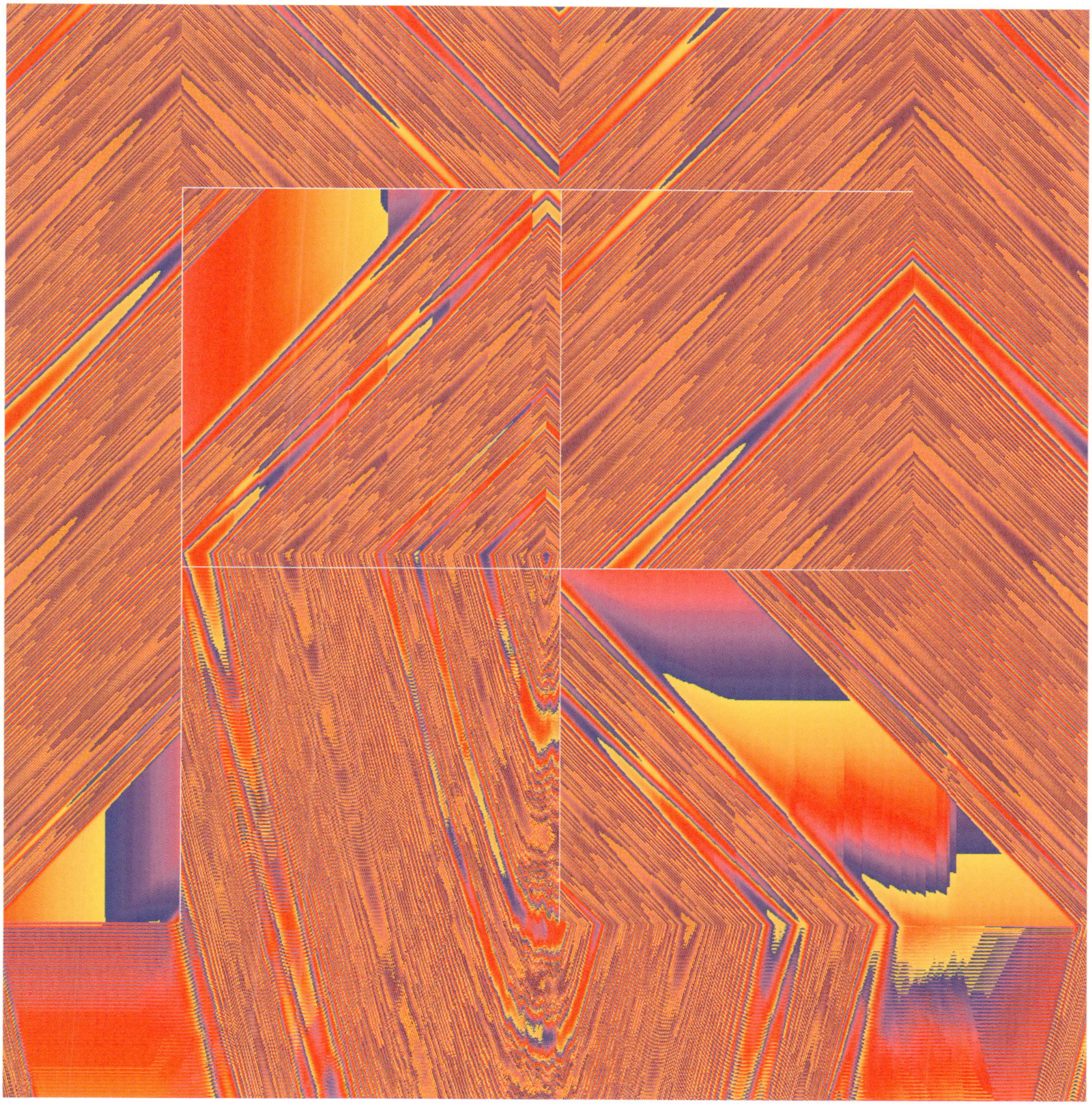

Six *frankensteinRebuilds* resulting from six different runs with the same input.

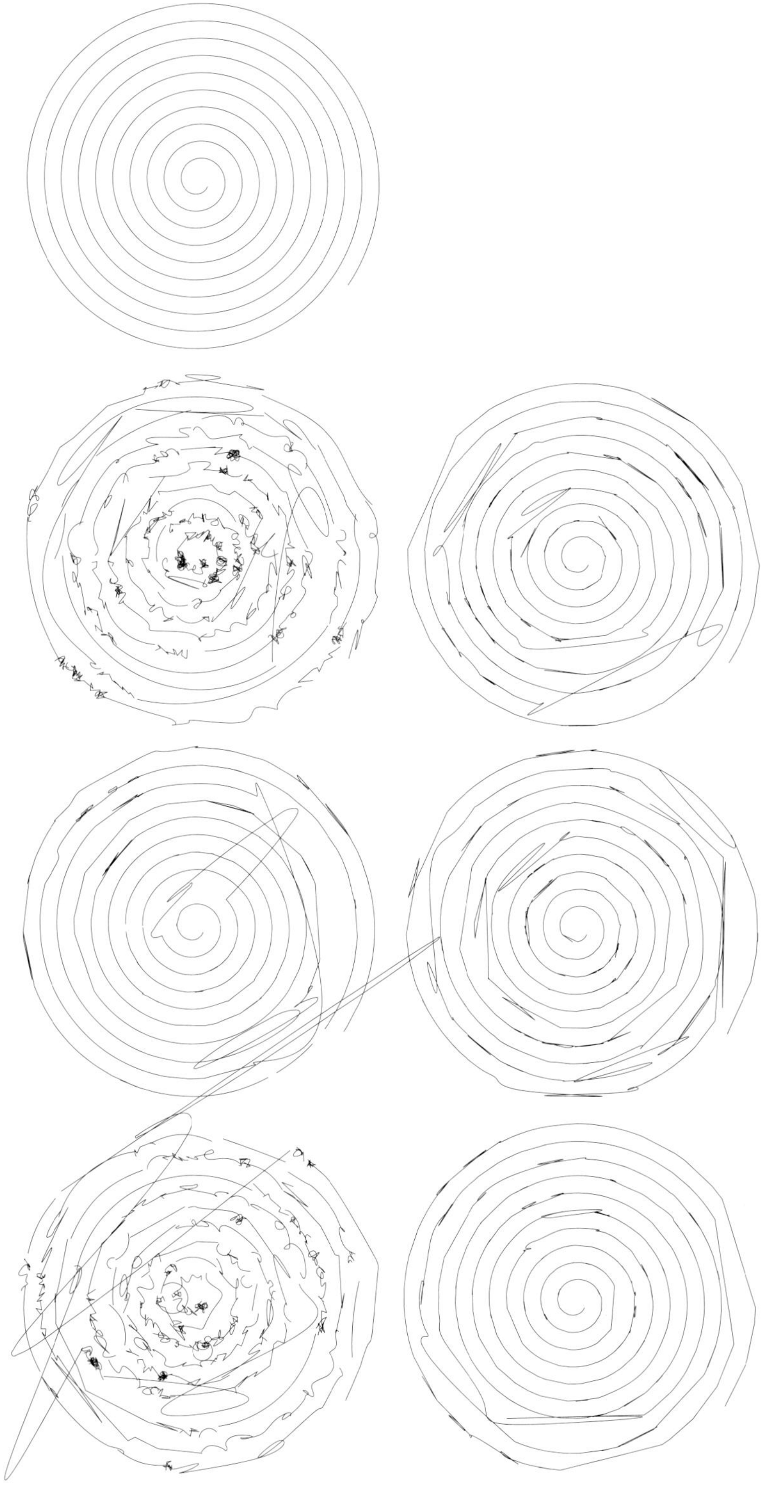

ABOVE AND OPPOSITE PAGE As an artificially-intelligent program plays Connect-4 against a human opponent, it records all the board states that have been considered. This is a drawing of those boards for one game.

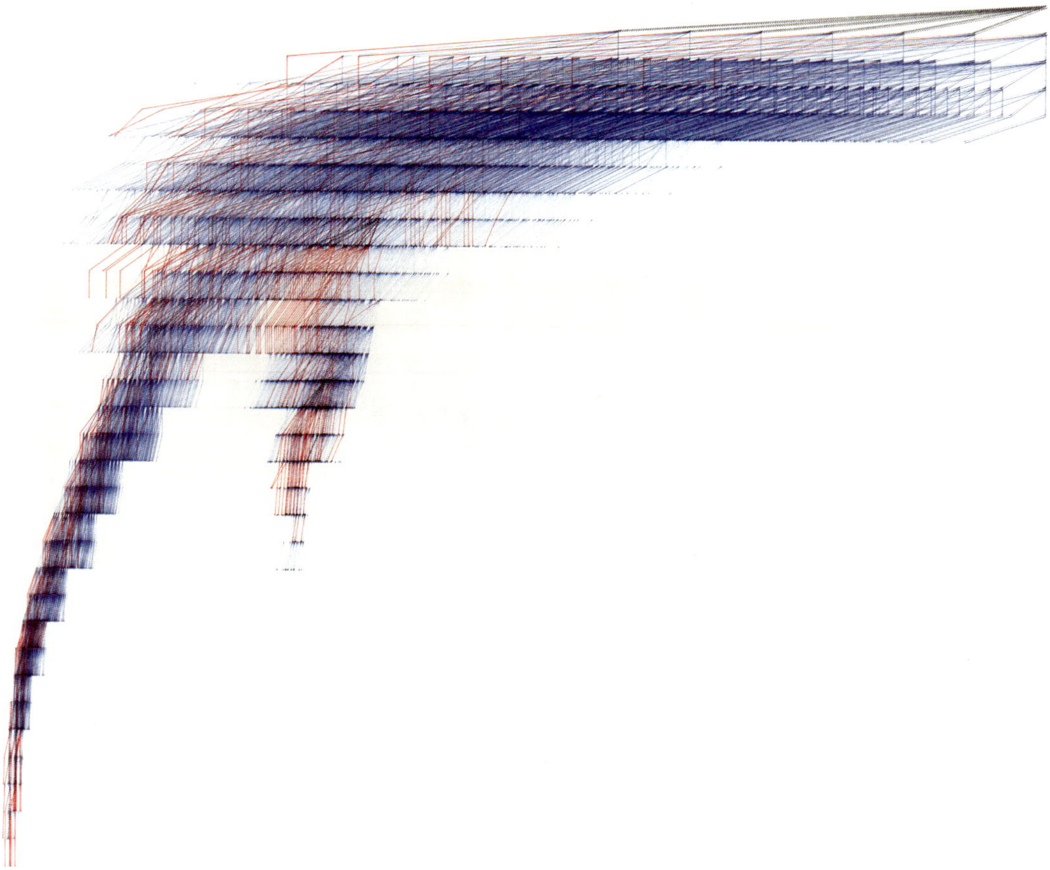

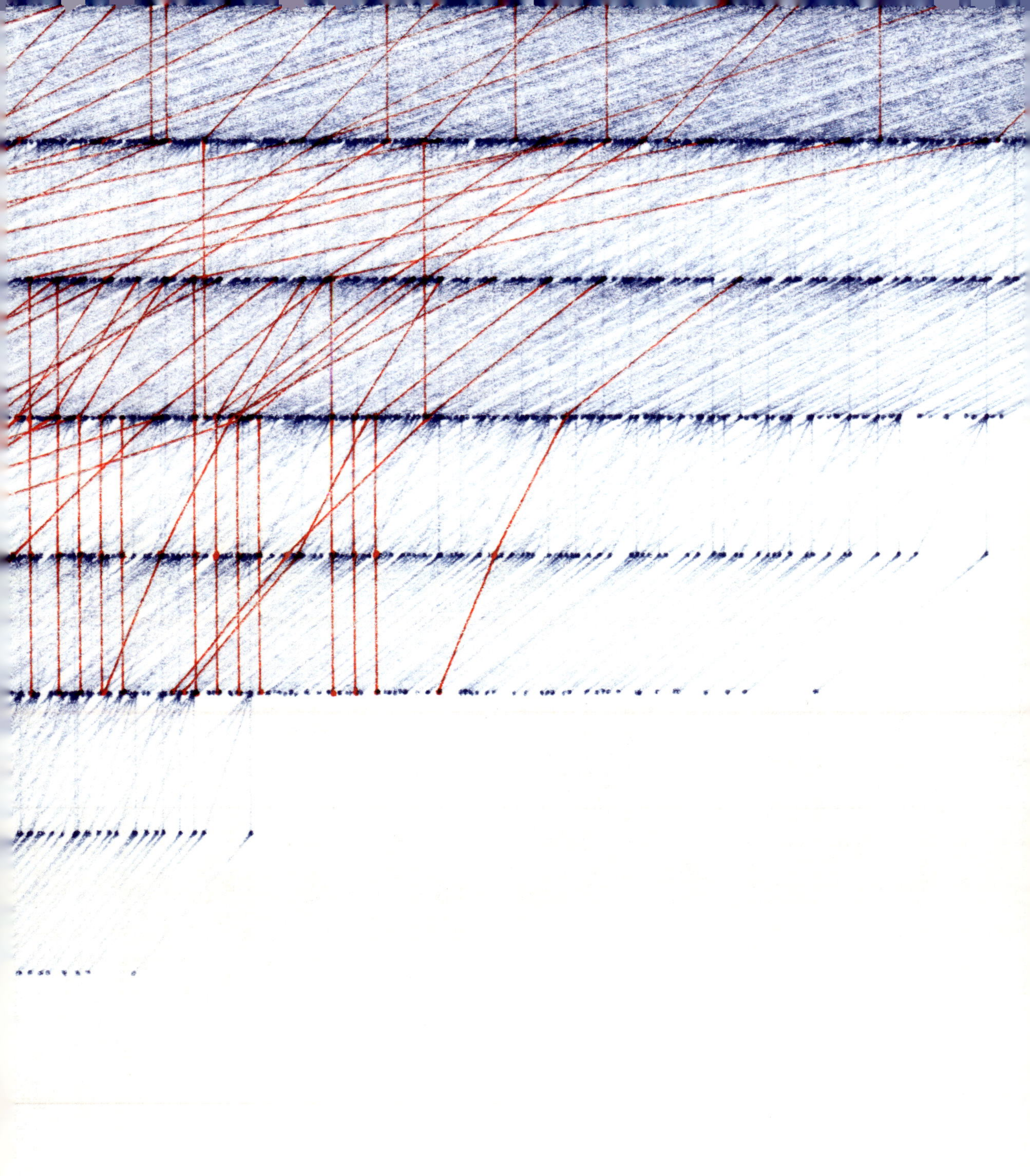

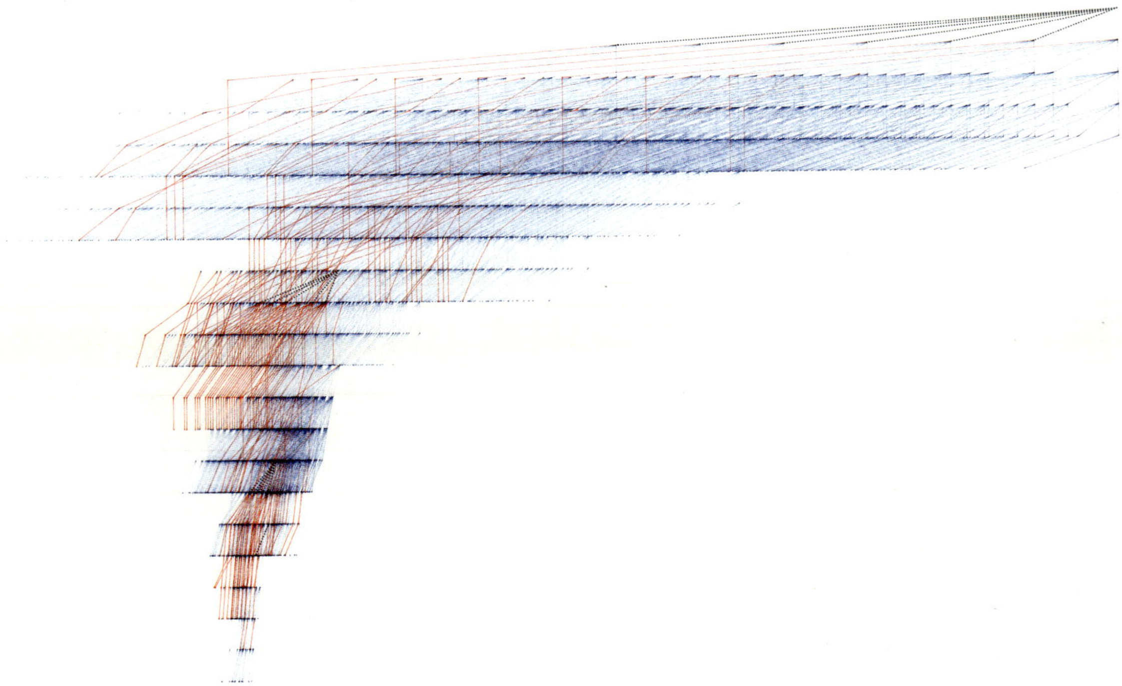

As an artificially-intelligent program plays Connect-4 against a human opponent, it uses a search tree to optimize the considerations of possible moves. This is a drawing of one such tree for one game.

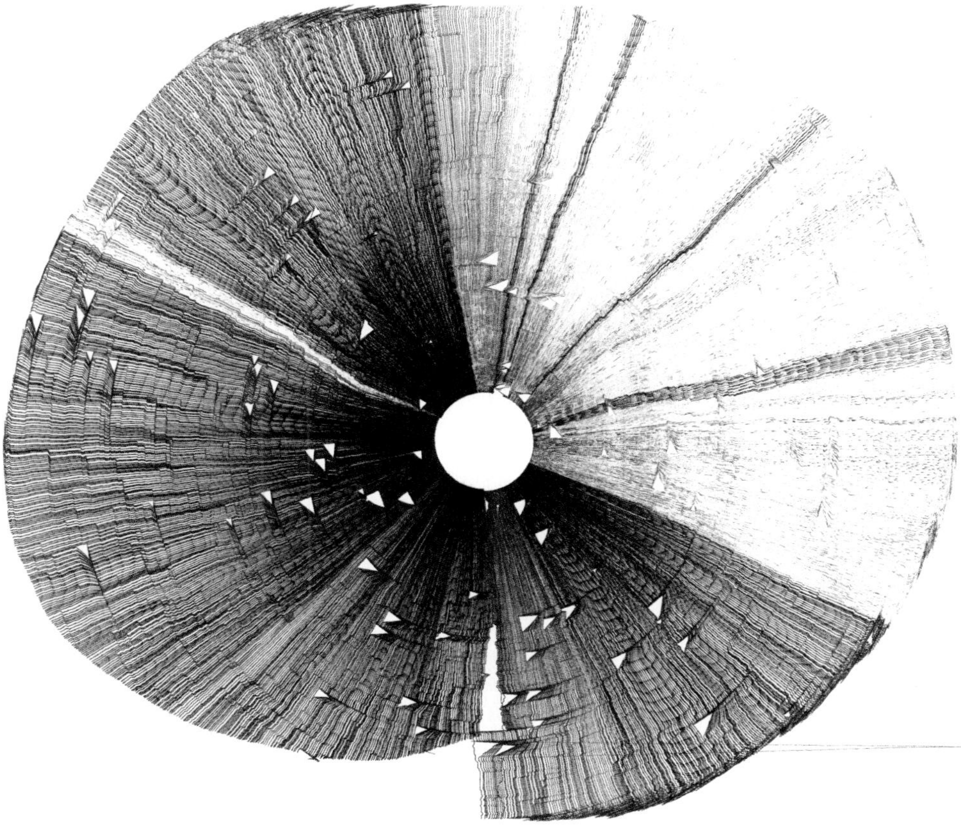

ABOVE AND FOLLOWING SPREAD A drawing resulting from a dumb algorithm that performs no calculation other can counting the length of tweets from a certain hashtag for one hour of a twitter stream.

Chapter 4
Form

Objects and Space / matter and machines

> "We choose to go to the moon in this decade and do the other things, not because they are easy, but because they are hard, because that goal will serve to organize and measure the best of our energies and skills, because that challenge is one that we are willing to accept, one we are unwilling to postpone, and one which we intend to win, and the others, too."
>
> —John F Kennedy[1]

Difficulty engenders innovation. Hard problems often bring out the best in us. How can we make drawing difficult? Matthew Barney's project, "Drawing Restraint" is built on the idea of self-imposed restraint. "I think as an athlete you understand that your body requires resistance in order to grow. It's something you take for granted ... I think when I was confronted with this idea of being in the studio and generating form, it was a way in which I could understand form being developed with a self-imposed resistance placed upon it, as it does in the body."[2] Computation brings its own kind of difficulty to drawing. This difficulty is intertwined with form and its co-conspirator in the domain of drawing: depth.

Depth & Projection

In architecture, we often assume that every drawing is the result of a projection of three-dimensional form onto a two-dimensional surface. In this chapter, we explore conceptions of depth that are just as rigorous, that allow more ambiguous relationships between objects in space and matter and machines. This approach to drawing uses projective representation as a way to speculate, interpret, analyze, and perceive, rather than a method to assert or communicate.

Perspective, orthographic, and oblique parallel projections are responsible for most of the drawing types we associate with the representation of architecture. Even if the drawing was not generated via projection, drawings are often keyed into a projection method, even if the lines were conceived casually on paper. For example, a "perspective" sketch might be drawn with the assumption that the lines can be associated with form via perspective projection. One might call these kinds of drawings "pseudo-projections." This kind of drawing can be rigorous and controlled, but are governed by rules that tend to reinforce the outcome of a projection rather than a method that involves actual projection. Two classic examples are the one-point perspective and the oblique axonometric. "One point perspective" refers to the single vanishing point that *results* when camera point, picture plane, and objects correspond in a particular relative orientation in linear perspective projection. Parallel lines in planes perpendicular to the picture plane appear on paper orthogonal to one another. Lines parallel to each other, but perpendicular to the picture plane appear on paper to intersect at a single vanishing point. This condition becomes an operable procedure when lines are drawn so that they behave the same way as those that resulted from actual projection. Establishing a vanishing point and then drawing allows one to draw a one-point perspective without projection. Can one sketch in this way and still implicitly understand projection? Perhaps. Can one draw a one-point perspective and reverse-project to arrive at a model of a scene? Yes. Most oblique axonometric projections are produced by first drawing a rotated plan and then extending lines vertically. This process can be measured and accurate to the extent that it replicates what would've resulted from actual oblique parallel projection. Pseudo-projections are not inherently bad, casual, or shortcuts necessarily. In fact, they can be generative in ways other than reverse projection.

Pseudo-projection rules often contain hints about depth cues, which will be explored a bit later. For now let's consider, how we can draw objects and space without projection, or even pseudo-projection. For many architects and designers, this question might seem strange. Why draw if that drawing can't be immediately associated with form? The answer lies in the fact that drawing without projection, if possible, would mean that the nature of objects and space could emerge from the drawing. It would mean that drawing is not a representation of something, but the direct space of our operations; It would mean that, when drawing, one could simultaneously draw things and draw the way we understand those things. It would mean that projection methods can be overlaid and interchanged. Some would argue that this approach eschews the notion of representation altogether because neither subject nor content would be fixed. The drawing would be the outcome rather than a medium to hold or transmit the outcome.

Many celebrate the end of representation, or avoid the term, for this very reason. Representation is treated as though it was the last bastion of vocational architecture. Representation can seem an explicitly technical procedure at times, as though given a three-dimensional form, there is a "right" way to represent it. Indeed, if architectural drawing was merely a question of getting known content from three dimensions to two dimensions, representation would seem quite tired. However, representation is yet another way for computation to productively disrupt and activate drawing. When drawing computationally, and without projection, representational systems are something to be designed (and even, perhaps, discovered), not imposed. Let's turn to another discipline, computer science, as a model for how architects, artists, and designer might think about representation, and apply that to drawing objects and space. We'll then consider how matter and machines play a role in disrupting and advancing conventional representation.

In computer science, for example, representation is often an interesting and open-ended question. In artificial intelligence, "representation of knowledge"[3] is itself a kind of sub-discipline, a necessary component of any system we might call intelligent. In AI, representations of knowledge and representations of the world do not always coincide. The classic AI example already mentioned is the game of chess: the knowledge of chess, and the processes by which move possibilities are computed, do not resemble the appearance of a chess board as perceived by humans. AI representation becomes even more interesting given experiments that involve seemingly intelligent behavior despite lack of representation.[4] We can take from computer science two over-arching charges to computational drawing in the arts: first, that representational systems can be authored and critiqued; second, that representational systems often are most enlightening when they don't correspond to the way we see and think about the word. That friction provokes reflection and innovation.

Depth is Inherently Difficult

Exercise 4.1 *Automatic Drawing*

Make what Psychologist David Maclagan would call an "automatic drawing."[5] Repeat until the perception of depth is unavoidable. If a class or a group is available, hold a group critique of automatic drawings in which depth is the only topic of discussion.

In chapter one, multiple anti-definitions of drawing were explored and drawing was considered not in terms of what it could be, but what it can't do. Considering *why* we draw is a similar pursuit. The positive reasons are vast and varied, but they often reduce to a consistent pattern: drawing is helpful because depth is difficult. Depth in drawing, on a practical level, is minute. Drawing media is inconsequentially thin. The paper of this book is about .0004 inches thick, and the thickness of the original paper of the drawings reproduced in this book is about the same. A drawing with around one million line segments is still around .0004 inches thick, with no measurable change in thickness from before to after the drawing process is complete. Any real thickness is a matter of perception. Depth perception is a matter well-studied[6] and in all 2-D image-based representation, various "depth cues" trigger our natural perception of space "in" an image. But in contrast to the advances in digital imaging, where the relatively low resolution pixel-based images advanced to become super-small in so called "retina displays" and virtual reality headsets that undermine the presence of the screen-as-distant-object in favor of an immersive experience, the drawing object reminds the viewer that it is there and it is flat. Depth can be implied, and our perception of depth can be triggered, but depth is in a constant, but productive, battle with flat reality. This may explain (along with the fact that, as Bruno Latour and Albena Yaneva explain,[7] a building is always moving, and the key representational challenge lies not in the modeling of the form, but in modeling the multi-dimensional space of building parameters) why various "draw in space" technologies have never matured beyond the stage of demonstrative novelty. Though counter to what we often value about technology, when drawing, often what is most productive is unintuitive, seamful,[8] and difficult.

Depth Cues

Though an amalgamation of instruments (paper, pens, and machines) drawing is not a technology. The distinction between instruments and technologies helps explain why so many debates about the digital computer replacing the drawing end in stalemate. Sure, digital media, especially digital modeling, allows for production, representation, and simulation not possible in the domain of drawing. But the counter argument for drawing is precisely the same—so much is not possible with drawing that we can borrow a McLuhan term and call it a helpfully cool medium.[9] The most important inhibiting feature of drawing is the difficulty of depth.

As we return to depth cues for a moment and take stock of a few specifically, we will keep in mind that we are not seeking technologies, tools, or methods to apply these depth cues. Rather, we're considering them as active frames of reference that can be imposed and revoked while drawing.

Occulation is perhaps the most straightforward of the depth cues. Objects obscure or block objects behind them as they overlap in a field-of-view. Perspective is another that has already been touched upon. Parallel lines tend to converge at vanishing points when viewed in perspective. Size is also a depth cue. Small objects appear farther away than closer objects. If a horizon is perceived, objects closer to the horizon line in the composition are perceived as more distant than those farther away from the horizon line. Fading can also be a depth cue as lighter lines appear farther as though they were engulfed in a fog. There are depth cues that relate to our common understanding of photography: curvilinear perspective (as parallel lines viewed through the side of a wide lens appear more curved than those through the center) and depth of field (where lines blur to a degree commensurate with their difference to a focal length).

All of these depth cues can be deployed without the need for actual projection, as we have explored previously. This approach is facilitated when we computationally author the characteristics of lines and the structure of drawing.

Exercise 4.2. *The depthy line.*

Take as a given a computational definition of a mark, such as one of the functions created in exercise 1.1. Augment this mark so that it appears three-dimensional. Avoid projection.

If one can control the movement from three-dimensions to two-dimensions, one can master the reverse.

Exercise 4.3 *Pursuit of flatness.*
Write a function that takes three-dimensional information (a collection of x, y, z coordinate values, for example) and structures it two-dimensionally without discarding three-dimensional information.

If one can code depth cues, one can conceive of and discover new spatial relationships.

Exercise 4.4. *Competing Cues.*
Choose two depth cues. Using one system of mark-making, create one drawing in which the two depth cues compete with one another to articulate different readings of depth. It might help to repeat this drawing a few times to allow one depth to dominate the other so that a precise balance can be cultivated.

Objects

In the previous chapter, the strategies discussed involved process. Likewise, so far in this chapter depth has been considered relative to lines and marks. The automatic drawings made in exercise 4.1 could be accurately described as "drawings of drawing" rather than drawing of content. In this kind of drawing, the content is the process. The drawing is its own world; nothing outside of that world need enter. This kind of drawing may become incredibly complex and detailed. Despite the suggestion that automatic drawings may be subconscious, it is nearly impossible to draw without some kind of indirect imagination, interpretation, and judgment. These behaviors tend to emerge because we cannot help but read into the drawing as we draw. Furthermore, once those behaviors emerge, so does content. We have also considered how computation affects the way we structure drawings and the methods we use to make marks in a drawing. Likely drawings that result from the recent exercises have created form. Now, we can return to something that was previously set aside: drawing with respect to the form of existing or known objects. It is important that this somewhat obvious approach to drawing come *after* depth cues and projection methods have been interrogated and critiqued. This allows for a drawing of objects (including discrete forms that might define inhabitable space) using computational methods that will actively transform those objects.

Let's consider drawing from life. This involves drawing what you see and observe in the world. It's certainly one of the most traditional kinds of drawing, and, in that, might seem a bad fit with the kind of progressive technological agendas that working computationally implies. However, new tools and new methods are perfectly poised to be challenged by old traditions.

Exercise 4.5. *Still life.* Set up some objects on a table. Draw the scene by editing and implementing functions for marks that you've already created.

Surfaces

As objects cohere in a drawing, depth cues are reinforced. For example, a rectangular prism, drawn as wireframe outlines, appears three-dimensionally as lines converge towards a vanishing point. As the formal nature of the shape resolves in our mind the perspective cue becomes nearly impossible to ignore. The depth cue fixes in a way that would not occur in a field of lines that do not correspond to the outlines of an object. Surfaces can play a similar role in depth cuing. Similar lines densely arranged can suggest a surface. These hatch lines can retain their legibility as individual and flat components of a drawing even as the surface cues readings of depth. As a result, surfaces are unique opportunities for computational drawing in that they sustain a threshold between legibility of objects and legibility of line in drawing. Apparent surfaces can emerge from a drawing to form objects and define space. Surfaces can also structure the geometry computationally, including as part of a projection method. Consider, for example, a surface used as a picture plane in the construction of a linear perspective. Surfaces can also be the subject of a drawing if modeled before projection. Though a common topological component of digital models, drawing surfaces via projection is a pre-digital cartographic technique for the rendering landform.[10]

Exercise 4.6 *Surface Scaffold.* Find or design a surface. Write an algorithm that measures and represents the surface in a drawing as a cartographer would, capturing and communicating every nuance of the geometry. Then, write an algorithm (or adapt the previous algorithm) to function as an anti-cartographer, as though the agenda is to undermine the conception of the surface, to make a measured drawing that is accurate, but that nonetheless distorts or otherwise misrepresents (even fabricates a different conception of) the surface.

Two and a half dimensional objects and pseudo-spaces

The personal computer substantially affected the way architects and designers conceive of and fabricate inhabitable matter. In the context of drawing, however, the pixel, and its relationship to depth is where we should focus our attention. In chapter one, the pixel was explored as a component of a kind of model—the digital image. But in considering the nature of pixels as immaterial, we must confront a casual myth: that a pixel-based image can become a drawing when it is printed. One might ask, why not? The result of the digital print is material. The color on the paper is made from real ink, and it is possible to interpret lines, forms, and depth. The issue is a one of dimensionality as well as structure. The file-print paradigm relies on a processing of the appearance of pixels as though they were flat even when the structure of that image includes a kind of depth. Many digital image formats are organized by layers. These two-and-a-half-dimensional images have a serialized depth—some layers are above others, but the depth is not measurable in the same way the x- and y-axes are measurable. Still, the order of layers can change the appearance of the image. This partial or half-dimension can manifest as a kind of temporal layering, even if the format doesn't organize pixels into layers. Consider, for example, an algorithm called *rectanglesOverRectangles* that fills a random rectangular area with white pixels and outlines the perimeter of the same area with black pixels.

```
A rectangle is defined in terms of positionX, positionY, width, and height
  y is set to positionY
  x is set to positionX
  while x is less than or equal to positionX+width
    set the pixel at (x, y) to black
    increase x by 1
  increase y by 1
  while y is less than positionY + height
    set x to positionX
    set the pixel at (x, y) to black
    increase x by 1
    while x is less than positionX+width
      set the pixel at (x, y) to white
      increase x by 1
    set the pixel at (x, y) to black
  set x to positionX
  while x is less than or equal to positionX+width
    set the pixel at (x, y) to black
    increase x by 1

fill the image with white pixels
while the numberOfRectanglesMadeSoFar is less than 1,000
  create randomValueA as a random number between -40 and the width of the image
  create randomValueB as a random number between -40 and the width of the image
  create randomValueC as a random number between 5 and 40
  create randomValueD as a random number between 5 and 40
  create a rectangle (randomValueA, randomValueB, randomValueC, randomValueD)
```

As this algorithm plays out, later rectangles will overlap earlier rectangles. This overlap, which is actually not an overlap at all but merely a replacement of certain pixel values with other pixel values, can be perceived as occlusion, and occlusion cues our depth perception.

No matter how many times a pixel is colored red, or however many layers of red pixels are on top of each other, the reds don't build up. In an RGB image, 100% red, 0% green, and 0% blue is as red as it gets. When printing a digital image, the pixels become ink droplets or toner, but a red dot translated from a red pixel is materially consistent regardless of the history of that pixel. But when drawing with ink, time and material are consequential. Even though the volume of ink is almost never enough to provide measurable depth, the behavior of the material ink as it interacts with the material paper participates in cuing and undermining depth. Ink affects paper and paper affects ink. While most digital printers (and the paper designed specifically for those printers) avoid ink spreading, or "bleeding" through the paper to achieve high resolution output, computer controlled pen plotters, like the ones used to make many of the drawing here, enable that kind of interaction. Ironically, pen-plotters, machines that move a physical pen in two axes across paper, were marketed as output devices for architectural and engineering technical drawings. Now, almost all have been re-appropriated by artists, designers, and architects who cherish them for the very qualities that made them obsolete.

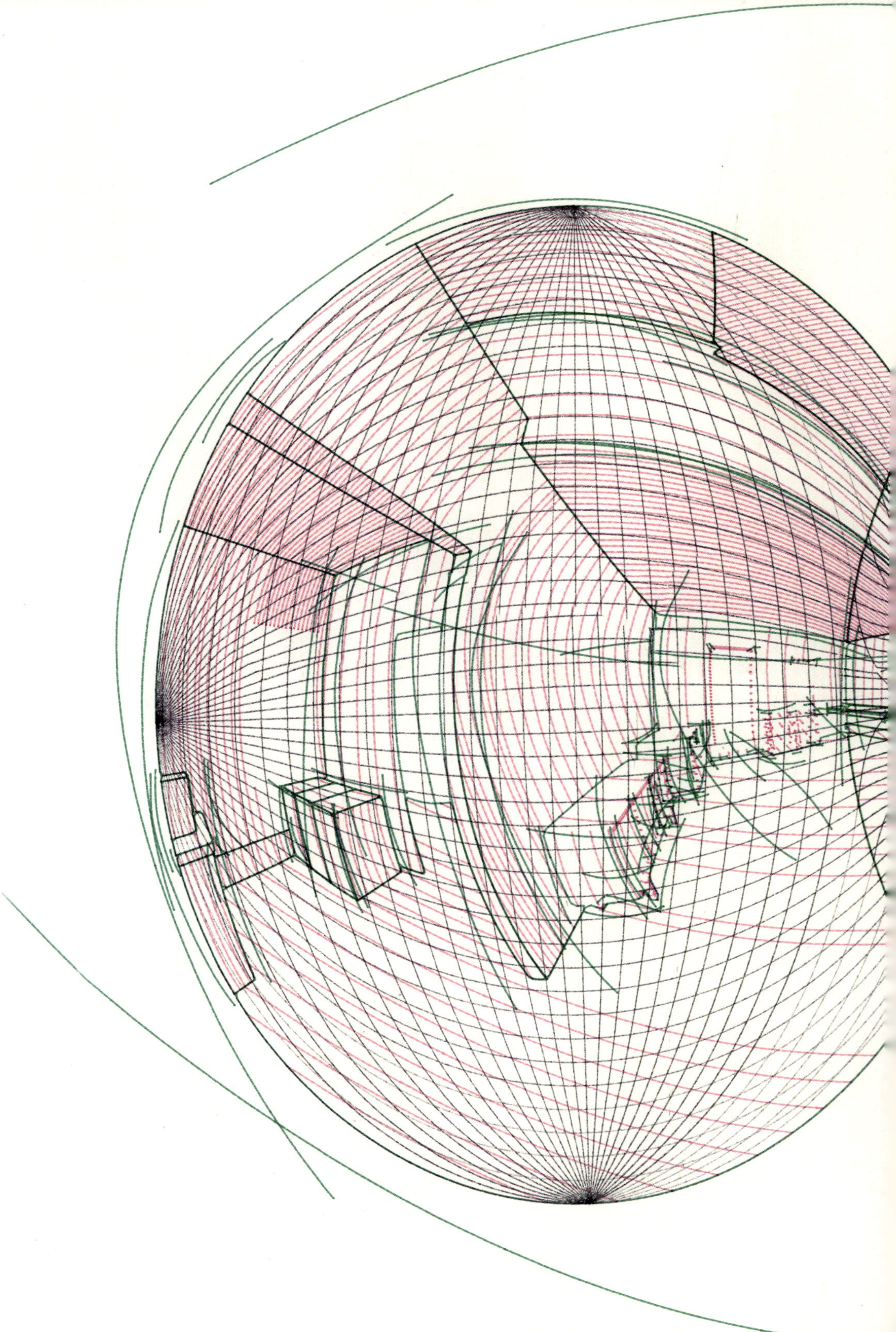

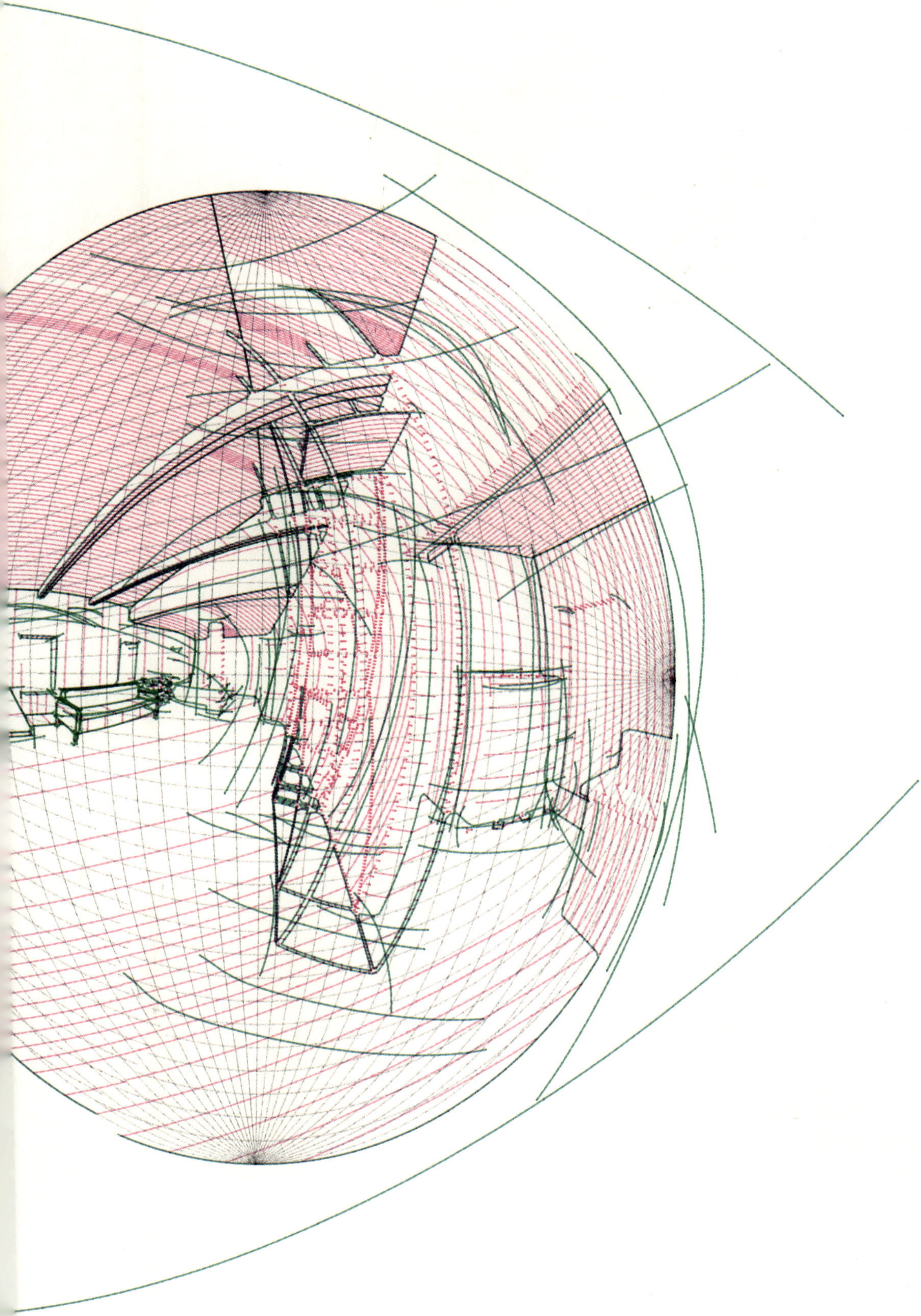

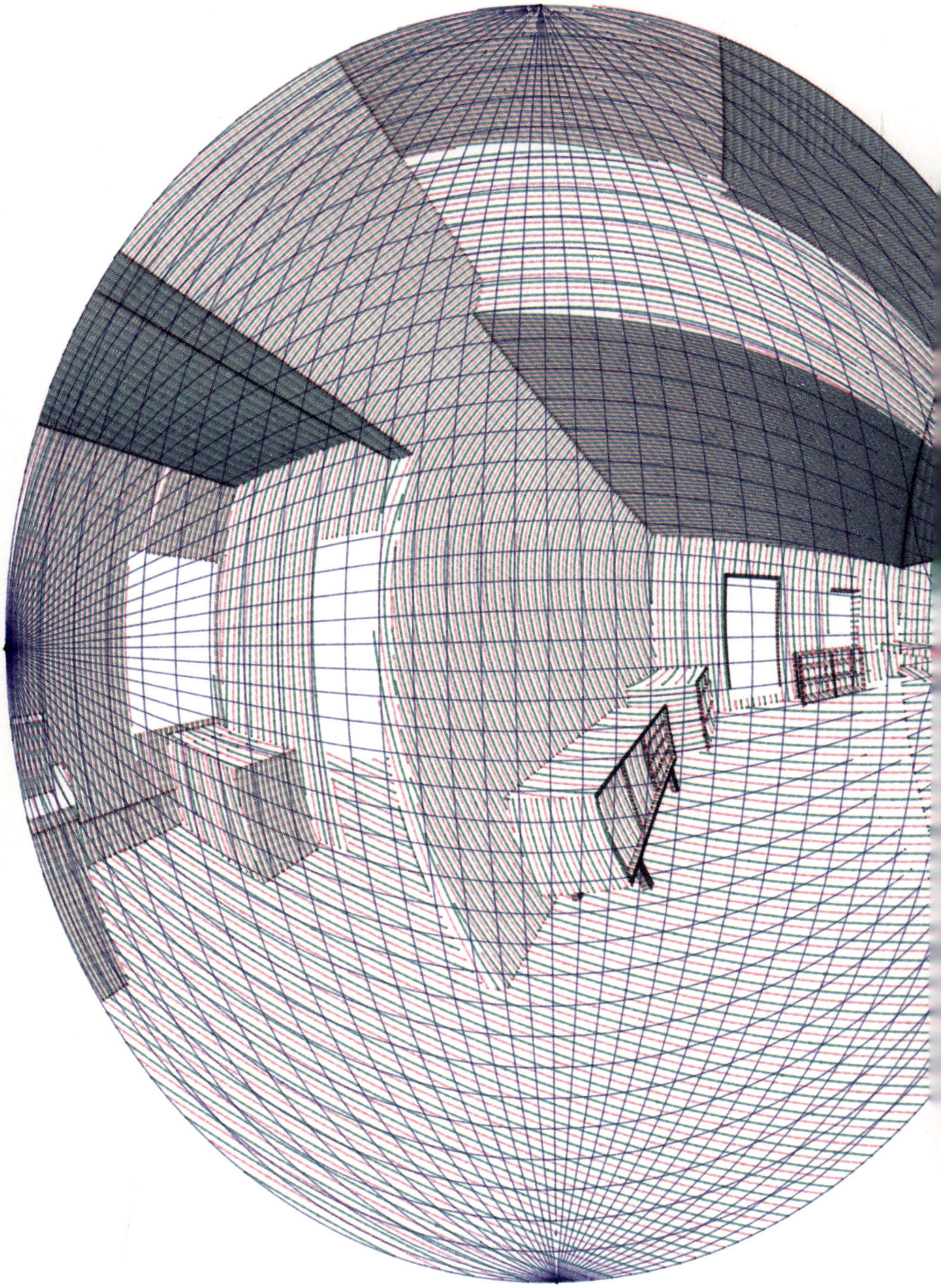

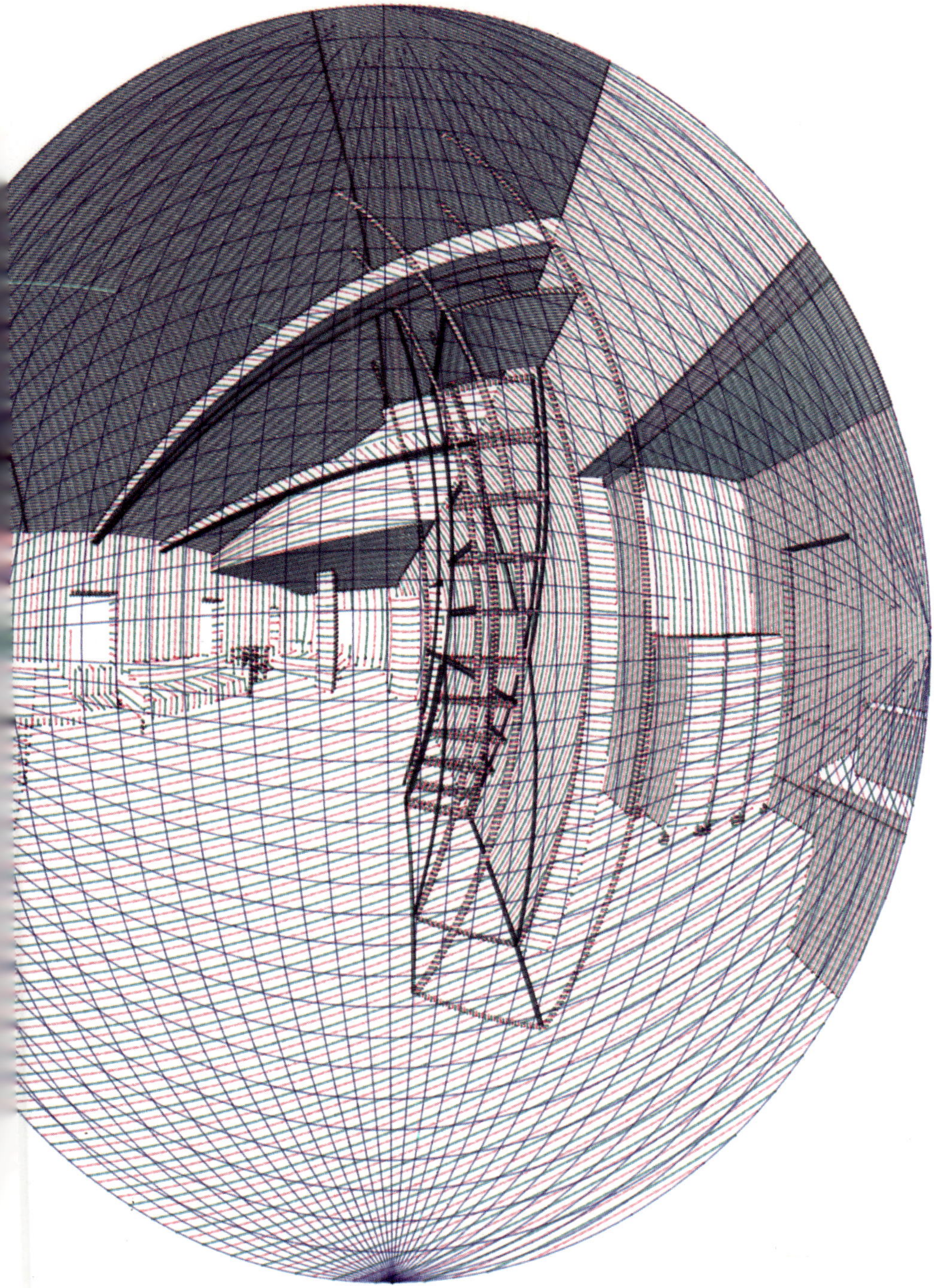

The Form of Ink

Bleeding ink leads to a few kinds of phenomena. First, each mark tends to be softened. The edges of the mark are not clearly defined, but tend to dissolve gradually. Lines drawn slower leave the pen in contact with the paper for longer, resulting in more transfer of ink, and thicker lines. Second, the ink from one mark can bleed into another causing them to blend. Third, because the ink is initially wet, later marks can spread the ink left by earlier marks. The paper itself changes its nature as it interacts with the tip of the pen and the ink as well. Softer, thicker papers will have very subtle troughs left by the pressure of the pen. New marks that cross the trough left by previous marks will be ever so slightly affected by the surface deviation. Many marks made over the same line can saturate the paper, weakening it. More marks, still, can cut through the paper.

This behavior of ink, when controlled, structured, and deployed purposefully, can be elevated to more than mere aesthetic stylization. As has already been mentioned, densely-spaced hatch lines can operate collectively to imply surface. Bleeding ink can contribute materially to this reading, as close parallel or nearly parallel lines can blend together into a smooth area of tone. A line drawn with variable speed may exhibit variable thickness, which may be perceived as closer (when the line is thick) and farther (when the line is thin). The overlap of two marks can create a third condition that reads as figure. It is also possible for the blending of the inks to dominate the drawing to the extent that the drawing looks completely different from a digital rendering of the same geometry.

Most significantly, the behavior of ink can allow lines to call attention to themselves as material on paper. This condition is analogous to the way singing simultaneously involves the sound of words and the meaning of words.[11] Outside of the realm of music, it can be very difficult to hear the sound of spoken word as direct stimuli, the meaning of the word invades our consciousness whether we want it to or not. The same goes for marks that form lines, shapes, and surfaces. To some extent, we cannot not see them. In a directly related but more chilling example, the J. G. Ballard short story "The Overloaded Man" tells the first person account of a man who developed the ability to "switch off" the meaning of objects. The character describes this dryly,

> "I may have stumbled on a means of repressing the photo-associative centers that normally identify visual objects, in the same way that you can listen to someone speaking your own language that none of the sounds has any meaning."[12]

As the character more regularly un-interperts houses, furniture, and even people, all of his world is reduced to raw stimuli. The result is madness.

Fortunately, we can look at a drawing and not go mad, even as the mark reasserts itself at the expense of the geometric form of the line, which also tends to undermine perception of depth. This ambiguity between dimensions is different than the type of ambiguity between various readings of lines. Any discussion of ambiguity inevitably returns us to Empson, the literary critic, and Stiny, the shape-focused mathematician. Stiny recounts the story of a "no-ambiguity" sign posted in an MIT computer science lab.[13] For Stiny, the sign becomes a proxy for the intractable difference between computer science's attendance to models and his own interest in the capacity for shapes to be perceived and operated on based on constantly shifting topological structures embedded in those shapes. Though Stiny's ambiguity discourse raises an important point about the limitation of digital computing, Empson's ambiguity types, despite being born of a completely different era and context, are of more interest here. In Empson's world of close-read literature, his discipline of interest, the intent of the author, the scope of the text, and the state of mind of the reader are all implicated in some of the ambiguity types, specifically, types five, six, and seven. The fifth type, in particular, can be applied most productively to computational drawing and can serve as a basis for a theory of representation. Empson explains that,

> "An ambiguity of the fifth type occurs when the author is discovering his idea in the act of writing, or not holding it all in his mind at once, so that, for instance, there is a simile which applies to nothing exactly, but lies half-way between two things when the author is moving from one to the other."[14]

The fifth type is not a matter of multiple interpretations of definitions (that kind of ambiguity is exhibited in types two through four) but rather it betrays a conflict in the author's mind. In this case, the author can refer to the computational structure of the lines while the mark on paper is analogous to the text. Empson notes that the construction of the words pull the reader back out of the narrative and force an awareness of language. Common in Shakespeare, this can manifest as the author winking to the reader. A material drawing functions in the same way, it may convey something, but it also may convey itself. The behavior of material—ink or graphite for example—sustains this ambiguity. This allows artists, designers, and architects to position representation not merely for communication or visualization of data or pre-defined subject matter but as active participant in content and matter. We can say that *Romeo and Juliet* does not just convey a love story, it is a love story, then we can also claim that a drawing does not just convey form, it is form.

Empson's close readings and obsession over the implications of language help understand why so much literature does not translate well. For example, Empson's ambiguity of the first type[15] often relies on the sound of the word, or the presence of a rhythm to contribute additional minor details. Even if a word in one language can be associated with a corresponding word in another, the relational meaning might not carry over. Just as we might easily argue that good literature resists translation, we can argue that artists, designer, or architect construct not only the drawing, but also the means of making the drawing—the apparatus. It means that the convenience of the software drivers that enable file-print kinds of output are unwelcome in their default state because they are translators from geometry to mark.

Notes

1. "Kennedy's Address at Rice University on Space Exploration." Archival Film, New York, NY: NBC Universal, 09/12/1962. Accessed Wed Nov 4, 2017 from NBC Learn: https://preview-archives.nbclearn.com/portal/site/k-12/browse/?cuecard=1249
2. Barney, Matthew. Matthew Barney on the Origins of "DRAWING RESTRAINT." May 13, 2010. Accessed August 10, 2017. https://www.youtube.com/watch?v=83WTxmkye04
3. Davis, Randall, Howard Shrobe, and Peter Szolovits. "What Is a Knowledge Representation?" AI Magaznine14, no. 1 (1993): 17–33.
4. *Eliza*, the computer that emulates a Rogerian psychotherapist was created in the '60s as a command-line interface. It actually involves no representation whatsoever of ideas or psychology and mostly turns words back on the participant. Many re-creations of Eliza are available today online. Another relevant, and much more powerful example of performance without a model is the work of Rodney Brooks. For example, Brooks, Rodney A. "*Intelligence without Representation*." Artificial Intelligence47, no. 1–3 (1991): 139–59. doi:10.1016/0004-3702(91)90053-m
5. Maclagan, David. *Line Let Loose: Scribbling, Doodling and Automatic Drawing*. London: Reaktion Books, 2014, 81.
6. Howard, Ian P., and Brian J. Rogers. Perceiving in Depth. New York: Oxford University Press, 2012.
7. Latour, Bruno, and Albena Yaneva. "GIVE ME A GUN AND I WILL MAKE ALL BUILDINGS MOVE: AN ANT'S VIEW OF ARCHITECTURE." Edited by Reto Geiser. *Exploratihighons in Architecture: Teaching, Design, Research*, 2008, 80–89.
8. MacColl, Ian, Matthew Chalmers, Yvonne Rogers, and Hilary Smith. "Seamful Ubiquity: Beyond Seamless Integration." UBICOMP 2002 Workshop.
9. McLuhan, Marshall. *Understanding Media: The Extensions of Man*. Cambridge: MIT Press, 1994. McLuhan at first describes hot verses cool in terms of high definition verses low definition writing, "A hot medium is one that extends one single sense in 'High Definition' ... A photograph is, visually, 'high definition.' A cartoon is 'low definition,' simply because very little visual information is provided." However, he goes on to extend this definition further to note that "Any hot medium allows for less participation than a cool one" because cool media require assertive interpretation. It's extended further still based on newness, which is hot, and traditional, which is cool. This would seem consistent in terms of a line of reasoning and colloquial usage, except that drawing would seem to be high-definition, but nonetheless cool in terms of requirement by the viewer/reader.
10. Imhof, Eduard. *Cartographic Relief Presentation*. Redlands, CA: ESRI Press, 2007, 222–234.
11. Ingold, Tim. *Lines a Brief History*. London: Routledge, 2016, 9. Ingold, in the context of notational lines in music, notes that, "the distinction that we – literate people – make between speech and song, and which seems obvious enough to us, would mean nothing to [pre-vocal people]. In both speech and song, for people at a stage of primary orality, it is the sound that counts."
12. Ballard, J. G. "The Overloaded Man" in *The Best Short Stories of J. G. Ballard*. New York: Picado, 2001, 116.
13. Stiny, George. *Shape: Talking about Seeing and Doing*. Cambridge, MA: MIT Press, 2006, 305.
14. Empson, William. *Seven Types of Ambiguity*. New York: New Direction Publ., 1980, 155.
15. Ibid., 2.

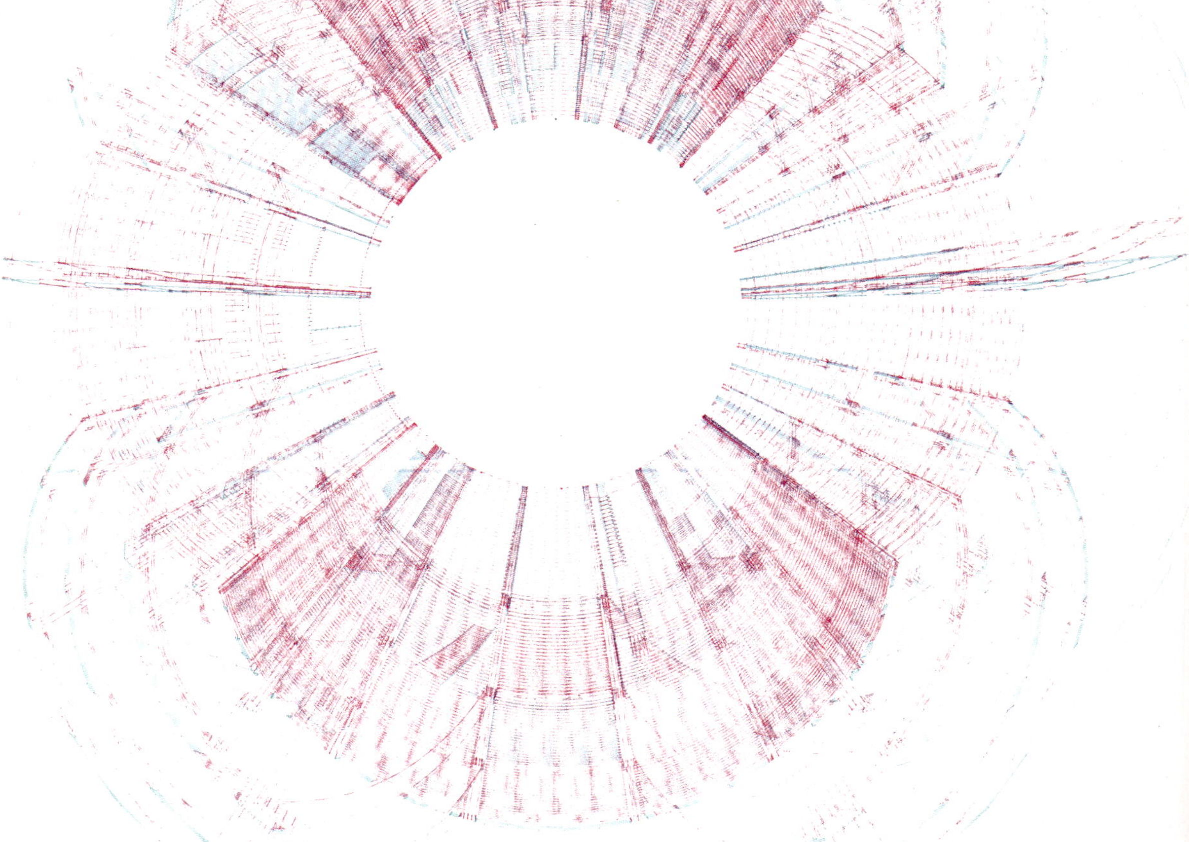

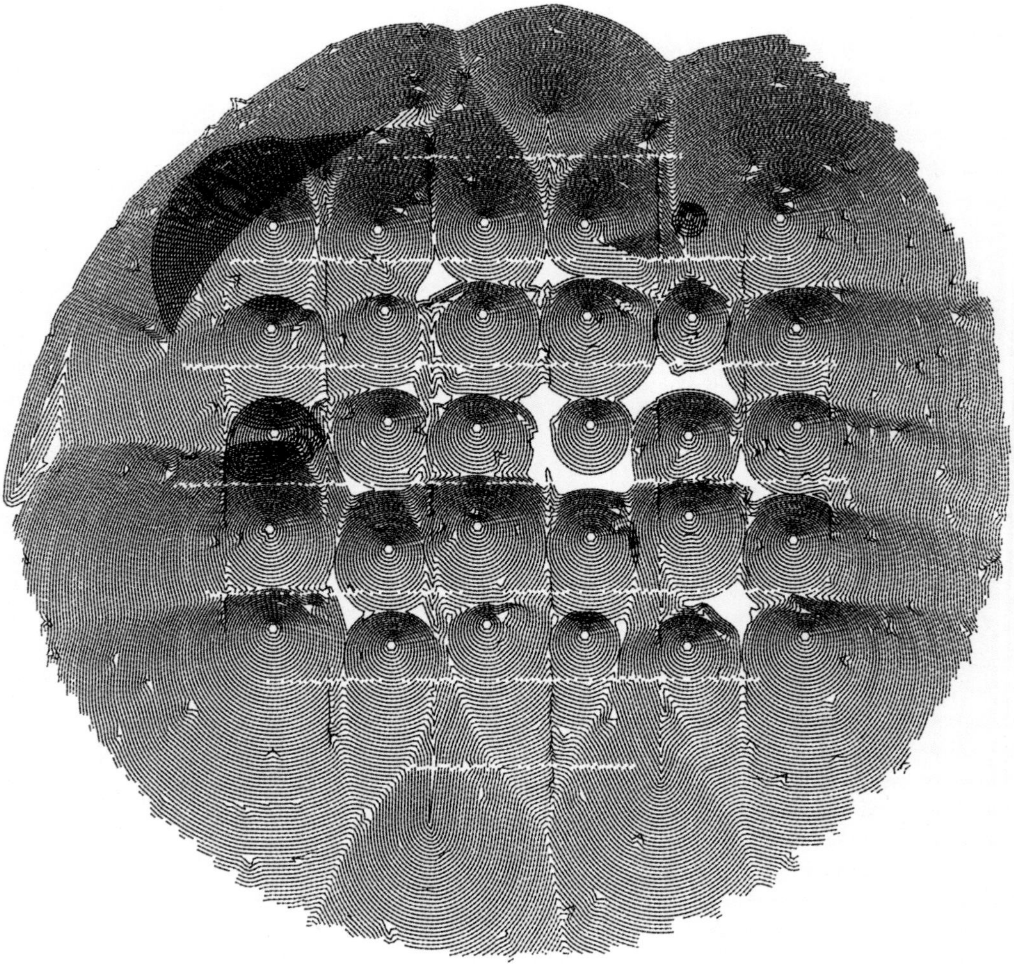

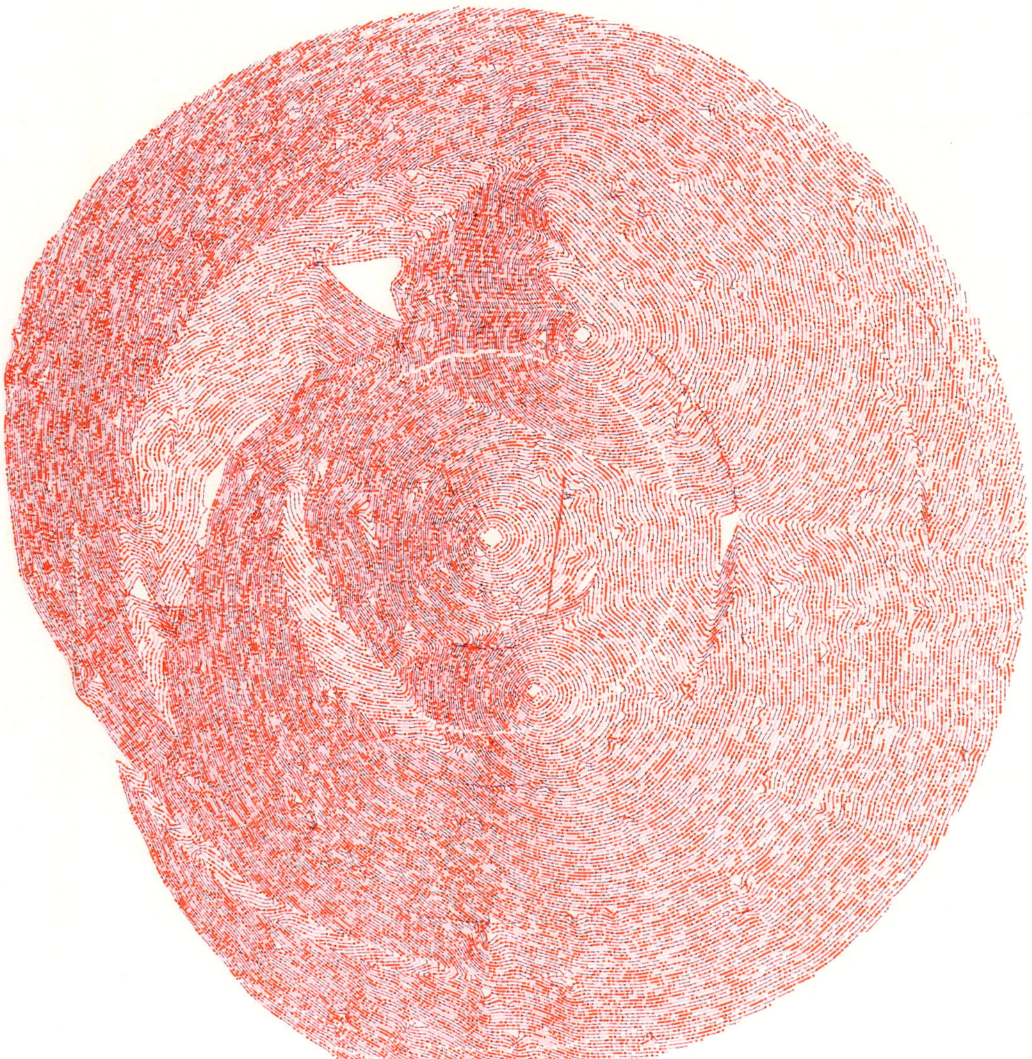

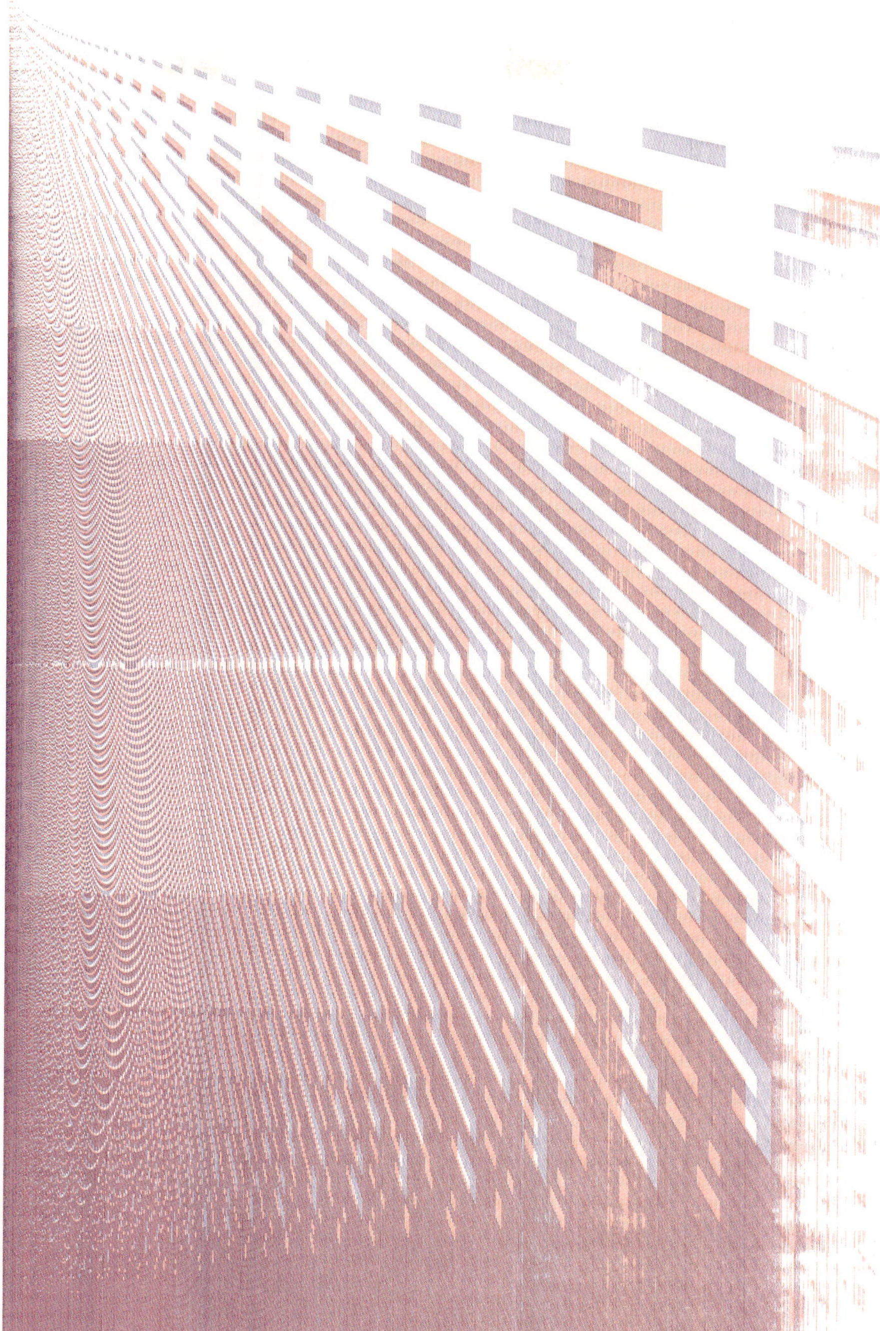

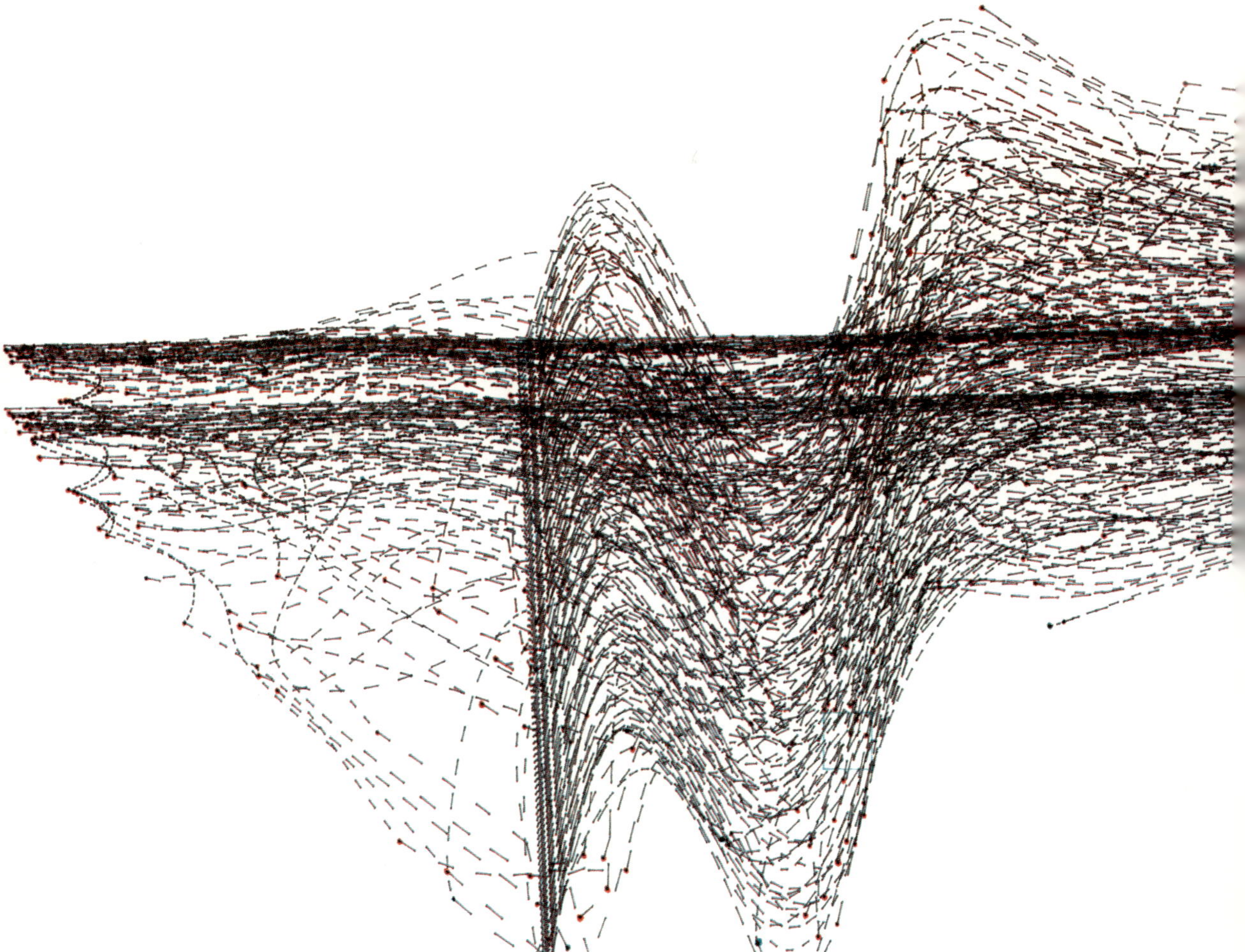

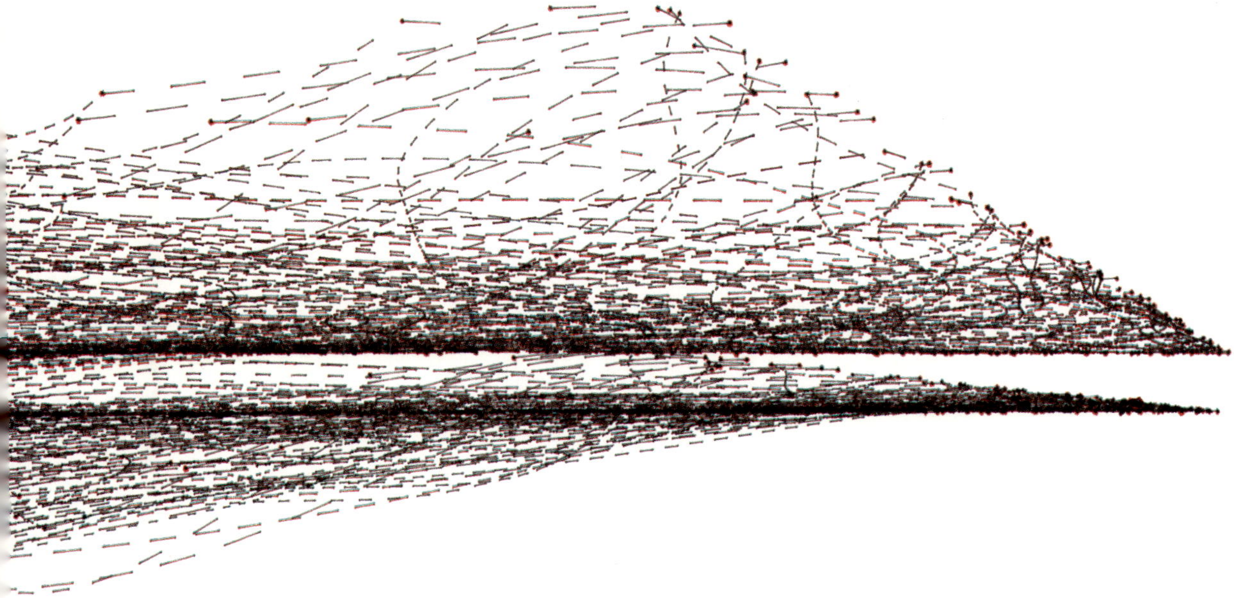

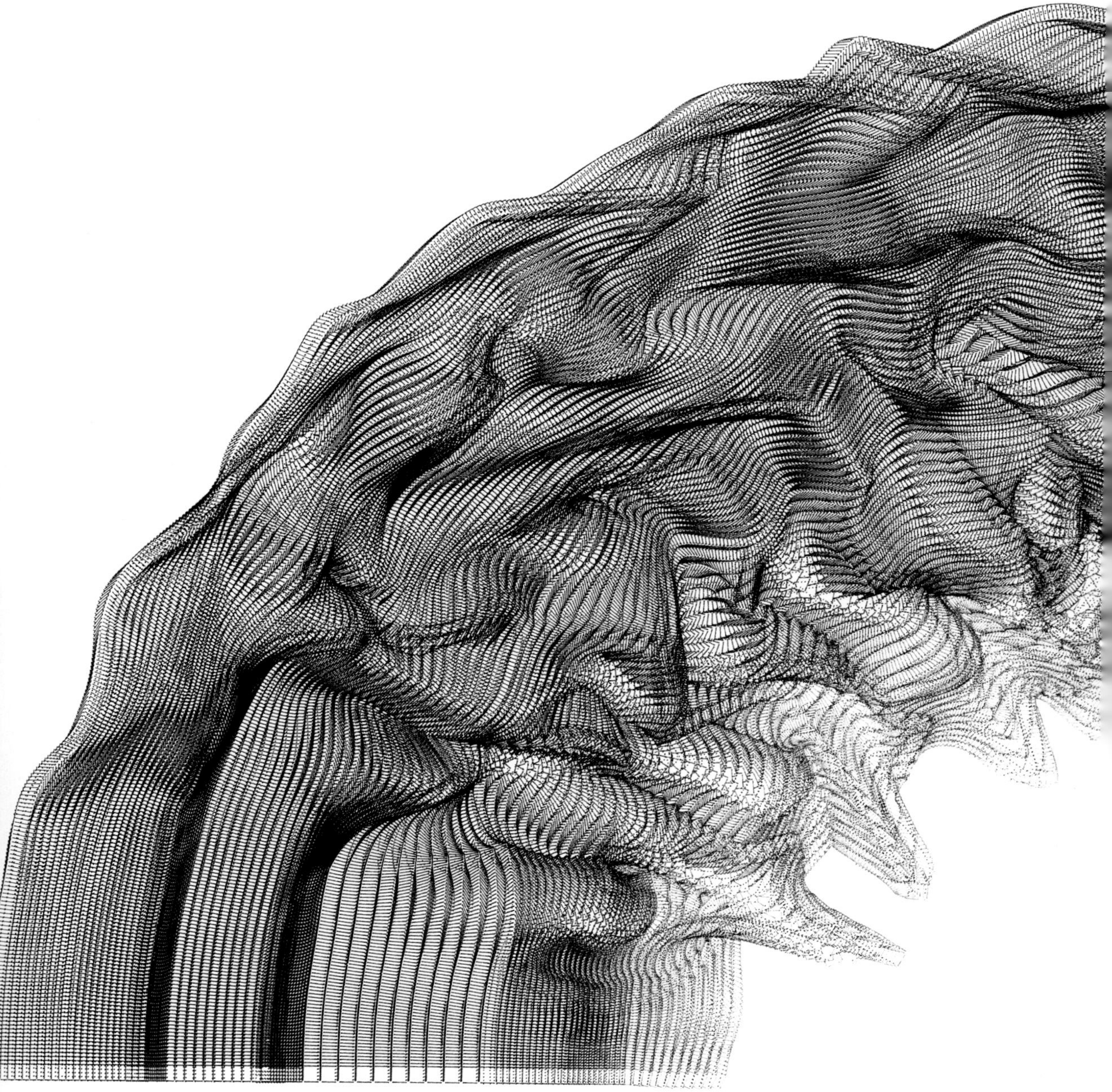

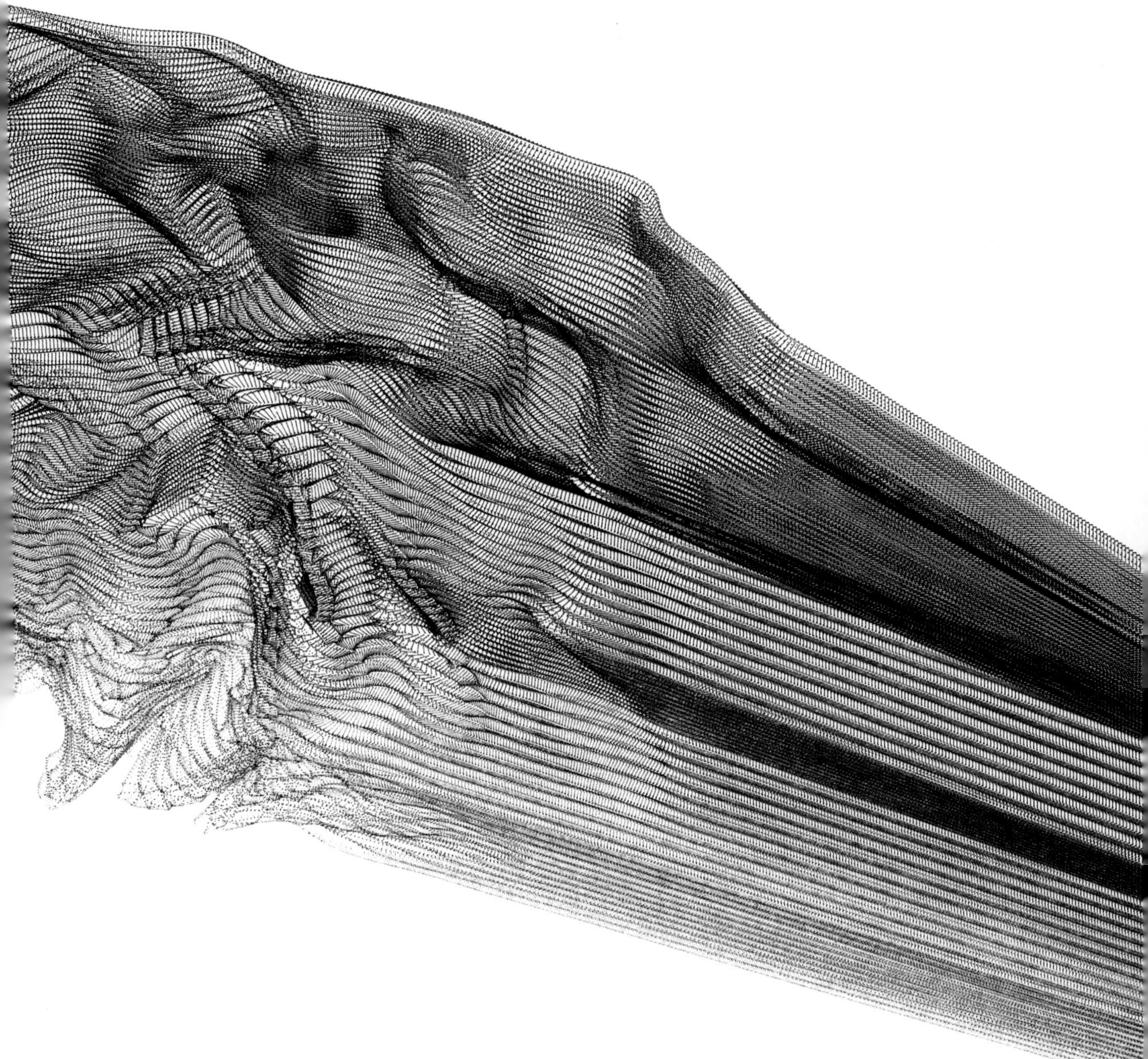

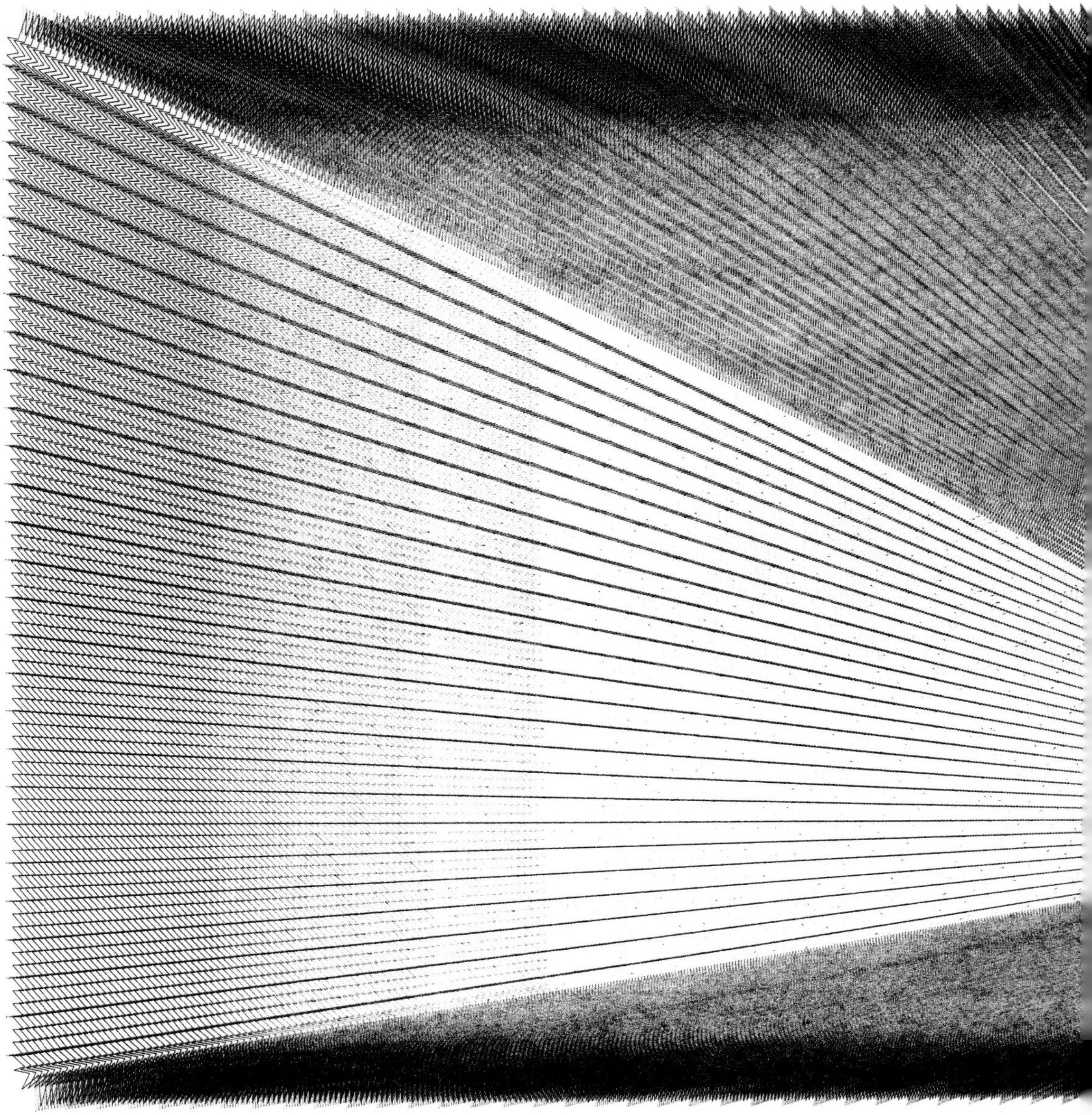

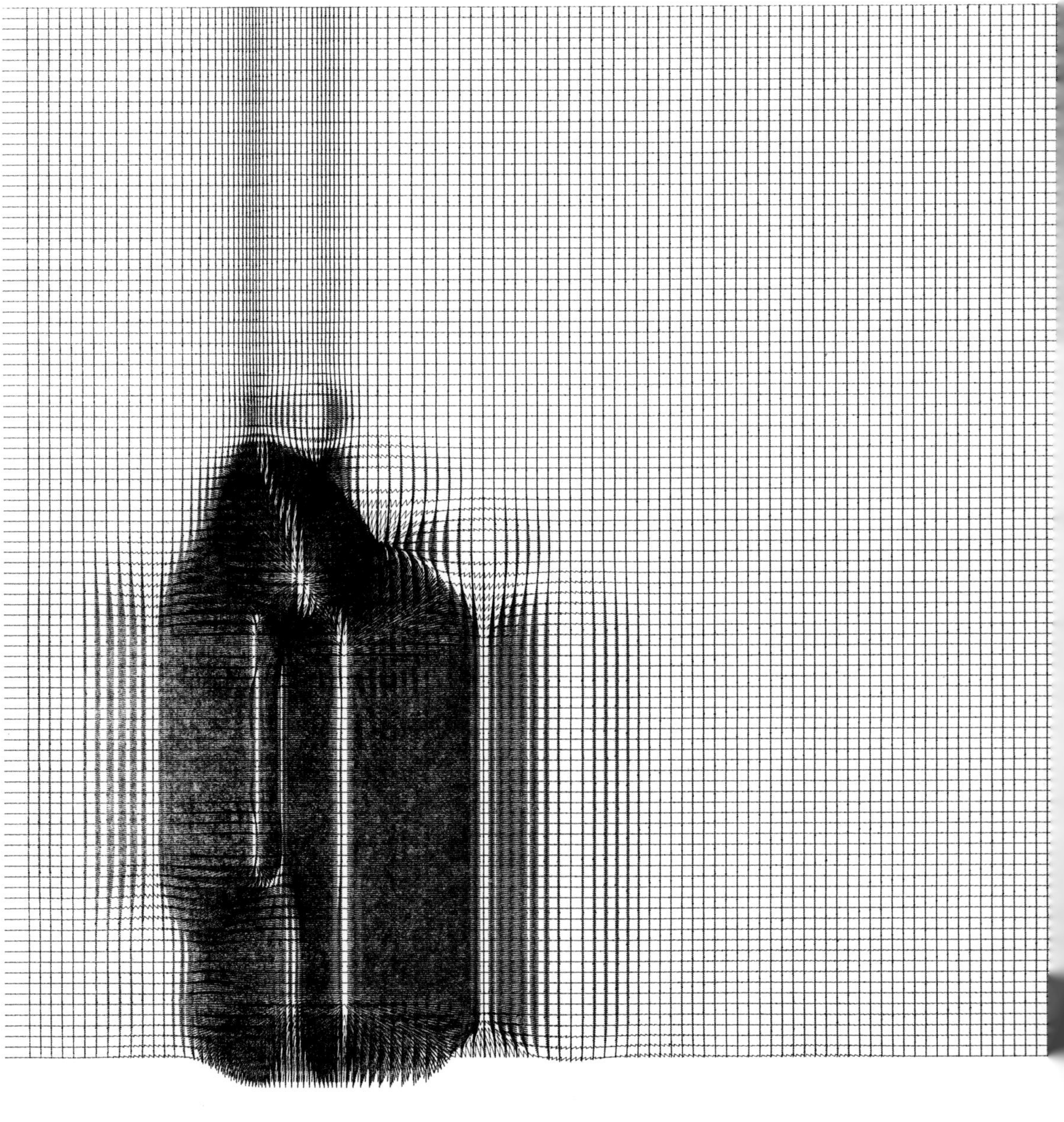

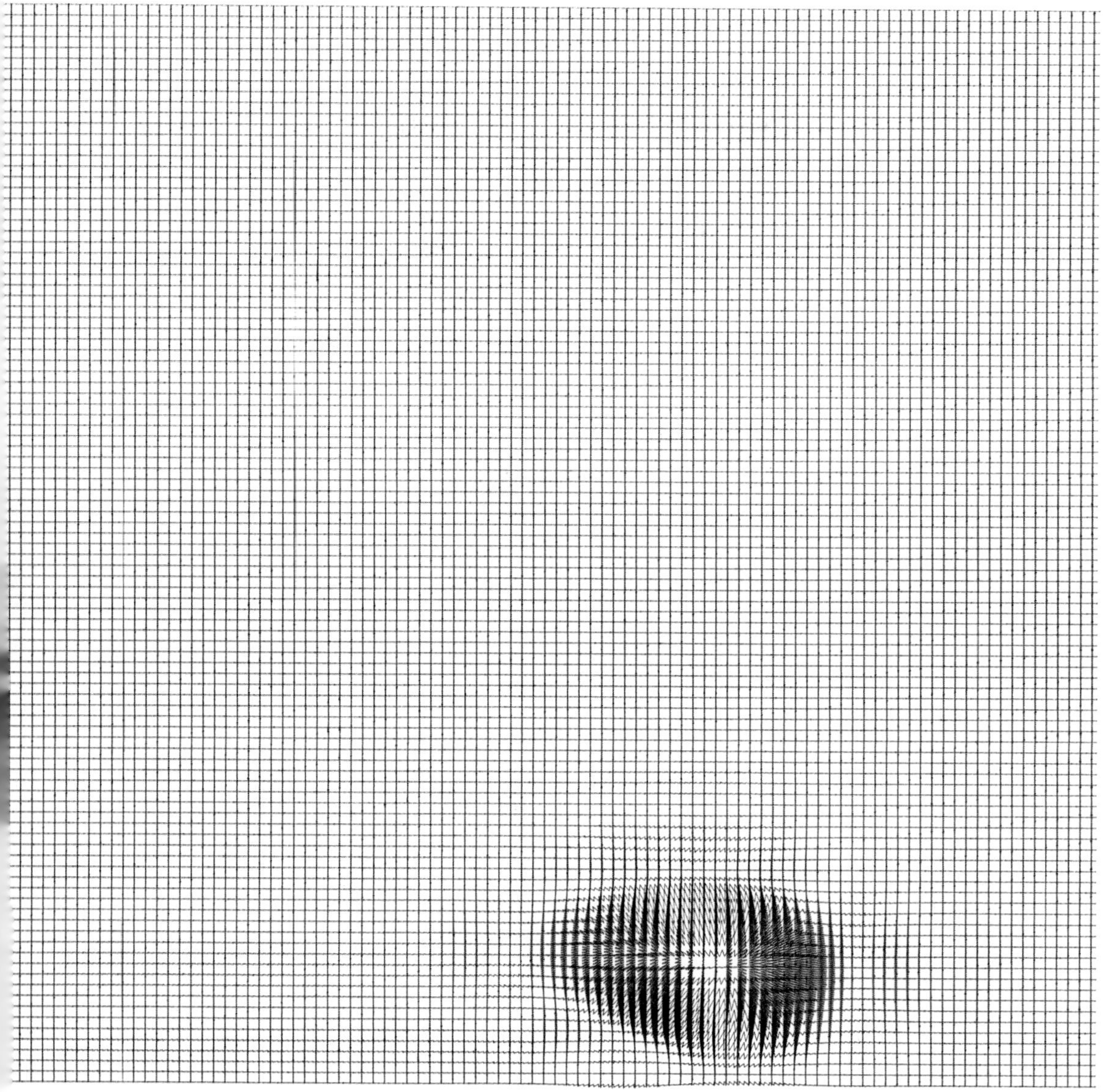

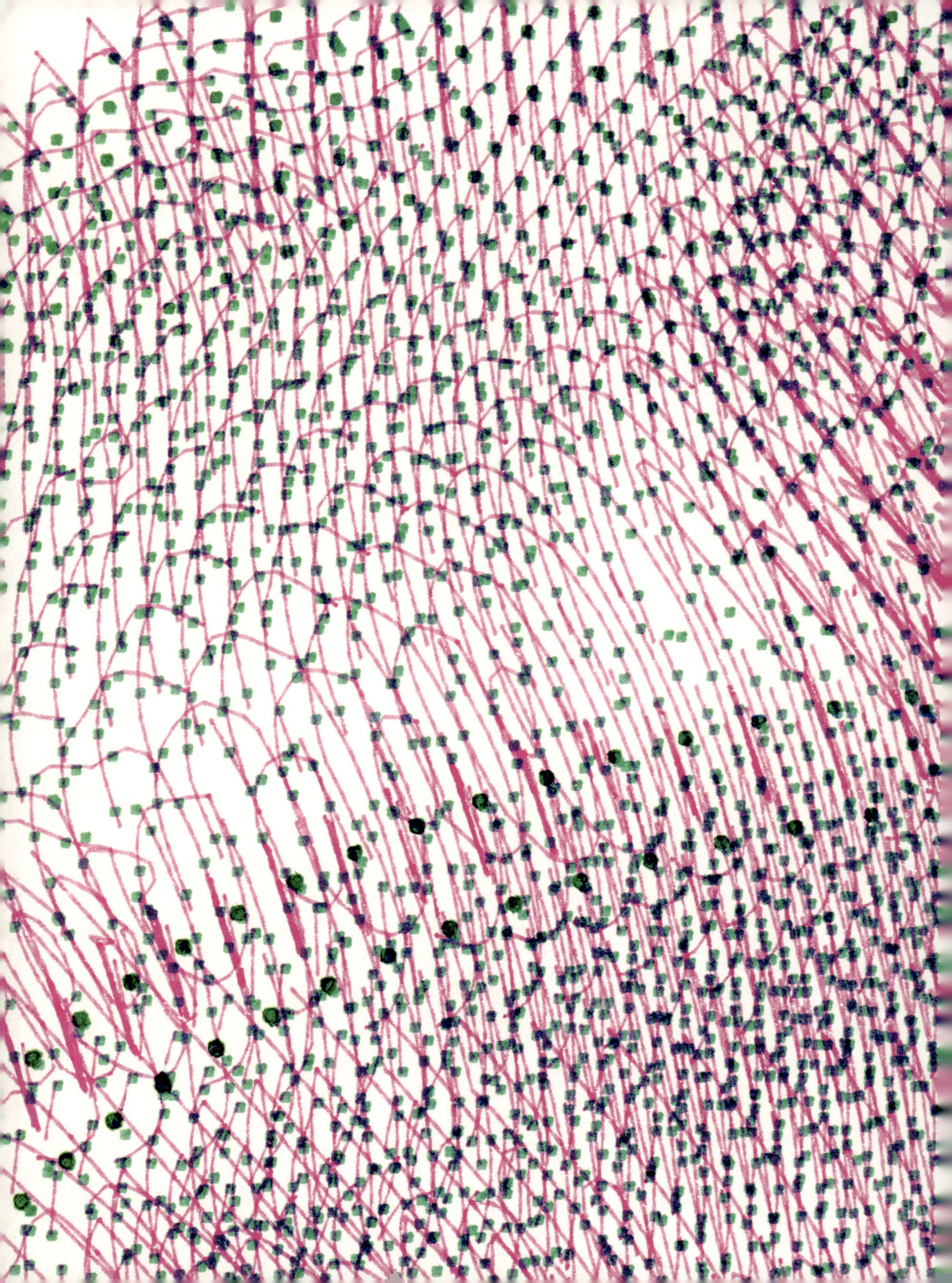

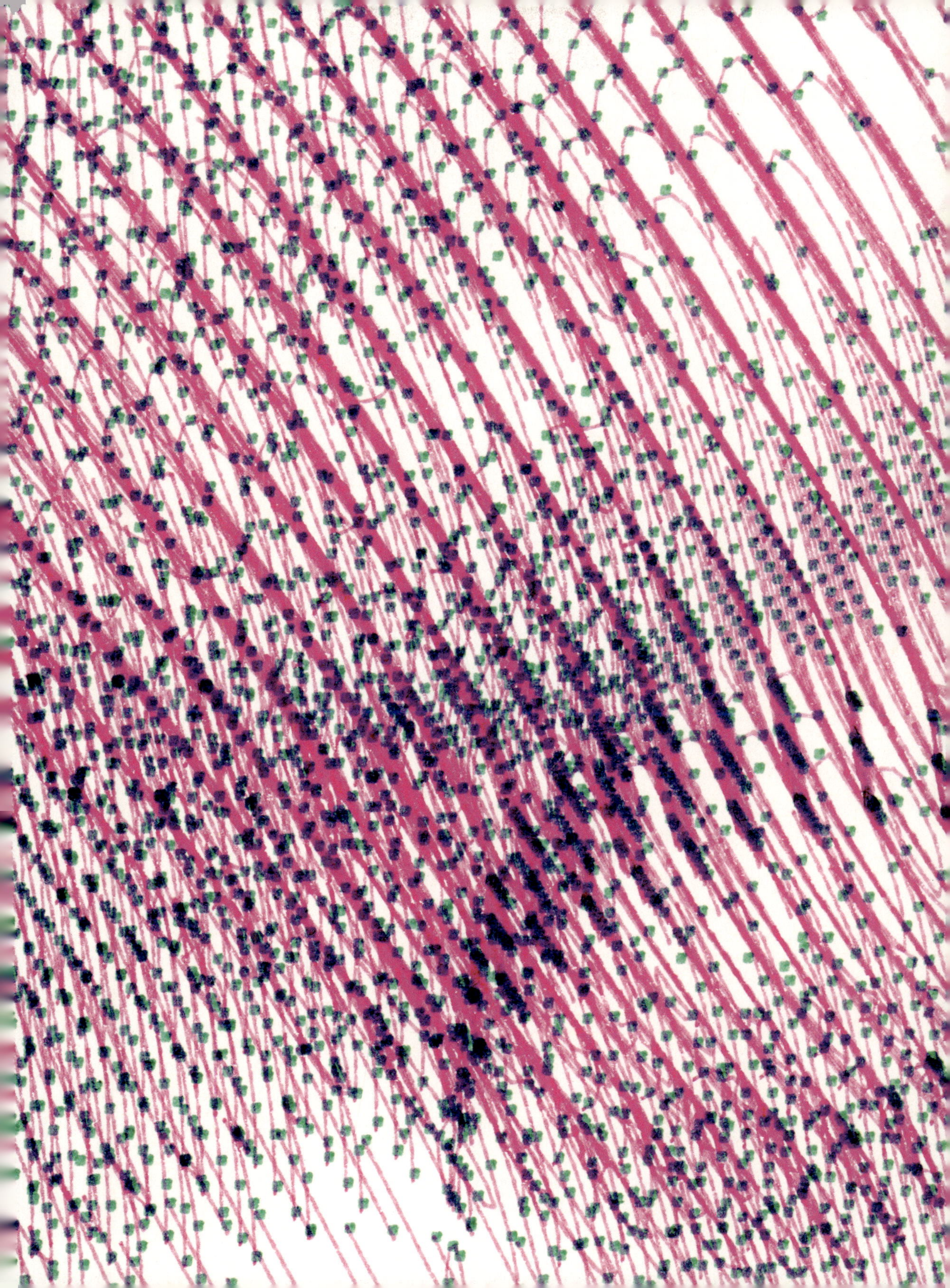

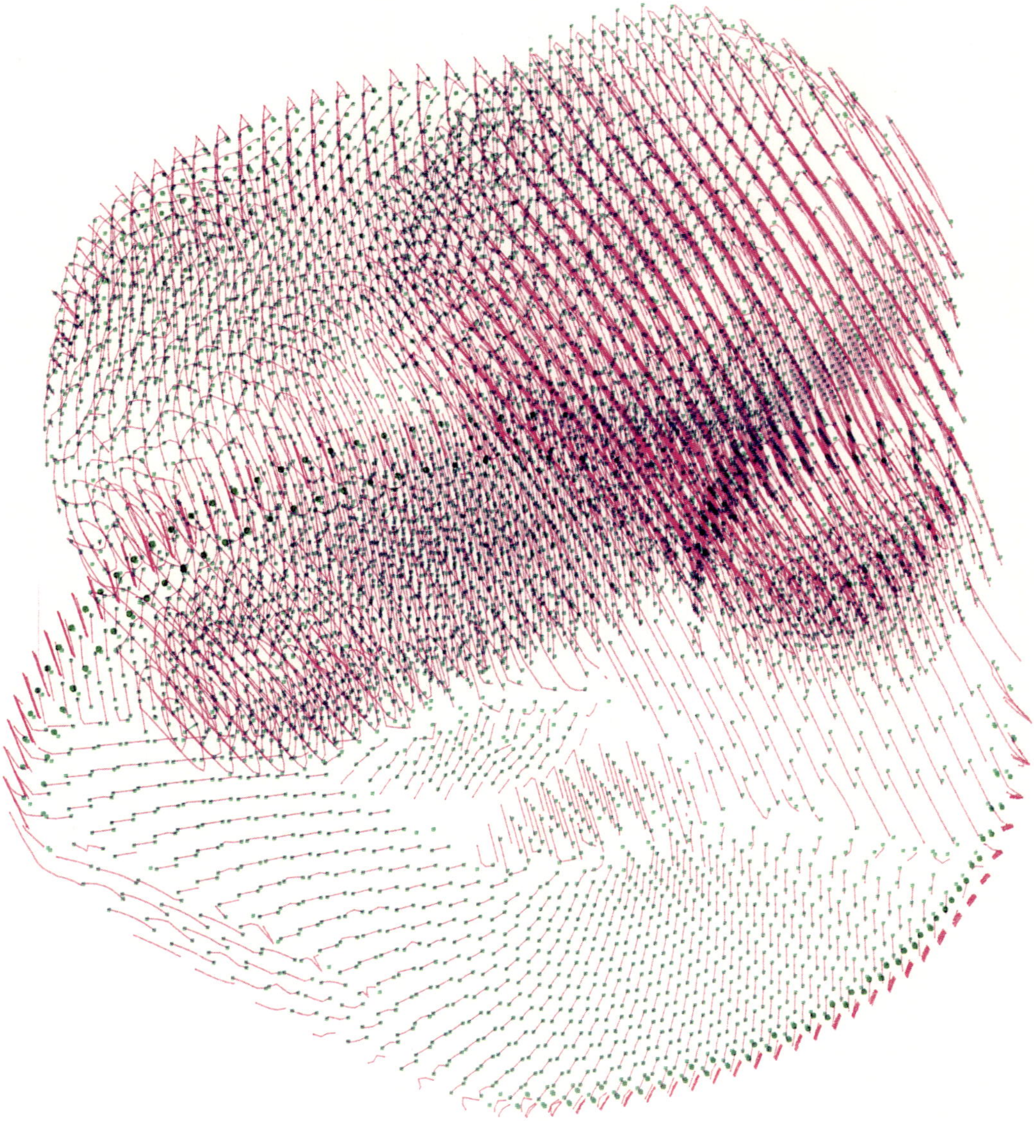

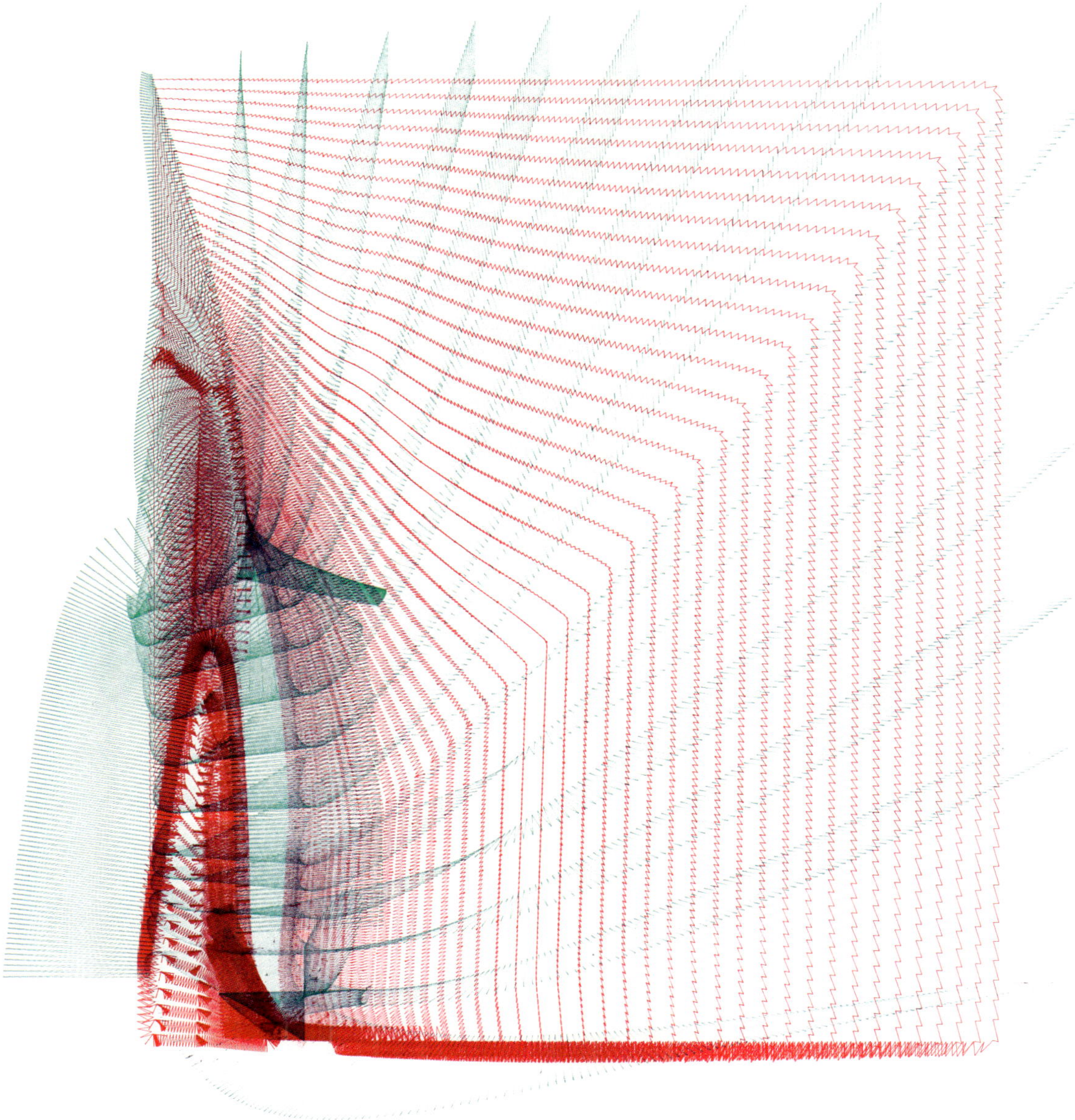

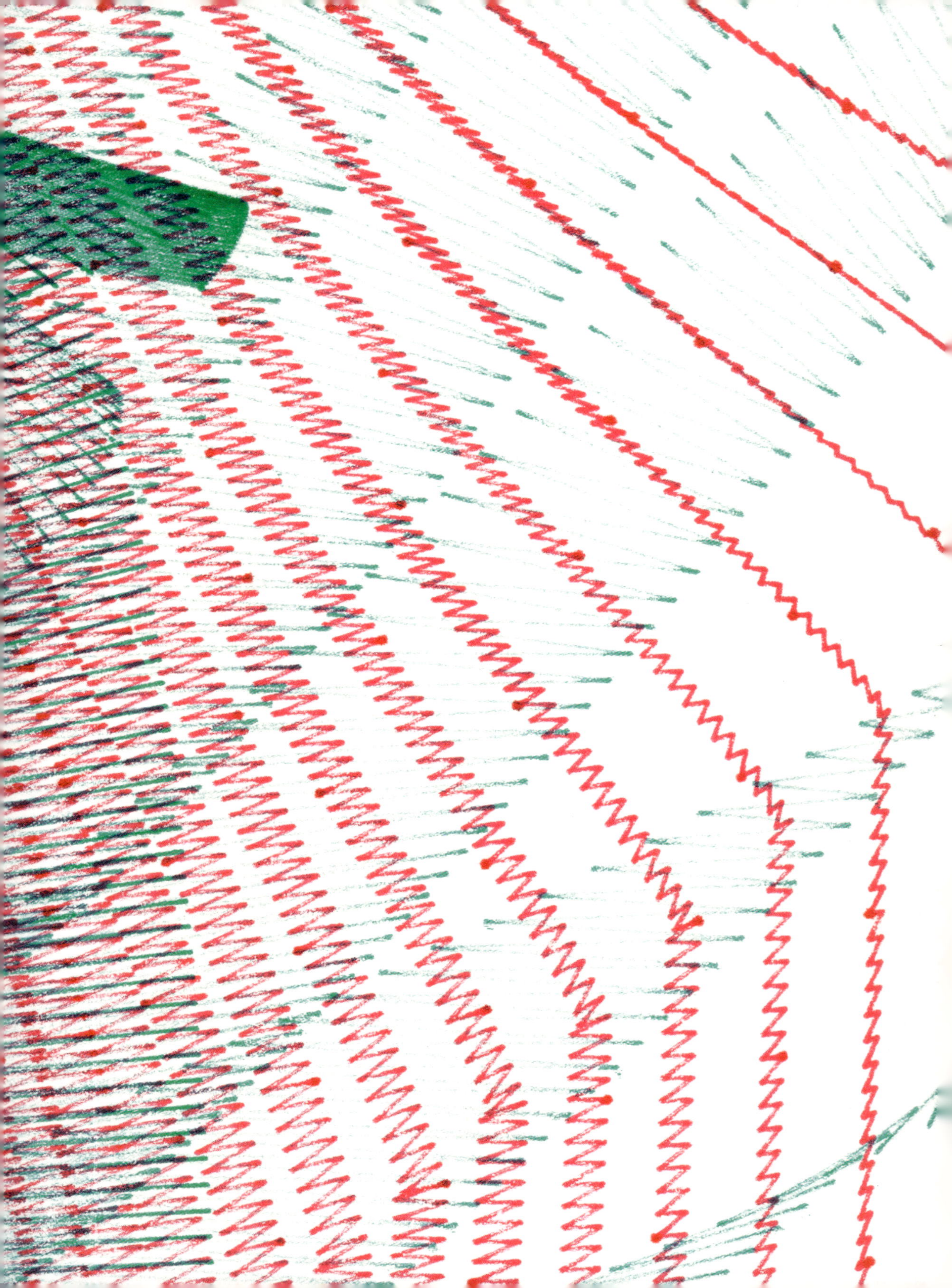

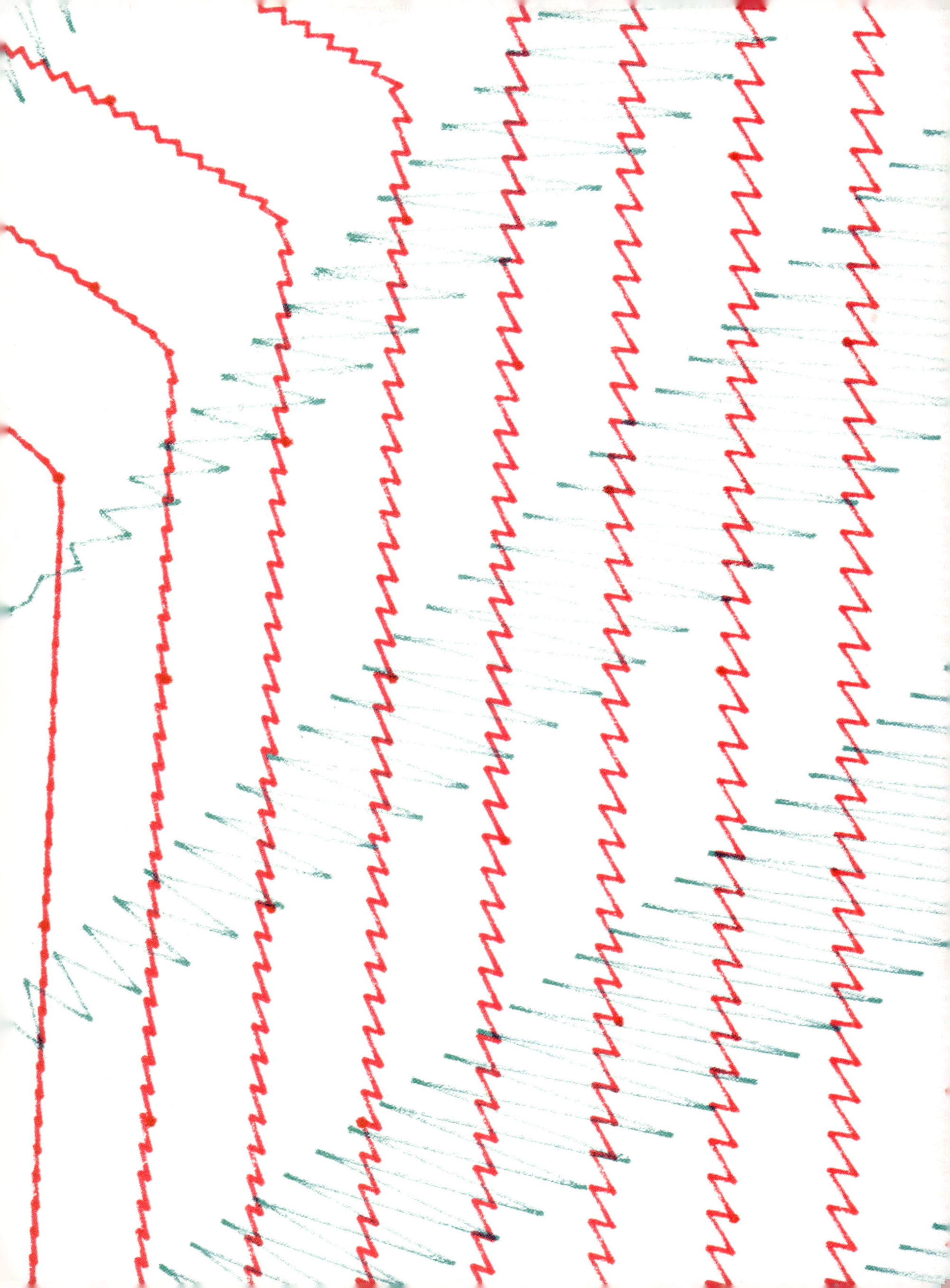

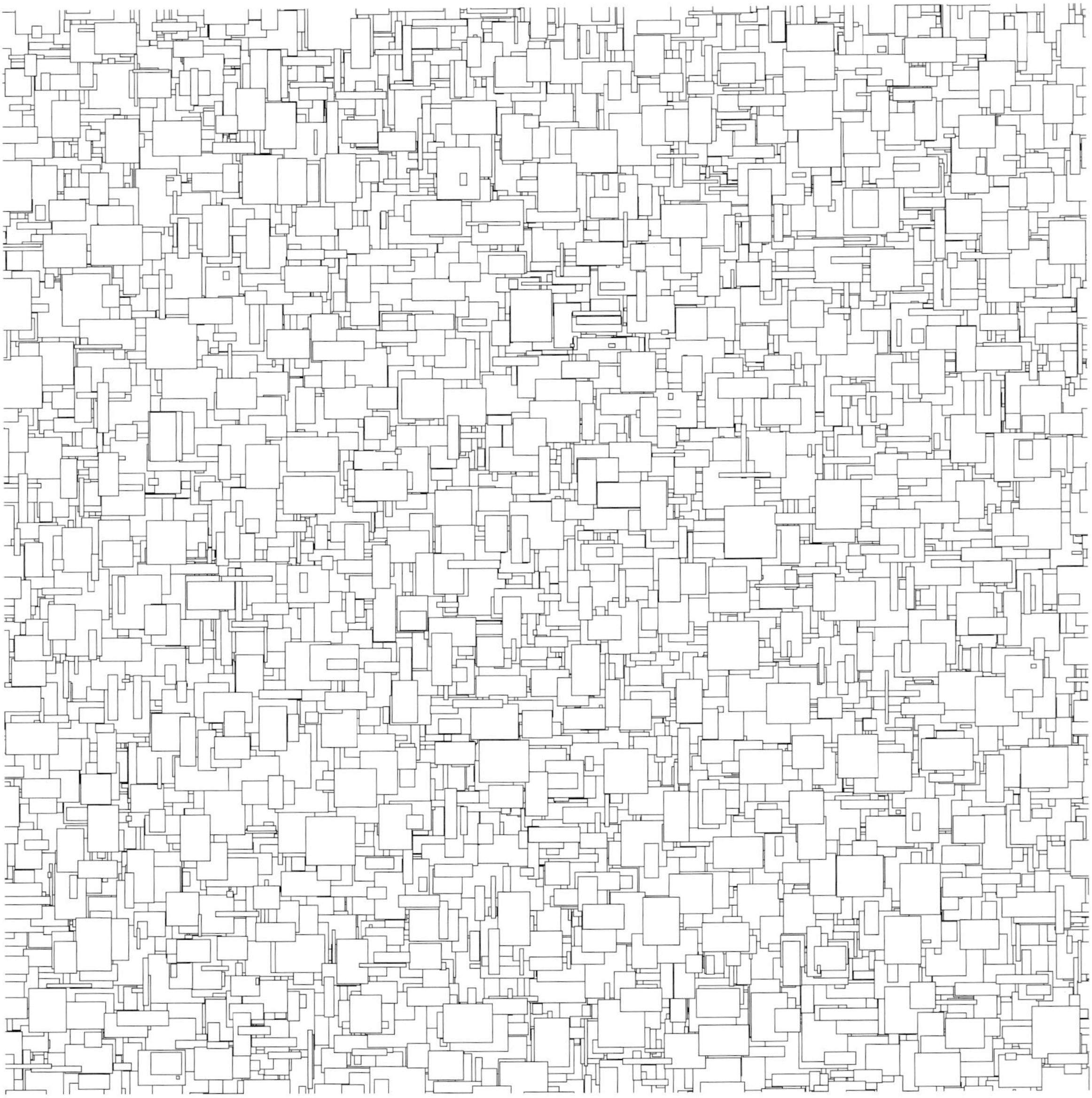

A *rectanglesOverRectangles* drawing.

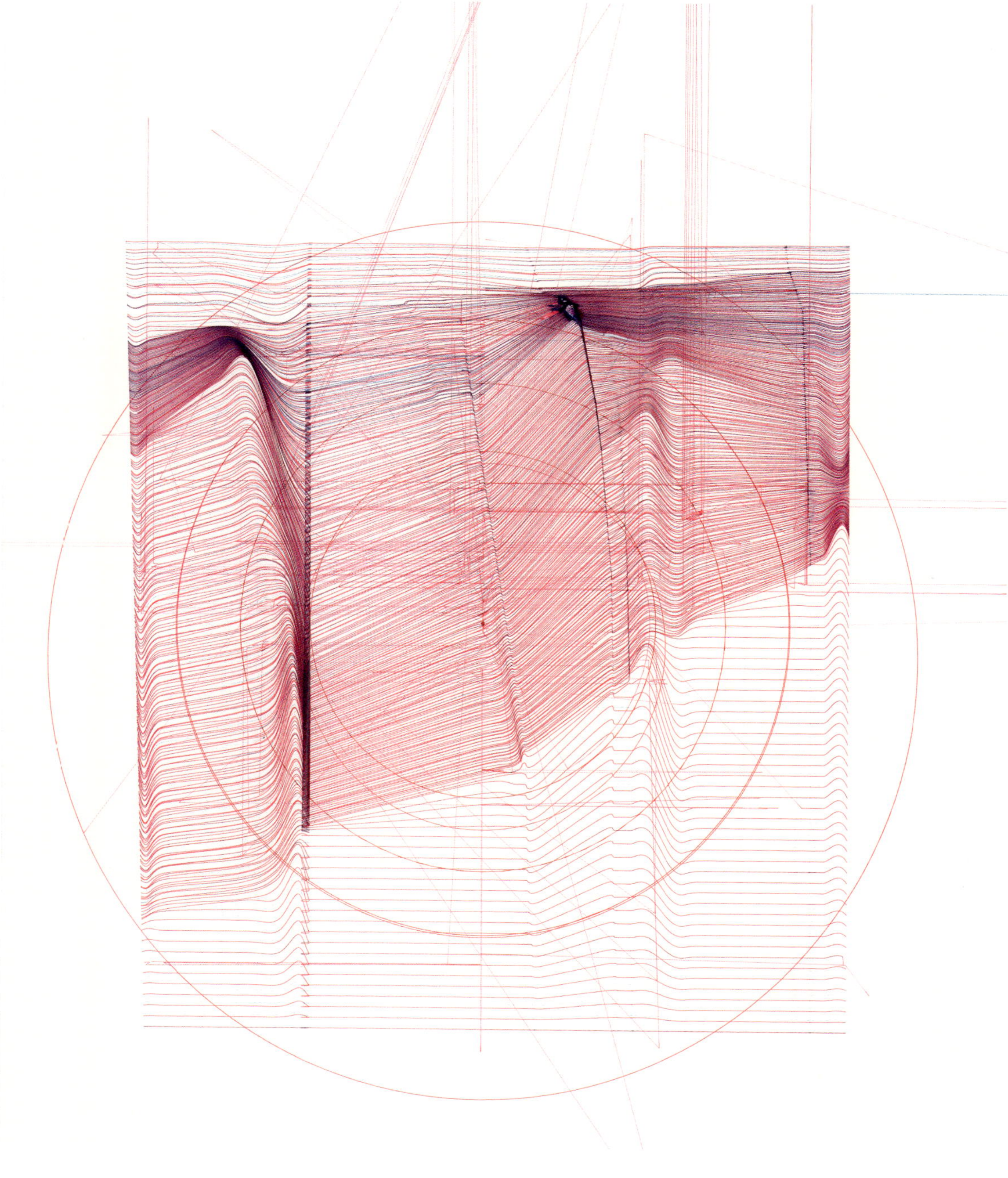

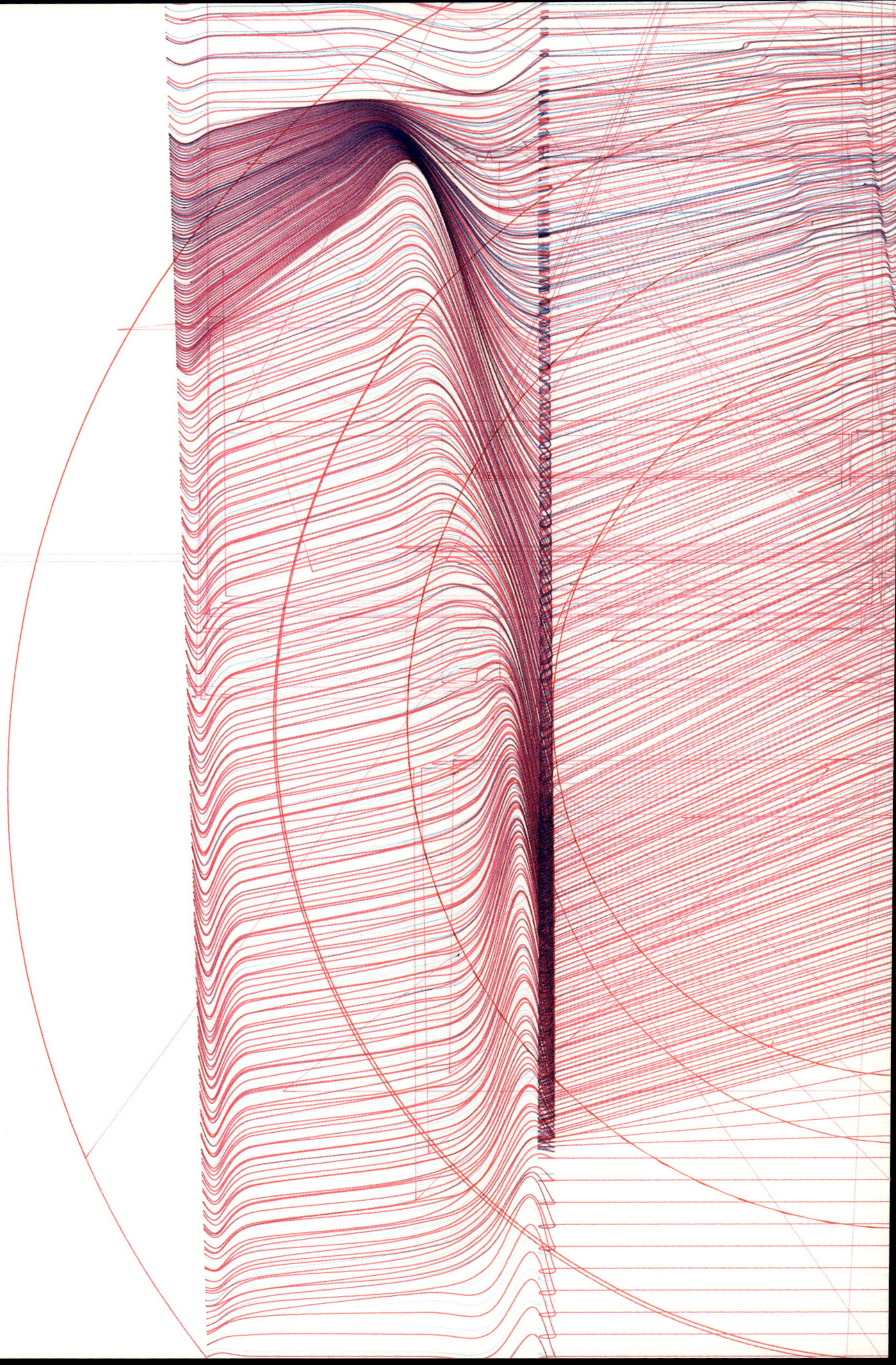

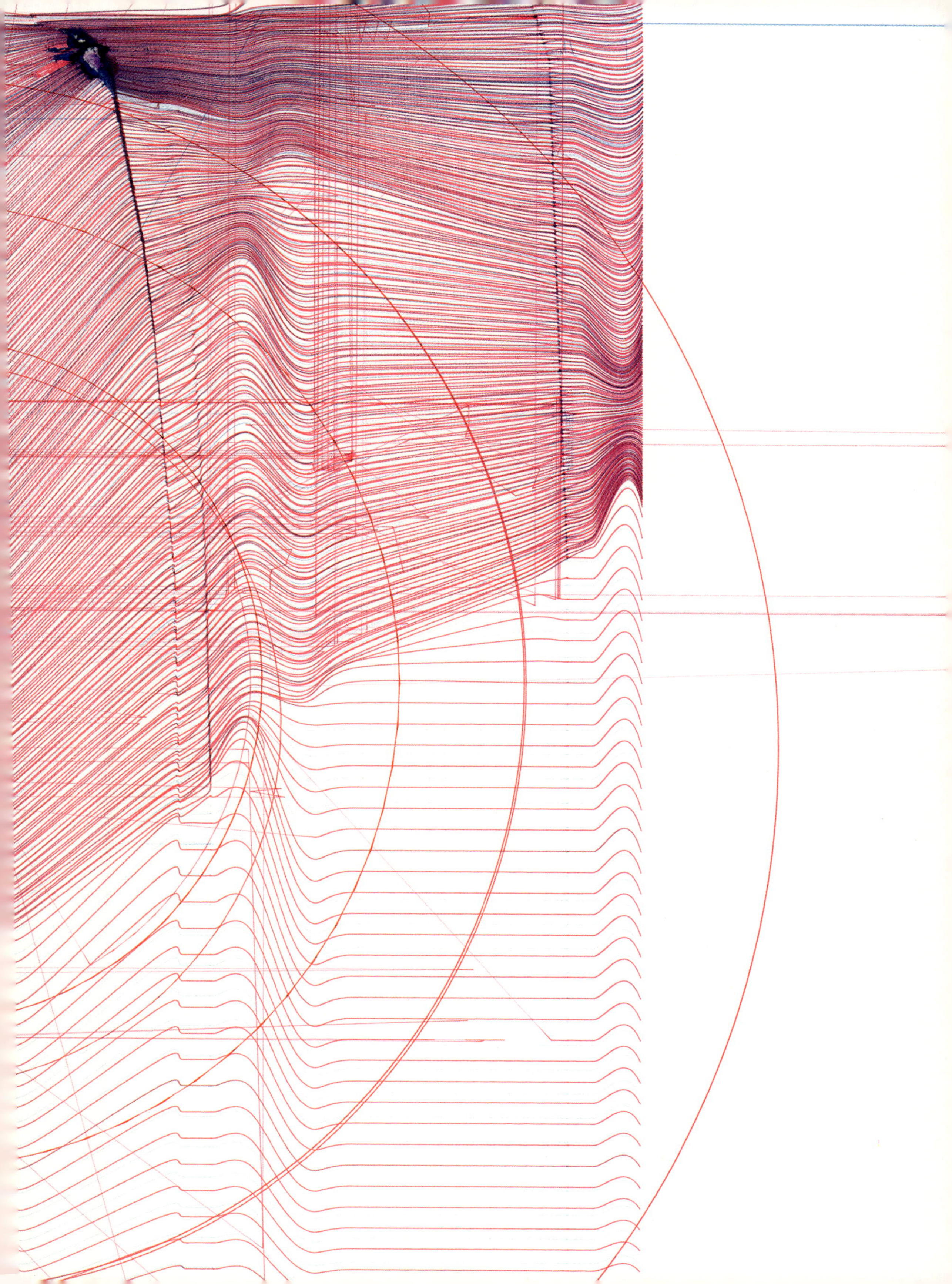

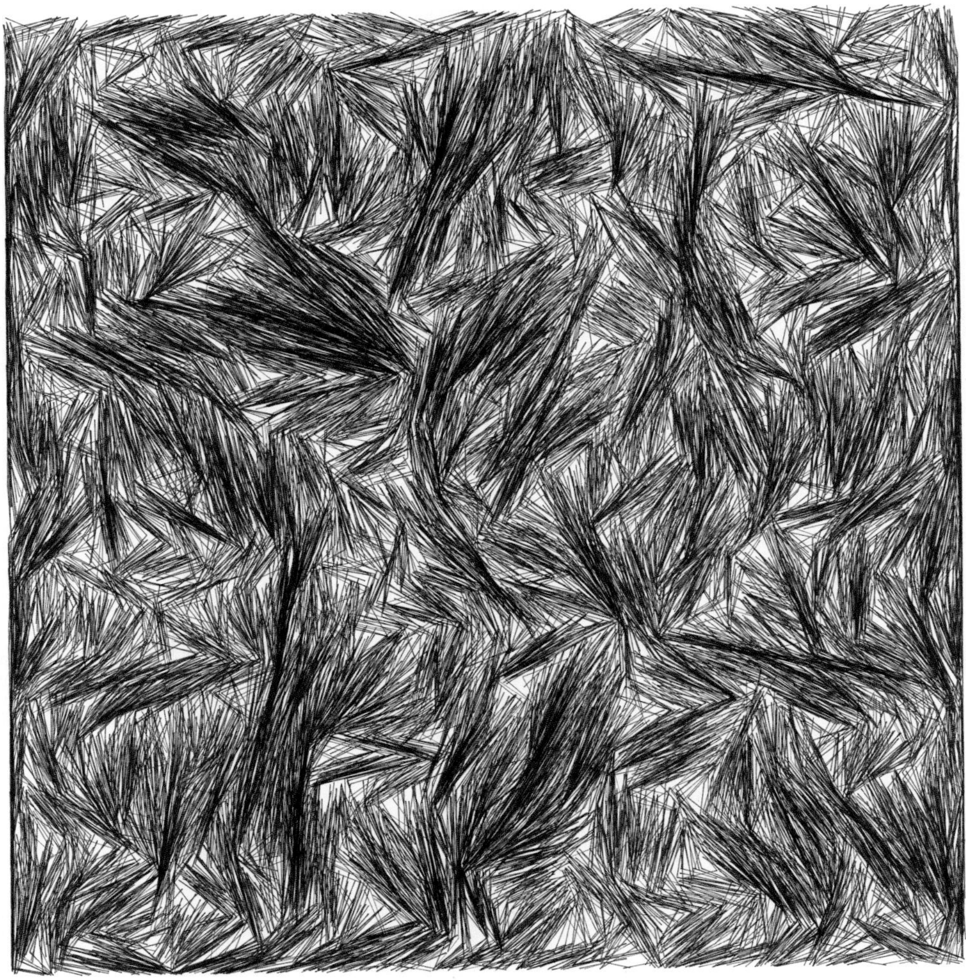

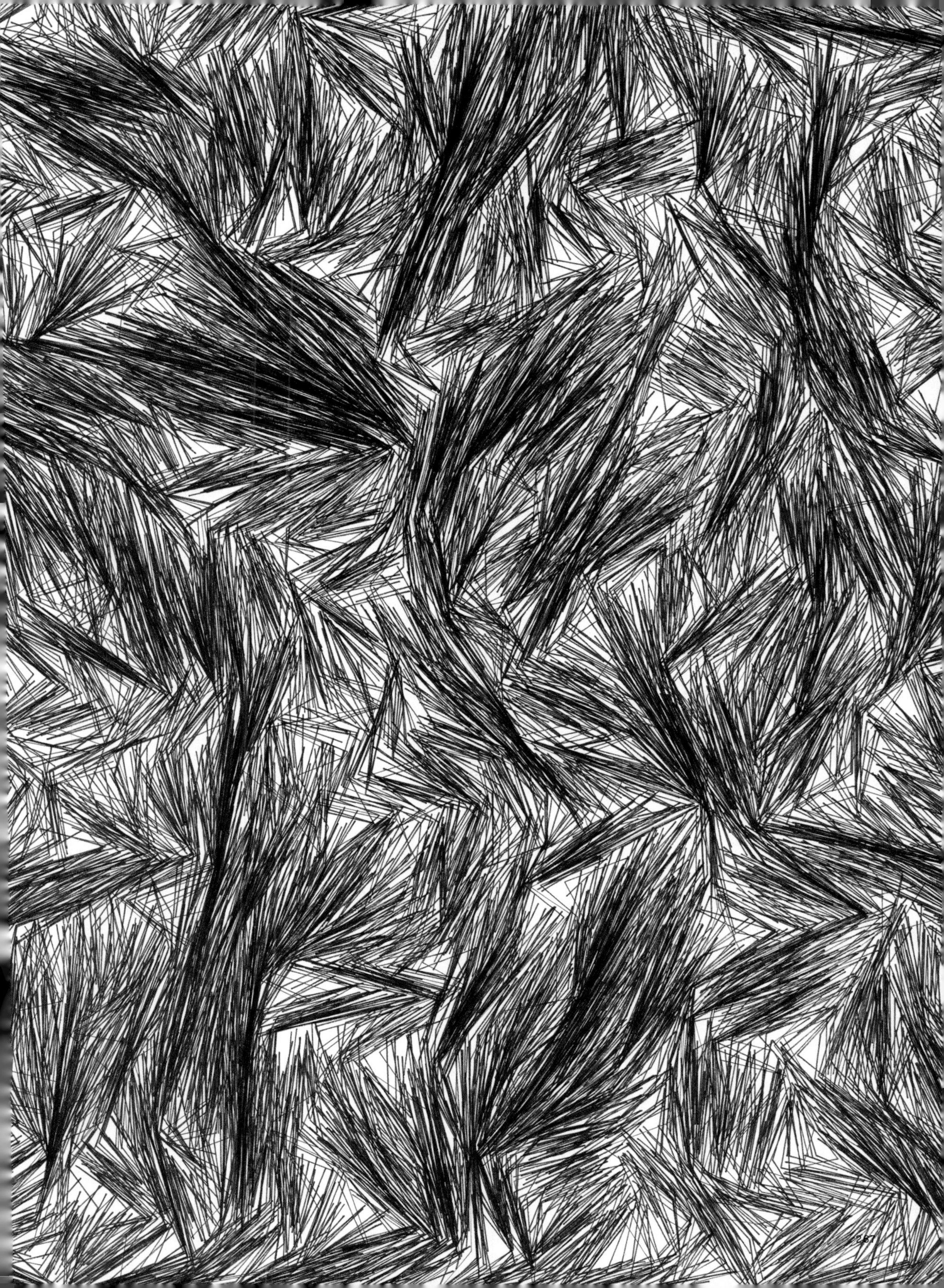

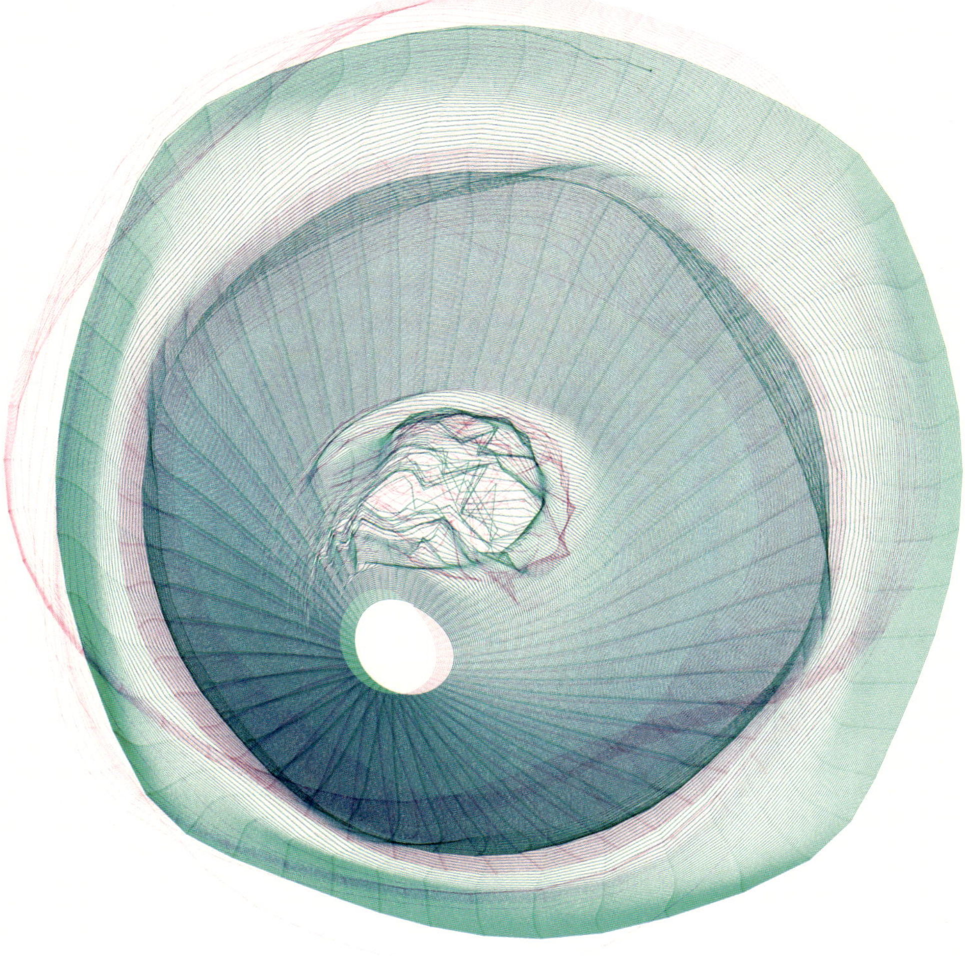

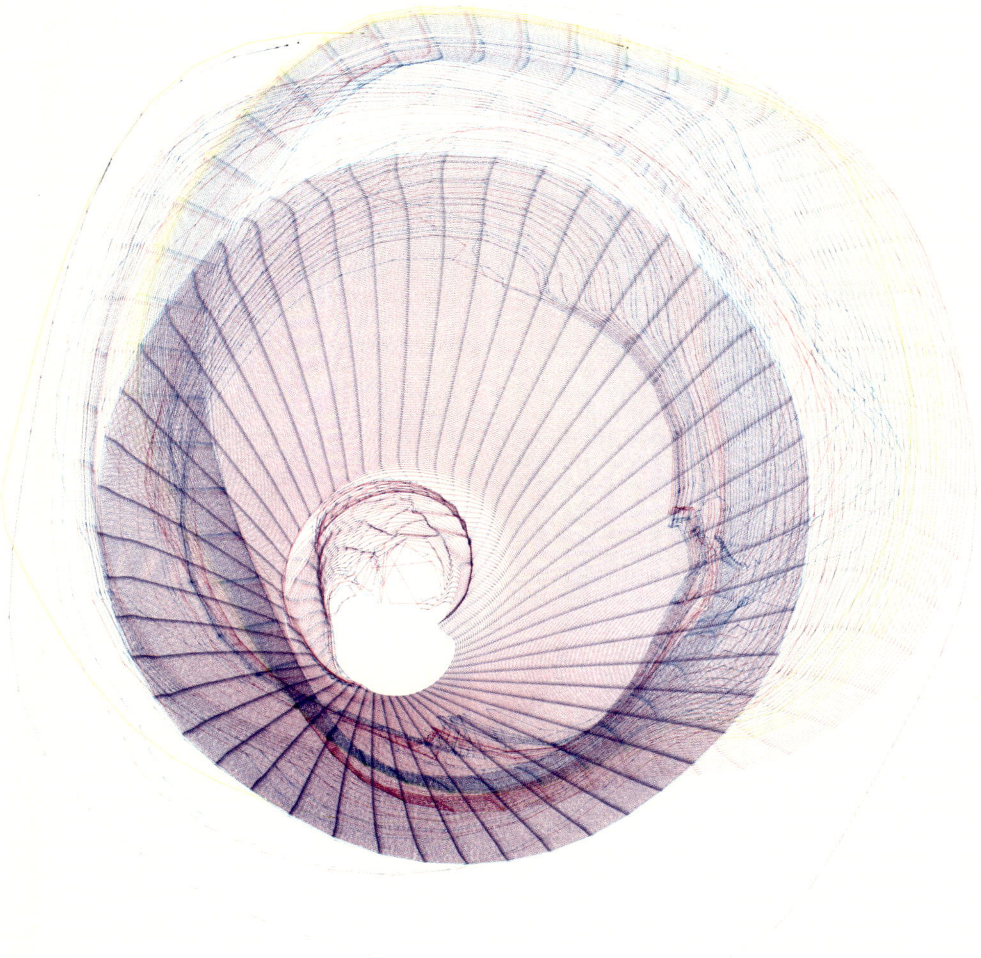

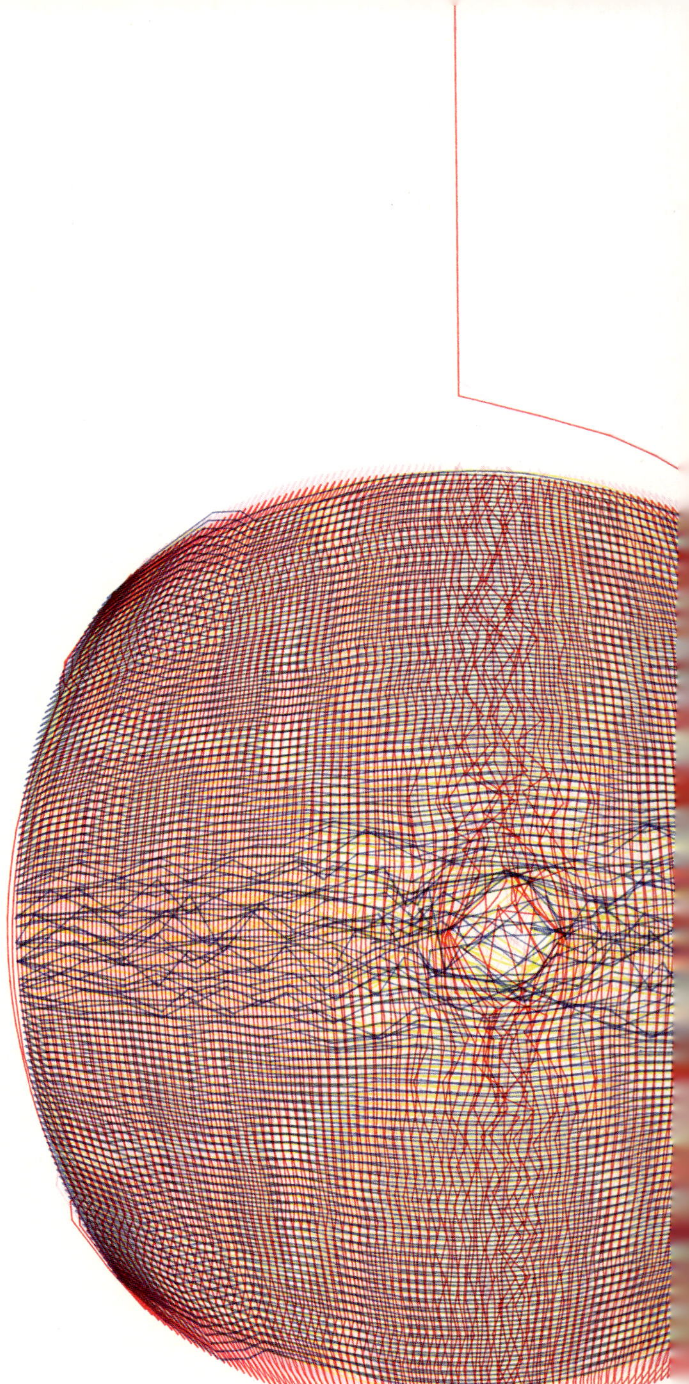

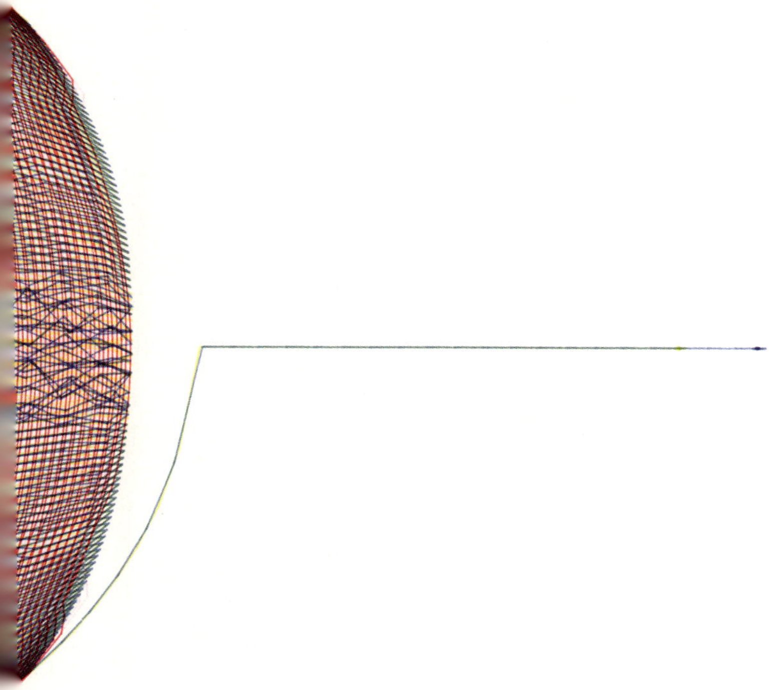

Chapter 5
Futures

Rather than predict the distant future, this final brief chapter will use the *Washington Post* style section "In/Out" list as a model for reflecting on where our culture is going. Every year since 1978 the *Post* uses a list of paired terms, one is out—as in out of fashion—and the other is in. Taken in the aggregate, these lists are more than a collection of passing trends, but a deep analysis of the direction and priorities of a nation. The list often positions macro economic trends along side matters of aesthetics and taste. The pairing is, of course, essential. Much more interesting than just what's trendy now is what that is replacing, mitigating, or undermining. Each diptych can be understood as defining a vector, the difference between what was once relevant and what is now relevant, and we can project that vector forward. In this way, taking the pulse of a culture also implicitly predicts the future.

The editors contextualize the items of the list with some observations that, in some cases, imply rather than assert some subtle but prescient predictions. Of course, a study of these lists often reveals profound fallacies, overconfidence, and pervasive intellectual bubbles on the cusp of bursting. For example, on January 1, 2016 the list proclaimed that "walls" were out and "ceilings" were in.[1] But it's more interesting to be wrong than to equivocate. So with those caveats in place, what follows is an out and in list for the near future of computational drawing in art, architecture, and design. This list will be the jumping-off point for three over-arching predictions for the future of drawing.

out : in

universal : customized

using software : making software

technology making computation invisible : technology making computation hackable

technologist : artisan

post-digital : digital artisanal

theory over craft : theory derived from craft

digital literacy : computational knowledge

digital vs. "by hand" : digital and "by eye"

digital vs. material : digital and material

digital vs. manual : analog and automated

algorithms enabling automation : algorithms enabling articulation

fixing bugs : exaggerating bugs

celebrating the accident : defining the accident

coding to make the world a better place : coding to make your work better

coding to make your life easier : coding to make your work harder

working fast : working slow

coding as research : coding as practice

drawing as practice : drawing as research

Still on Paper, Still Difficult, Slower, Longer

Addressing the question, "What is the future of drawing?" is difficult, because the future of drawing doesn't look much different than its past. Much like the question, "What is the future of voting?" addressing what might be possible quickly leads to an inquiry of what *should* be possible. Like voting, the discipline of drawing is inherently resistant to technological advancements because the limits of paper media are beneficial. In voting, paper ballots provide a material record that transparently resists digital hacking. Paper ballot voting is beneficial because of what can't be done, or can't be done easily. The same is true for the technology of drawing. Like electronic voting machines, three-dimensional drawing interfaces, or virtual and augmented reality tools that allow for drawing in space, may receive attention, but they peak as demonstrations. Fixing the inherent limitations of drawing does not advance drawing. Instead, the future of drawing will not see a paradigm shift, but rather it will advance and expand its duration, scale, indirection, and range of human engagement. Technology, specifically computational technology, will not alleviate the difficulty of depth, automate the production of drawing, or make the interfaces of drawing more convenient or seamless. In some cases, the seams will be greater, the difficulty more palpable, and the process more layered and less direct. In other cases, the different ways we draw will cause cultural, theoretical, and conceptual shifts.

Craft

The future of drawing will see a renewed focus on craft. If a move to a "post-digital" era suggests that architecture and design graduate from the topic of the digital, a focus on drawing will push the pendulum back to a "post-post-digital" era that is again comfortable with the notion that novel techniques can open the door to new theories and ideas. Though unlikely that purely digital projects will themselves garner much attention, when considered alongside drawing rather than opposed to drawing, architects, designers, and artists will find that the digital media well has not run dry. Indeed, many post-digital projects avoided discourse about the digital at their peril. Ironically, these projects can accidentally converge with one another. Granting digital media status as a given allowed workflows to become normalized without critique. Thus, post-digital, can describe a position, and, unfortunately, an aesthetic. What will the post-post-digital era look like? It will see an acceptance of digital expertise, but will expect that such expertise bring humor, critique, messiness, and artistry to the digital landscape.

Drawing Discipline

The future of drawing will be disciplinary. For much of the history of drawing it has been understood as part of other disciplines—as in drawing for architecture. We discuss how painters draw differently than illustrators or sculptors, but the hybridization of computation with drawing will give renewed energy to the prospect that drawing can be understood as its own discipline. This certainly aligns with some recent trends in academia and curatorial institutions that have cultivated drawing departments, concentrations, centers, and institutes. This prediction runs in parallel to the previous assertion that we will see a renewed focus on craft. One expectation of an autonomous discipline is a reflection on methods. Computer scientists, for example, do not merely make advancements to engineering or technology, but they reflect on the nature and methods of computing. This is, of course, not to imply that disciplinary autonomy makes drawing separate from other disciplines. Rather, drawing, like computing, can function as a space for research: it can sustain a process for asking and answering questions; for hypothesizing and positing without the expectation that it provides a utility for other disciplines.

Making and Re-making Technology

The future of drawing will focus on how authors make technology for their practice rather than use technology made by others. Relatedly, those who write code will be celebrated not just for what they enable others to do, but will be expected to create themselves. For a short time, knowing how to write code extended one's functional capacity far beyond the norm. Computational skill involved significant expertise and likely involved understanding difficult programming language.[2] But today, advances in software have greatly broadened access to computational tools. Programming languages are critiqued, evolved, and championed based on legibility, elegance, access, and pleasure. Today, computation allows artists, architects, and designers to write code that creates, adjusts, customizes, or hacks tools for their own practice. The distinction between engineer and user is as irrelevant as those terms are outdated in creative fields. As recently as a few years ago, many computational research projects focused on making tools for others. Thus they aimed to generalize the application of a novel technique. Today, the focus can shift to coding that bridges between scales, media, and formats.

We can look forward to a future that celebrates the code written by artists, architects, and designers code for its strangeness, quirkiness, or capacity to make us think rather than impress with something marketable to a wide audience. This future also means that the chasm between the impersonal "make a tool for others" and the hyper-personal "my work is a reflection of myself" is dramatically narrowing. Both ways of working will thankfully soon become untenable and indefensible in the context of computational drawing. Instead, artists, designers, and architects will make work that acknowledges their own role in making that was not previously possible. At the same time, their methods will be open to analysis, critique and discourse.

Notes

1. Contrera, Jessica. "The 2016 In/Out List." The Washington Post. January 1, 2016. Accessed January 3, 2018. https://www.washingtonpost.com/graphics/lifestyle/year-in-review-in-out-list/2016/
2. I know of one researcher who earned their Ph.D in the mid '90s who successfully lobbied the School of Design with which they were affiliated with to allow their study of an Assembly programming language to satisfy the foreign language requirement of the Ph.D program. Such an argument held water in part because an architect-programmer was a novel proposition. Additionally, Assembly languages are so low-level and technical that months and even years of education is typically necessary before one could be considered fluent. Today, high-level languages are immediately accessible. Their ease of use has made them so mainstream that they would certainly not qualify as a language by most academic standards.

Appendix

Some computational drawing resources are listed here. Because this book aims to be neutral with respect to specific resources, readers should treat this text as neither endorsement nor review. All are available online, many for no cost. URLs and version numbers have not been listed only for the purposes of avoiding this list quickly becoming obsolete.

Processing. A complete programming environment for artists and designers. Very well suited for the first-time programmer. The default programming language is JAVA, but there is also a Python mode, which may be of interest to those looking to transition to scripting or use Python to control a pen plotter.

P5JS. Processing for the web in Javascript. Excellent starting point for those interested in web-based programming. The p5.serial library enables communication over serial port, which theoretically opens the door for controlling pen-plotters.

OpenFrameworks. A C++ toolkit for creative coding. The most powerful option.

Python Libraries (collections of code that may be useful for those programming in Python outside of an environment like Processing or existing software)

Chiplotle. Control vintage HLGP pen-plotters of the kind manufactured by Hewlett Packard, Roland, and others in the '80s and '90s. This library is used in making many of the drawings included in this book.

Pygame. Advertised as a library for making arcade games, this library is nonetheless widely used by artists, scientists, and others to create static and interactive pixel-based graphics. All the pixel images in this book were made with Pygame.

OpenCV. Handles image processing and live video feeds svgwrite. A library for creating .svg (web-friendly vector format) files

Turtle graphics. Turtle graphics has a history that precedes Python, but has been ported to Python. Though originally designed with the young pupil in mind, the relative method of drawing may be of practical and conceptual interest to many.

Pyglet. A multi-media library that can be used for 2-D drawing or 3-D interactive Open-GL programming.

Software applications that allow scripting (programming to control the software, usually executed from within the software).

Rhinoceros. 3-D modeling and drafting software. The Python and C# libraries are extensive. Many of the drawings in this book involved content that flowed in and out of Rhinoceros.

Blender 3D. Open source 3-D modeling and animation.

Maya. Python API (Application Programming Interface).

Index

10Print, 84–85
7 Types of Ambiguity, 90
Abstraction, 34
Accident, 175–76, 278
Algorithm, 32, 35
Ambiguity, 80–81, 90, 231–32
Anti- aliasing, 32
Architecture, 11–12, 173, 217, 223
Artificial Intelligence, 178, 204, 210
Autographic drawing, 114
Automatic Drawing, 114, 218
Autonomous drawing, 114
Ballard, J.G., 230
Barney, Matthew, 215
Carpo, Mario, 29
Chess, 35, 80, 217, 231
Choose your own adventure, 86
Craft, 280
Creativity, 174–76
Depth, 216, 218–20, 222–23
Difficulty, 215, 218, 279
Diffusion, 115, 150–53
Digital model, 20
Digital turn, 30, 222
Discipline, 15, 281
Drafting, 16
Drifting-Dash-Polyline, 38
Drifting-Dash-Polyline, 63–65
Drunken-Ant-Path, 37, 62
Empson, William, 90, 231
Errors, 175–76
Eye, 179
Flood Fill, 176–77, 181, 183, 185, 187–99
Frankenstein-Rebuild, 177, 200–01
Frascari, Marco, 80
Function, 34
Gershenfeld, Neil, 114–15
Grid-Segments, 84
Handmade, 29, 179, 278
Hatch, 33, 92
Horizon, 79, 92, 219
Ink, 225, 230
Intelligence, 178
Kennedy, John F, 215
LeWitt, Sol, 32
Library (of code), 34
Line, 79–80, 82–83, 90–115, 184, 216, 230
Literature, 86, 90, 230–32
Mark, 34, 79–80
Material, 106, 225, 230
McLuhan, Marshall, 29
Media, 29–30, 80, 114, 173
Occulation, 219
Outline style, 92
Paper, 182, 184, 225, 230, 279
Perlman, Elliot, 90
Petherbridge, Deanna, 15
Pixel, 25, 30, 32, 223
Poetry, 34, 86
Projection, 216, 226–29
Rectangles-Over-Rectangles, 224–25, 260
Representation, 85, 217
Riley, Bridget, 182
Scheer, David Ross, 175–76
Seeing, 25, 179
Shakespeare, 231
Shape Grammars, 80
Sketching, 16, 216
Software, 80, 82, 86, 174, 278
Sorting, 32, 40–49
Space-Filling-Line, 83
Squiggle, 36, 50–52
Still life, 221
Stiny, George, 80–82, 85, 231
Surface, 222
Sutherland, Ivan, 81–82
Time, 102, 179, 279
Two and a half dimensional, 223
Variably-Thick-Line, 37, 54–57
Vector Graphics, 32

Published by Applied Research and Design Publishing, an imprint of ORO Editions.
Gordon Goff: Publisher

www.appliedresearchanddesign.com
info@appliedresearchanddesign.com

Text by Carl Lostritto
Project Manager: Jake Anderson

Book Design by Pablo Mandel
www.circularstudio.com

Typeset in Dala Moa, Nitti, and Nitti Grotesk

10 9 8 7 6 5 4 3 2 1 First Softbound Edition

ISBN: 978-1-957183-45-9

Color Separations and Printing: ORO Group Ltd.
Printed in China.

AR+D Publishing makes a continuous effort to minimize the overall carbon footprint of its publications. As part of this goal, AR+D, in association with Global ReLeaf, arranges to plant trees to replace those used in the manufacturing of the paper produced for its books. Global ReLeaf is an international campaign run by American Forests, one of the world's oldest nonprofit conservation organizations. Global ReLeaf is American Forests' education and action program that helps individuals, organizations, agencies, and corporations improve the local and global environment by planting and caring for trees.